John Disturnell

The Traveler's Guide

To the Hudson River, Saratoga Springs, Lake George, Falls of Niagara and Thousand Islands

John Disturnell

The Traveler's Guide
To the Hudson River, Saratoga Springs, Lake George, Falls of Niagara and Thousand Islands

ISBN/EAN: 9783743442719

Manufactured in Europe, USA, Canada, Australia, Japa

Cover: Foto ©Andreas Hilbeck / pixelio.de

Manufactured and distributed by brebook publishing software (www.brebook.com)

John Disturnell

The Traveler's Guide

THE
TRAVELER'S GUIDE

TO THE

HUDSON RIVER,

SARATOGA SPRINGS, LAKE GEORGE,

FALLS OF NIAGARA AND THOUSAND ISLANDS;

MONTREAL, QUEBEC,

AND THE

SAGUENAY RIVER;

ALSO, TO THE

GREEN AND WHITE MOUNTAINS,

AND OTHER PARTS OF

NEW ENGLAND;

FORMING THE FASHIONABLE NORTHERN TOUR THROUGH THE

UNITED STATES AND CANADA.

WITH MAP AND EMBELLISHMENTS.

———✿———

COMPILED BY J. DISTURNELL.

———✿———

New York:
PUBLISHED BY THE "AMERICAN NEWS COMPANY,"
121 NASSAU STREET;
AND FOR SALE BY A. WILLIAMS & CO., BOSTON; DAWSON & BROTHER, MONTREAL; AND BY BOOKSELLERS GENERALLY.

Entered, according to Act of Congress, in the year 1864, by

JOHN DISTURNELL,

In the Clerk's Office of the District Court of the United States for the Southern District of New York.

DAVIES AND ROBERTS,
STEREOTYPERS,
118 *Nassau-st.*, *N. Y.*

TO THE READER.

The arrangement of the PICTURESQUE TOURIST will be found to differ, in some respects, from works of the same class.

The general object of this book is to furnish a convenient and faithful guide for strangers, whether traveling on business, or for pleasure, or health, through the northern section of the United States and the Canadas.

The city of New York, as being the principal commercial emporium in the country, and the chief center of resort, in the first instance, for distant travelers, whether native or foreign, is chosen as the point from which the tourist is supposed to commence his excursion. Starting thence, this Guide will conduct him along the principal lines of travel North and West. Northward he will proceed up the Hudson River, through the flourishing cities at the head of navigation, to the famous Springs at Ballston and Saratoga—thence to Lake George, and by the way of Lake Champlain into Canada. Westward, over the line of the *New York Central Railroad*, through the rich midland and western counties of the State of New York, to Niagara Falls and Buffalo—thence northerly through Canada, passing over Lake Ontario and down the St. Lawrence to Montreal, Quebec, and the Saguenay River,—returning by the way of the WHITE MOUNTAINS of New Hampshire, Portland, Boston, etc. ; or by the more direct route *via* Lake Champlain, Lake George, and Saratoga Springs to Troy and Albany—noticing, on each route, the places and scenery most worthy of the attention of the tourist, either for memorable events or for local attractions, and aiming, in the accounts of them, more at simple accuracy than at embellished description. Such are the scope and design of this Traveler's Guide.   J. D.

NEW YORK, *June*, 1864.

CONTENTS.

	Page
TABLE OF DISTANCES, etc., from the city of New York to the principal Cities in the Northern States and Canada.	13
New York and Harlem Railroad Route	15
Hudson River Railroad Route	17
TOUR FROM NEW YORK TO ALBANY, TROY, etc., *via* Hudson River	19
Jersey City—Hoboken—Weehawken—Manhattanville	20
Fort Washington—Fort Lee—Palisades—Spuyten Duyvel Creek	21
Yonkers—Hastings—Dobbs' Ferry—Piermont	22
Tappan Bay—Irvington—Tarrytown	23
Nyack—Rockland Lake—Sing-Sing	24
Croton, or Teller's, Point—Haverstraw—Verplanck's Point	25
Caldwell's Landing—Peekskill	27
Mahopac Lake—Fort Independence—Highlands	28
West Point—U. S. Military Academy	29
Coldspring—Beacon Hill	31
Crow's Nest—Cornwall—Newburgh	32
Fishkill—Matteawan—Glenham	33
New Hamburgh—Milton—Poughkeepsie	34
New Paltz—Hyde Park	35
Esopus Meadows—Rondout—Kingston	36
Rhinebeck—Barrytown	37
Tivoli—Saugerties—Catskill	38
Catskill Mountain House—Pine Orchard	39
City of Hudson	40
Columbia Springs	41
New Lebanon Springs—Coxsackie	42
Stuyvesant—Coeymans—Overslaugh	43
City of Albany	44
New York Central Railroad	47

CONTENTS.

	Page
Albany Ninety Years Since	49
City of Troy—West Troy	50
Lansingburgh—Waterford—Cohoes Falls	53, 54

HUDSON RIVER STEAMBOATS 55
   Clermont, or Experiment Boat 57

TOUR TO SARATOGA SPRINGS, LAKE GEORGE, ETC.:
   Railroad Routes—Ballston Spa 59
   Saratoga Springs 60
   Analysis of the Principal Springs 61–69
   Route to Lake George, Lake Champlain, etc. 70

WESTERN TOUR:
   City of Schenectady 71
   Amsterdam—Fonda—Johnstown—Palatine Bridge 73
   Sharon Springs 74
   Cooperstown—Richfield Springs 75
   Fort Plain—St. Johnsville—Little Falls 76
   West Canada Creek—Herkimer—Mohawk 77
   City of Utica 78
   Trenton Falls 79
   Whitesborough—Oriskany 81
   Rome—Oneida Depôt—Canastota 82
   Chittenango—Cazenovia—Syracuse 83
   Geddes—Liverpool—Onondaga Salt Springs 84
   Camillus—Jordan—Skaneateles—Auburn 86
   Weedsport—Port Byron—Montezuma 87
   Cayuga Lake 88
   Cayuga Village—Springport 89
   Levanna—Aurora 90
   Sheldrake Point—Ithaca 91

LAKES OF WESTERN NEW YORK:
   Oneida Lake—Onondaga Lake 92
   Otisco Lake—Cayuga Lake—Seneca Lake 93
   Canandaigua Lake 94
   Crooked Lake—Chautauque Lake 95

Seneca Falls 96
Waterloo—Geneva 97
Clyde—Lyons 98
Newark—Palmyra—Clifton Springs 99
Canandaigua—Rochester 100
Avon Springs 103
Batavia—Attica—Brockport 104
Albion—Medina—Lockport 105
Niagara Falls 106
City of Buffalo 107

CONTENTS. vii

Page
BUFFALO TO NIAGARA FALLS, TORONTO, ETC.:
Fort Erie—Grand Island—Navy Island—Chippewa—
Falls of Niagara—Clifton—Queenston—Brock's Monument—Niagara—Fort George....................109-113

NIAGARA RIVER:
Its Rapids, Falls, Islands, and Romantic Scenery—
Grand Island—Tonawanda—Iris, or Goat Island....114-118

CATARACT OF NIAGARA:
American Fall—Canadian, or Horse Shoe, Fall—Suspension Bridge—Whirlpool and Rapids—Maid of the Mist—
Niagara Falls Village—Lewiston—Youngstown.....119-126

LAKE ONTARIO:
Beautiful Mirage, Route, etc....................127, 128

STEAMBOAT ROUTES:
Lake Ontario and River St. Lawrence Steamers....129, 130

TRIP FROM LEWISTON TO OSWEGO, KINGSTON, AND OGDENSBURGH:
Fort Niagara—Charlotte, or Port Genesee—Genesee
River—Great Sodus Bay—Little Sodus Bay—Oswego.131-138

RAILROAD AND STEAMBOAT ROUTE FROM SYRACUSE TO
NIAGARA FALLS, via OSWEGO..................... 139

OSWEGO TO KINGSTON, OGDENSBURGH, ETC.:
Port Ontario—Salmon River—Sacket's Harbor—Black
River—Chaumont Bay—Cape Vincent—Clayton, or
French, Creek—Alexandria Bay—Well's Island—Morristown—Ogdensburgh........................140-144

TRIP FROM NIAGARA AND HAMILTON TO TORONTO AND
KINGSTON, CANADA:
Port Dalhousie—Welland Canal—St. Catherine's—HAMILTON—Oakville—Port Credit—TORONTO—Oshawa—
Port Hope—Cobourg—Duck Island—Amherst Island—
KINGSTON.......................................145-154

KINGSTON TO BELLEVILLE AND PORT TRENTON:
Bay of Quinté—Fredericksburg—Picton—Belleville—
Port Trenton—River Trent—Rice Lake...........155-157

LIST OF AMERICAN AND BRITISH STEAMERS...........158-161

CANALS OF CANADA—Trade and Navigation.........160-162

TRIP FROM KINGSTON TO MONTREAL:
Thousand Islands—Wolfe, or Grand, Island—Gage Island—Howe Island—Carlton Island—Grindstone Island—
Admiralty Islands—Amateur Islands—Brockville—Prescott—Ogdensburgh—Windmill Point—Gallop Rapids—
Matilda—Waddington—Williamsburg—Louisville—

	Page
Long Saut Rapids—Cornwall—St. Regis—Lake St. Francis – Coteau du Lac—Cedar Rapids—Beauharnois—Caughnawaga—La Chine Rapids—St. Lawrence River and Rapids	163–176

RAILROAD ROUTE FROM MONTREAL TO TORONTO, *via* GRAND TRUNK RAILWAY:
St. Anne's—Isle Perot—Vaudreuil—Cornwall, etc...177–179

MONTREAL:
Grand Trunk Railway, etc......................180–185

TRIP FROM MONTREAL TO OTTAWA CITY, ETC.:
St. Anne's—Lake of the Two Mountains—Carillon—Point Fortune—Grenville—Rideau Falls—Chaudiere Falls—City of Ottawa—Aylmer—Arnprior—Pembroke.....186–190

OTTAWA RIVER:
Chaudiere Falls, etc...........................191–196

LAKE GEORGE:
Caldwell—Falls of Ticonderoga, etc............197–200

LAKE CHAMPLAIN:
Mississquoi Bay, etc..........................201–203

LIST OF STEAMERS running on Lake Champlain—Table of Distances—Whitehall, etc....................204–206

TRIP FROM WHITEHALL TO ROUSE'S POINT, ETC.:
Ticonderoga—Crown Point—Port Henry—Westport—Fort Cassin—Split Rock—Essex—BURLINGTON—Port Kent—Keeseville—Au Sable River—Port Jackson—PLATTSBURGH—Battle of Plattsburgh—Cumberland Head—Chazy—Isle au Motte—Alburgh—Highgate Springs—Nississquoi Bay—Rouse's Point—St. John's, Canada—Chambly Canal......................207–230

TABLE OF DISTANCES:
Montreal to Albany, Portland, Quebec, Toronto, etc. 231, 232

TRIP FROM MONTREAL TO QUEBEC:
Longueuil–Rapids of St. Mary—Varennes—Sorel, or William Henry—Lake St. Peter—Three Rivers—Richelieu Rapids—Cape Rouge—Wolfe's Cove...........233–237

QUEBEC:
The Citadel—Plains of Abraham—Wolfe's Monument—Gen. Montgomery.............................237–246

VICINITY OF QUEBEC:
Cape Rouge—Falls of Lorette—Falls of Montmorenci—Falls of St. Anne—Lake St. Charles—Point Levi—Chaudiere Falls..................................247–250

CONTENTS. ix

                  Page
TRIP FROM QUEBEC TO THE SAGUENAY RIVER, ETC. :
 Island of Orleans—St. Patrick's Hole—Madam Island—
 Cape Tourment—Grosse Island—St. Thomas—Crane
 Island—Isle aux Coudres—Murray Bay—Kamouraska—
 Red Island—River du Loup—Kakouna—Tadousac..251-259

SAGUENAY RIVER :
 Tête du Boule—St. Louis Island—Eternity Point and
 Cape Trinity—Tableau—Ha-Ha, or Great Bay—Chicou-
 timi—Lake St. John............................260-265

TRIP TO MURRAY BAY, TADOUSAC, HA-HA BAY, ETC..266-268

ANTICOSTI :
 Gulf of St. Lawrence, etc........................269-271

RAILROAD AND STEAMBOAT ROUTES.................... 272

GRAND PLEASURE EXCURSION :
 New York to Niagara Falls, Toronto, Montreal, etc. 273-275

TRIP FROM MONTREAL TO QUEBEC AND RETURN.......276-279

MONTREAL TO BOSTON AND NEW YORK..............280, 281

ROUTES OF TRAVEL from Montreal to Boston and New York 281

ROUTE from Montreal and Quebec to the White Mountains,
 and Portland, Me.................................. 282

WHITE MOUNTAINS OF NEW HAMPSHIRE..............283-286
 Height of the Principal Mountains................. 287

ROUTES to Lake Winnipisiogee and the White Mountains. 288

PORTLAND, City of 288-289

RAILWAY STATIONS in Boston........................ 290

RAILROAD ROUTES Diverging from Boston...........291-293

STEAMBOAT AND RAILROAD ROUTES from New York to the
 White Mountains................................... 294

ADVERTISEMENTS...................................... 295

LIST OF ADVERTISEMENTS.

	Page
New York and Albany Steamers (People's) Evening Line.	295
New York and Troy Steamers, Evening Line	296
New York and Albany Steamers, Morning Line	297
New York, Stonington, and Boston Line Steamers	298
Lake George Steamer	299
Lake Champlain Steamers	300
Lake Ontario and St. Lawrence Steamers	301
Lake Huron and Superior Line Steamers	302
Ottawa River Mail Steamers	303
Montreal and Quebec Steamers—Saguenay River	304
New York Central Railroad Lines to Buffalo, Niagara Falls, etc.	305
Albany and Troy to Saratoga Springs, Montreal, etc	306
Albany and Troy to Rutland, Burlington, Montreal, etc.	307
Great Western Railway of Canada	308
Grand Trunk Railway of Canada, etc	309
Sea-Bathing Pleasure Excursions	311
Boston to Portland *via* Eastern Railroad	312
Boston to Portland *via* Boston and Maine Railroad	313
Boston to the Green and White Mountains, Montreal, etc., *via* Vermont Central Railroad	314
Boston to Portland, Eastport, and St. Johns, N. B., *via* International Line Steamers	315
Hotels in the City of New York	11
" Saratoga Springs, etc	318
" Lake George	319
" Montreal, Quebec, Ottawa City, etc	320
" Boston	322
Congress Spring Water, Saratoga Springs	323
Empire Spring Water, " "	324

PRINCIPAL HOTELS IN THE CITY OF NEW YORK.

Name.	Proprietors.	Location.
Astor House	Stetson & Co.	Broadway, cor. Vesey St.
Bancroft House	M. L. & A. W. Bordwell.	Broadway, cor. 20th St.
Bond Street House	Charles Plinta	665 Broadway.
Brandreth House*	J. Curtis & Co.	Broadway, cor. Canal St
Brevoort House*	Albert Clark.	11 Fifth Avenue.
Clarendon	Kerner & Birch.	62 Union Place.
Commercial Hotel		78 Cortlandt St.
Cortlandt St. Hotel		28 Cortlandt St.
Dey Street House*	Charles W. Clickener	54, 56, and 58 Dey St.
Earl's Hotel		Canal St. cor. Centre.
Everett House		4th Avenue, cor. 17th St.
Fifth Avenue Hotel	Hitchcock, Darling & Co.	192 Fifth Avenue.
French's Hotel*		Chatham St., op. C. Hall.
Girard House*	Smith & Willard	129 Chambers St.
Howard Hotel	Lynde & Lamb	B'way, cor. Maiden Lane
International Hotel*	William H. Gilson	Broadway, cor. Franklin
Lafarge House	Henry Wheeler	673 Broadway. [St.
Libby House	M. Martin	58 Warren St.
Lovejoy's Hotel*		34 Park Row.
Manhattan Hotel	N. Huggins	Murray St., near B'way.
Merchants' Hotel	Clarke & Schenck	37, 39, & 41 Cortlandt St.
Metropolitan Hotel	S. Leland & Co.	580 Broadway.
National Hotel	Jesse Foster.	3, 5, & 7 Cortlandt St.
New York Hotel	Hiram Cranston	721 Broadway.
Pacific Hotel		172 Greenwich St.
Park Hotel		Cor. Beekman & Nassau.
Powers' Hotel		17 and 19 Park Row.
Prescott House	Frederick Diez	B'dway, cor Spring St
Spingler House	E. E. Balcom	5 and 7 Union Square.
St. Nicholas Hotel	Spotts & Hawk	Broadway.
Stevens' House*	Lyman Fisk	25 Broadway.
United States		Cor. Fulton & Water sts.
Washington Hotel*		1 Broadway.
Western Hotel	D. D. Winchester	9 Cortlandt St.

* Kept on the European Plan.

RAILROAD DEPOTS IN THE CITY OF NEW YORK.

New York, New Haven, and Boston R.R. Dépôt, Fourth Avenue, corner 27th Street.
New York and Harlem, to Albany, etc., Fourth Avenue, corner 26th Street.
Hudson River Railroad Dépôt, Warren Street, and 30th Street.
Erie Railroad, to Dunkirk, etc., foot Chambers Street.
Atlantic and Great Western, " " "
New Jersey Railway, to Philadelphia, etc., foot of Cortlandt Street.
New Jersey Central, to Easton, etc., foot of Cortlandt Street.
Pennsylvania Central Railroad, " " "
Morris & Essex Railroad, foot of Barclay Street.
Flushing and New York Railroad, James Slip and Hunter's Point, L. I.
Long Island Railroad, James Slip and Hunter's Point, L. I.

Lines of Steamers connecting with Railroads.

Fall River Line Steamers, Pier No. 3, North River.
Stonington Line Steamers, foot of Cortlandt Street.
Norwich Line Steamers, Pier No. 39, North River.
New Haven & Hartford Line, Peck Slip, East River.
Albany Morning Line, foot of Desbrosses Street, North River
Albany Evening Line (People's), foot Cortlandt St., " "
Troy Evening Line, foot of Liberty Street, " "
Newburgh and Poughkeepsie Line, foot of Jay Street, North River.
Camden & Amboy Line, foot of Barclay Street, North River.

TABLE OF DISTANCES, ETC.,

ROM THE CITY OF NEW YORK TO THE PRINCIPAL CITIES IN THE MIDDLE, NORTHERN, AND EASTERN STATES, AND CANADA.

ROUTES.	Miles.	H.	M.
EW YORK to NEWARK, N. J., via New Jersey Railroad...	9	0	30
Elizabethtown, " " ...	15	0	45
New Brunswick, " " ...	31	1	15
TRENTON, " " ...	58	2	30
PHILADELPHIA, via Phil. and Trenton R. R..	88	4	30
WILMINGTON, Del., via Phil. and Balt. R. R.	116	6	30
Havre de Grace, Md., " " "	150	8	00
BALTIMORE, " " " "	186	9	30
WASHINGTON, D. C., via Balt. and Ohio R. R.	225	11	30
EW YORK to HARRISBURG, Pa., via Philadelphia.........	194	9	00
Altoona, Pa., via Pennsylvania R. R.	324	15	00
PITTSBURGH, Pa., " "	441	20	30
CLEVELAND, O., via Pittsburgh.............	580	25	00
EW YORK to Goshen, via New York and Erie R. R	60	3	15
Port Jervis, " " "	89	4	00
Deposit, " " "	178	7	30
Great Bend, Pa., " " "	201	8	30
BINGHAMTON, " " "	216	9	00
Owego, " " "	238	9	45
ELMIRA, " " "	274	11	00
Corning, " " "	292	11	45
Hornellsville, " " "	333	13	30
BUFFALO, via Buffalo Division	424	18	00
DUNKIRK, via New York and Erie R. R.....	460	19	00
CLEVELAND, O., via Dunkirk................	602	25	00
CINCINNATI, O., via Cleveland	857	34	00
CHICAGO, Ill., via Cleveland and Toledo	957	37	00
EW YORK to Poughkeepsie, via Hudson River R. R.	75	2	45
Hudson, " " "	116	4	00
ALBANY, " " "	144	5	00
Schenectady, via New York Central R. R...	161	6	30
UTICA, " " " ...	239	9	30
Rome, " " " ..	253	10	20
Syracuse, " " " ..	292	12	00
Oswego, " " " ..	327	13	30
ROCHESTER, " " " ..	373	15	15
Batavia, " " " ..	406	16	20
BUFFALO, " " " ..	442	17	30
Lockport, " " " ..	429	17	00
NIAGARA FALLS, " " " ..	447	18	00
HAMILTON, Ca., via Great Western R. R. ..	490	21	00
TORONTO, " " " "	528	23	00
DETROIT, Mich., " " "	677	28	00
CHICAGO, Ill., via Michigan Central R. R....	960	37	00
EW YORK to ALBANY, via Hudson River R. R...........	144	5	00
TROY, " "	150	5	15
Saratoga Springs, via Albany and Troy.....	182	7	30
Lake George, via Saratoga Springs.........	211	10	00

2

TABLE OF DISTANCES, ETC.

Routes.	Miles.	H.	M.
New York to Whitehall. *via* Saratoga & Whitehall R. R.	223	9	00
Burlington, *via* Lake Champlain	300	16	00
Plattsburgh, " "	325	17	80
Rouse's Point. " "	350	19	00
Montreal. Ca., *via* Cham. and St. Law. R.R.	395	21	00
New York to Chatham Four Corners, N. Y. & Harlem R.R.	130	4	30
Albany, " " "	152	5	30
Troy, " " "	158	5	45
N. Bennington, Vt., *via* Troy & Boston R. R.	190	7	00
Rutland, " " " "	242	8	30
Burlington " *via* Rutland & Bur. R.R.	309	11	30
Rouse's Point, *via* Vermont & Canada R. R.	364	14	00
Montreal, Ca., *via* Cham. & St. Law. R. R.	408	16	00
New York to New Haven, Conn., *via* Railroad	76	3	00
Hartford " "	112	4	45
Springfield Mass., " "	138	5	45
Boston. *via* Western Railroad *.	236	9	00
Greenfield, *via* Connecticut River R. R.	174		
Bellows Falls, Vt., " " "	222		
Windsor, " " " "	248	15	00
White River Junction, *via* Verm. Cent. R. R.	262		
Wells' River, *via* Conn. & Pass. River R. R.	302	18	00
White Mountains. N. H., *via* White Mountain Railroad	342	22	00
New York to New London, Conn., *via* Steamer	115	7	30
Norwich. " "	127	8	00
Worcester. Mass. *via* Steamer and Railroad	186	10	80
Boston, " "	231	12	30
Nashua N. H.. *via* Wor. and Nashua R. R.	232		
Manchester, N. H., *via* Concord Railroad	249		
Concord, " " "	267	15	00
Wier's Station N. H. (Lake Winnipisseogee)	300	16	30
Plymouth N. H., *via* Boston Con. & Mont. Railroad	318		
Wells' River, Vt.. *via* Boston. Con., & Mont. Railroad	360	20	00
Littleton. N. H.. *via* White Mountain R R .	380		
White Mountains N. H.. *via* Stage	400	24	00
New York to Stonington Conn. *via* Steamer	125	8	00
Providence, R. I., *via* Steamer and Railroad	175	10	00
Boston, " "	218	12	00
Lawrence. Mass., *via* Boston & Maine R. R.	244		
Dover, N. H.. " " "	286		
Portland, Me. " " "	330	18	00
South Paris, Me., *via* Grand Trunk Railway	378		
Gorham N. H., " " "	421		
White Mountains, N. H., *via* Stage	428	24	00
New York to Newport R. I., *via* Steamer	160	10	00
Fall River, Mass. "	178	11	00
New Bedford, *via* Steamer and Railroad	204	12	00
Boston, " "	232	12	80
Salem Mass. *via* Eastern Railroad	248		
Newburyport, " "	268		
Portsmouth. N. H., " "	288		
Portland, Me. " "	339	19	00
Augusta, " *via* Kennebec & Portl. R. R.	399		
Bangor, " *via* Penobscot & Kenn. R. R.	469	24	00

NEW YORK AND HARLEM RAILROAD ROUTE.

DEPÔT, CORNER 4TH AVENUE AND 26TH STREET, NEW YORK.

THIS Railroad extends from the station in Centre Street, and runs through Broome Street, the Bowery, and Fourth Avenue to the outer depôt, corner Twenty-sixth Street; at Thirty-second Street it enters the deep cutting into the solid rock, at Murray Hill, which is covered over to Forty-first Street, and then proceeds to YORKVILLE, 5 miles, where is a *tunnel* under Prospect Hill, which is about 600 feet long, 24 feet wide, and 21 high, cut through solid rock; from thence it runs through HARLEM, 7 miles, crossing Harlem River over a substantial bridge, entering the county of Westchester at MOTT HAVEN, where is a thriving settlement, and several extensive manufacturing establishments.

MORRISANIA, ten miles, is a continuous settlement, which may justly be considered as the suburbs of New York. Here is a population of about 5,000, most of whom are connected with business in the city.

FORDHAM, 12 miles, is another village pleasantly situated on the line of the railroad. Here is located *St. John's College*, a Roman Catholic institution, standing on a slight eminence called Rose Hill. Thus far there is almost a continuous settlement on both sides the railroad, affording many delightful sites for suburban residences.

WILLIAMS' BRIDGE, 14 miles from New York, lying on the west bank of a small stream called Bronx River, is the station from whence diverges the *New York and New Haven Railroad*, extending eastwardly 76 miles to New Haven, Conn. This road forms in part the great railroad route from New York to Hartford, Springfield, Boston, etc.

WHITE PLAINS, 26 miles from the city, is a handsome village situated near the spot where was fought a sanguinary battle during the war of the Revolution, when this section of country was considered the *neutral ground*, extending north from King's Bridge, over the Harlem River, to Verplank's Point, near Peekskill. This quiet village is now the county seat of Westchester County, and contains besides the public buildings many handsome edifices, and several flourishing institutions of learning—this section of country, extending northward through the counties of Westchester and Putnam, being considered extremely healthy, abounding in pure water, and blessed with an invigorating climate

CROTON FALLS, 51 miles, is situated on Croton River, above the dam and reservoir from which the city of New York is supplied with pure and wholesome water. Here is a small village surrounded by hills extending northward through Putnam County. Passengers bound for *Lake Mahopac*, a few miles westward, here leave the cars and proceed by stage.

DOVER PLAINS, 80 miles from New York, is pleasantly situated in the east part of Dutchess County, about 20 miles from Poughkeepsie. The surrounding country is hilly, while on the east lies the range of high hills dividing the waters of the Hudson from those of the Housatonic River.

AMENIA, 88 miles from New York, is a small village, surrounded by hills and some good land.

BOSTON CORNERS, 103 miles from New York, now attached to Columbia County, N. Y., formerly belonged to Massachusetts. Here the Taghkanic Mountains on the east rise to a considerable height, being a spur of the Green Mountains of Vermont, running south through Dutchess and Putnam counties to the Hudson River, there being termed the " Highlands," or Matteawan Mountains. This range of mountains or highlands forms the dividing ridge between the waters that flow east into Long Island Sound from those flowing west into the Hudson River; in an extended point of view running from Westchester County to the confines of Canada.

CHATHAM FOUR CORNERS, 131 miles from New York, is the present terminus of the New York and Harlem Railroad. The Lebanon Springs Railroad, when finished, will extend north to the Vermont State Line. Through this village runs the Albany and West Stockbridge Railroad, forming a branch of the *Western Railroad* of Massachusetts; also, the Hudson and Boston Railroad, run by the above company, thus forming direct and speedy routes of travel from Albany and Hudson to Springfield, Worcester, Boston, etc

Over the Albany and West Stockbridge Railroad passengers are now conveyed from Chatham Four Corners to Albany, a farther distance of 22 miles; making a total distance from New York to Albany by this route of 153 miles. At EAST ALBANY it connects with the great lines of travel North to Saratoga and Montreal, and West to Buffalo and Niagara Falls. For Table of Distances, etc., see pages 13 and 14.

HUDSON RIVER RAILROAD ROUTE.

DEPÔT, COR. WARREN ST. AND COLLEGE PLACE, NEW YORK.

THIS important Railroad extends through Hudson Street, Canal Street, and West Street, to the outer depôt at Thirty-first Street; from thence it runs along the west shore of the island of New York to MANHATTANVILLE, 8 miles. Here is a village surrounded by high and picturesque grounds, where are located many handsome private edifices.

FORT WASHINGTON, about 9 miles from the city, stands on elevated ground, commanding a fine view of the Hudson and East rivers, and the surrounding country. In this vicinity the rock excavation is over a quarter of a mile in length, on the line of the railroad, the cutting being between 40 and 50 feet deep for a considerable distance. Here, also, at Fort Washington Point, is erected a telegraph pole, from which extends several wires across the Hudson River, to the *Palisades* on the Jersey shore, above Fort Lee.

SPUYTEN DUYVEL CREEK, 13 miles from Chambers Street, is a continuation or branch of Harlem River, dividing the island of New York from Westchester County. Here is a draw-bridge for the convenience of navigation—this stream being susceptible of improvement so as to allow vessels to pass through into the East River or Long Island Sound, going through *Hell-Gate*.

YONKERS, 17 miles from New York, is delightfully situated on the east bank of the Hudson, here doubly interesting from its romantic and picturesque beauties. The bold and abrupt eminence called the "Palisades" stands on the Jersey side, while the hilly and rolling country of the opposite side, where runs the line of the railroad, gives a great charm to this locality. The village contains many fine residences, several churches, hotels, and stores. It may be regarded as a suburb, as most of its inhabitants are connected with business in the city of New York.

HASTINGS, 20 miles; DOBBS' FERRY, 22 miles; IRVINGTON, 25 miles, and TARRYTOWN, 27 miles from New York, may all be justly considered as suburban villages, most of their inhabitants being closely connected in business pursuits with the city of New York.

SING SING, 32 miles, is another handsomely situated and healthy location, being closely connected with the city of New York, both by water and railroad communication. The *Sing Sing State Prison*, located here, contains about 1,000 inmates.

PEEKSKILL, 44 miles, is another romantic and thriving village, lying in the immediate vicinity of the Hudson River and "*Highlands.*" The latter here assumes a mountain-like appearance, running northward for several miles, through which the river finds a tortuous passage, passing WEST POINT, 52 miles; COLD SPRING, 52 miles, to FISHKILL LANDING, 60 miles north of New York. Here is a steam ferry, connecting Fishkill with Newburgh on the opposite shore. On winding through the "Highlands," several *tunnels* are entered and passed in quick succession, giving the traveler a vivid idea of the uneven and rocky section through which the track of the railroad passes. At one time water may be seen on both sides the track, when the next moment the fierce locomotive plunges out of sight under a mountain brow—with the majestic Hudson on the one side, and the frowning hills or mountains on the opposite side, rising from 1,000 to 1,500 feet above the water's edge. The longest tunnel on the route occurs a short distance above Fishkill.

The City of POUGHKEEPSIE, 75 miles above New York and 70 miles below Albany, situated on east side of the Hudson, is a large and growing place, where the passenger trains of cars usually stop for a few minutes, affording an opportunity to partake of a hasty meal.

HYDE PARK, 81 miles; RHINEBECK, 91 miles; TIVOLI, 100 miles; OAK HILL, opposite Catskill, 110 miles, are speedily reached and passed by the ascending train of cars, affording the traveler a grand view of the *Catskill Mountains* on the opposite side of the river.

The City of HUDSON, 116 miles from New York and 29 from Albany, is an old and interesting locality, being favorably situated at the head of ship navigation on the river. The *Hudson and Boston Railroad* extends eastward from this place to the New York State Line, connecting with the *Western Railroad* of Massachusetts.

COXSACKIE STATION, 123 miles; STUYVESANT, 126 miles; SCHODACK, 133 miles; CASTLETON, 136 miles, and EAST ALBANY, 144 miles, are the next stations reached. At the latter passengers alight for Albany—crossing the Hudson River in a steam ferry—while those going to TROY, 6 miles farther, or are bound northward, remain in the cars, soon arriving at the latter city.

For further information, see Albany and Troy, described in another part of this work.

TOUR
FROM
NEW YORK TO ALBANY, TROY, ETC.,
VIA
HUDSON RIVER.

During the season of navigation on the Hudson, which usually extends from about the 20th of March to the fore part of December, numerous steamboats leave the city of New York every morning and evening, for various places on both shores of the river. The boats of the largest class, nowhere excelled for comfort and speed, run through to Albany and Troy, about 150 miles, in ten to twelve hours running time; others touch at the principal villages on the way, to land and receive passengers. Usual fare through, $2 00, including berths in the night boats.

To the traveler for pleasure and health, the day boats are the most desirable, particularly in hot weather, when a night's confinement in a crowded cabin is very oppressive; and they furnish a fine opportunity to enjoy the varied and beautiful scenery of this noble river.

The panoramic view on leaving the city is extensive and grand. Seaward it embraces parts of Long Island and Staten Island, with the "Narrows;" the spacious Bay of New York, studded with Governor's, Bedlow's, and Ellis's islands: the Jersey shore on the west, with its settlements and cultivated fields; and on the east the city itself, with its long ranges of wharves and shipping, its spires, and its masses of architecture; and as the boat rounds out upon the bosom of the majestic river, and springs forward on her upward course, the view, crowded with striking contrasts and full of life and action, is one of rare beauty and interest.

JERSEY CITY, opposite the lower part of New York, and HOBOKEN, a mile north, are seen to great advantage as the steamboat leaves the wharf. At the former place commences the *New Jersey Railroad* and the *New York and Erie Railroad.* The latter place is a delightful and favorite resort of the citizens of New York during the warm summer season, when the commodious steam ferry-boats are crowded every afternoon with parties of both sexes, seeking refreshment from the heated and thronged streets of the city, in that charming retreat.

WEEHAWKEN, on the Jersey shore, north of Hoboken, and 3 miles from New York, a high, wooded cliff, with its bold, rocky bluffs partly vailed with trees and partly bare, and a handsome villa on its summit, is one of the finest points in the scene as you move up the river. At the foot of this cliff, and on the margin of the river, a small obelisk of white marble for many years marked the spot where Alexander Hamilton fell in his fatal duel with Aaron Burr, on the 12th July, 1804. The monument, however, has long since been removed.

BULL'S FERRY, 2 to 3 miles farther north, on the same shore, is a place of considerable resort, being connected with the city by a steam ferry.

BLOOMINGDALE, on York Island, 5 miles from the City Hall, is a scattered settlement, in which the most prominent object is the *Orphan Asylum*, which, as seen from the river, with its green lawn extending to the water's edge, and surrounded by a fine grove, presents a pleasing aspect.

About 3 miles farther up the island, or 8 miles from the City Hall, is the *Lunatic Asylum*, a stately pile standing on elevated ground.

The next conspicuous object on the island, and visible from the Hudson, is MANHATTANVILLE, about a mile and a half east of which, toward the East River and near Hell-Gate, is the village of HARLEM.

FORT WASHINGTON, 2 miles north of Manhattanville, is elevated 238 feet above the river, being the highest point on the island of New York. The old fort was captured by the British and Hessians, in the disastrous campaign of 1776, when some two or three thousand Americans were either killed or taken captive, and thrown into the prison-ships at the Wallabout Bay, Brooklyn, where the United States now have an extensive Navy Yard.

FORT LEE, on the Jersey shore, 10 miles from New York, is a place of considerable interest, and between it and that city a steam ferry-boat plies daily. The site of the old fort is on the brow of the Palisades, a short distance from the river, and elevated about 300 feet above it. It was surrendered to the British in 1776, immediately after the capture of Fort Washington.

The PALISADES, the most striking and peculiar feature of the scenery on either side of the Hudson, commence a little north of Wechawken, and on the same shore. This descriptive designation has been given to a majestic range of columnar rock, varying in height from 100 feet to 350 feet, and walling in the Hudson as far as Piermont, a distance of 20 miles. Just above Fort Lee, they rise almost perpendicularly from the water's edge; and as the channel of the river, for the whole 20 miles, runs near the west side and along the base of these majestic cliffs, they are seen to great advantage from the deck of the passing steamboat.

SPUYTEN DUYVEL CREEK flows into the Hudson 13 miles north of the City Hall of New York, and connects with the Harlem River on the east, thus separating the island of New York from Westchester County. It is crossed by the track of the *Hudson River Railroad*, where is a draw-bridge. KINGSBRIDGE, on the great post-road from New York to Albany, crosses this creek about a mile from its mouth, near which, on the north bank, is the site of old *Fort Independence*. Here commences a succession of beautifully situated country residences, looking out upon the river, and across it to the Palisades; the shore itself being marked by a succession of narrow valleys and ridges running back with a gradual ascent to the north and south range of highland, which separates the waters flowing into the Hudson from those which pass off to the East River and Long Island Sound. As you advance up through Westchester, this north and south ridge becomes more elevated and rocky. It is, in fact, the commencement of that extensive and lofty range which soon enlarges itself into the "Highlands," or Fishkill Mountains, farther north swells into the still loftier Taghkanic group, and finally attains its highest grandeur in the Green Mountains of Vermont.

YONKERS, 17 miles north of New York, is a thriving village in Westchester County, at the mouth of Sawmill River. It contains many fine dwelling-houses, about 12,000 inhabitants, and is the summer resort of many citizens of New York, being easily reached by railroad, or the steamboats which ply daily between that city, Sing Sing, and Peekskill. It is surrounded by very pleasant scenery, and commands a fine view of the Hudson and the Palisades.

HASTINGS, 3 miles north of Yonkers, is a convenient landing-place, at which the smaller steamboats touch to receive and discharge passengers.

DOBBS' FERRY, 22 miles north of New York, is the name of a village, where is a convenient steamboat wharf. This was an important point in the military operations of the Revolutionary war. A ferry communicates with the opposite shore at the foot of the Palisades, a little north of the boundary line between the States of New York and New Jersey; and from this point northward both sides of the Hudson are in New York.

PIERMONT, formerly known as *Tappan Landing*, or the "Sloat," is on the west shore of the Hudson, 24 miles from the city of New York. It has become a place of importance as the *terminus* of a branch of the New York and Erie Railroad. The line of this great work, from New York to Dunkirk, on the shore of Lake Erie, is 460 miles long. At Piermont a substantial pier, more than a mile long, has been constructed, extending from the shore to the channel of the Hudson. A steamboat plies daily between this place and New York, and connects with the cars running on the railroad. At this point, also, the Palisades terminate on the north by an abrupt hill. This *hill* and the extensive *pier* already mentioned, being the two most distinguishing features of the place, they have been appropriately combined to form the name of *Piermont.*

Two or three miles west from the river is the old village of TAPPAN, memorable as having been for a time the head-quarters of Washington and the American army during the Revolution, and the place where Major Andre was executed, on the 2d of October, 1780.

TAPPAN BAY—or, as it was usually called in earlier times, *Tappan Sea*—being an expansion of the river, commences at Piermont and extends northward to Croton, or Teller's Point, a distance of 10 miles, with an average width of about 3 miles. On the eastern shore of this bay, in the midst of a beautiful landscape, is the favorite country residence of Washington Irving. Nowhere on either shore of the Hudson is the scenery more distinguished for its picturesque beauty, having the Palisades in full view at the southwest; at the west and north a fine range of hills stretching away to the grand mountain masses of the "Highlands," with the broad river between.

IRVINGTON, 25 miles, is the name given to a small settlement about 3 miles north of Dobbs' Ferry.

The village of TARRYTOWN is beautifully situated on the east bank of the river, overlooking Tappan Bay, 27 miles north of the city of New York. It contains about 450 dwelling-houses and 3,000 inhabitants. Steamboats running to New York touch daily at this place. Immediately north is BEEKMANTOWN, where is the *Irving Institute*, a school of much celebrity, and a venerable Dutch Reformed Church, erected about the middle of the seventeenth century. Tarrytown is famed as being the place where Major Andre was captured, while watering his horse, on his return from West Point, and from a personal interview with the traitor, General Arnold. Immediately north

Palisades.—Hudson River.

of this village, also, is the famous *Sleepy Hollow*, where Washington Irving laid the scene of his entertaining legend of that name.

NYACK, on the western side of the bay or river, is a pleasant and thriving place, between which and New York a steamboat plies daily. Here Tappan Bay spreads to its greatest width, presenting a noble expanse of water.

ROCKLAND LAKE, 2 or 3 miles northwest of Nyack, is a picturesque sheet of the purest water, from which large quantities of ice are annually sent to the New York market.

SING SING, 32 miles from New York, is handsomely situated on the east bank of the Hudson River. It has four landings, from which steamboats and vessels ply daily to and from the city, affording a pleasant excursion. The main part of the village is situated on high and uneven ground, rising 180 feet above tide-water, and overlooking Tappan and Haverstraw bays, the Hudson and Croton rivers, and the surrounding country, including a distant view of the Palisades and the Highlands. Sing Sing was incorporated in 1813, and now contains about 3,500 inhabitants. This village derives its name from the Indian words "*Ossin-Sing*," meaning in their language the *place of stone*. It is now celebrated for its marble quarries, which are worked to a great extent by the State Prison convicts, who have here erected two large prisons, a keeper's house, and several ranges of workshops, from materials found on the State farm: where is also located a silver mine, which was worked to some extent previous to the Revolution, and a copper mine which has been more recently worked. The marble found in this vicinity is of a medium quality, and almost inexhaustible; large quantities are annually quarried and sent to the city of New York and other places. Here is to be seen a beautiful viaduct, over which is conveyed the acqueduct for supplying the city of New York with pure and wholesome water.

The MOUNT PLEASANT STATE PRISON is situated about half a mile south of the village of Sing Sing. The prison grounds consist of 130 acres of land, lying between the villages of Sing Sing and Sparta, being bounded on the east by the Highland turnpike, and on the west by the Hudson River, which here affords a depth of twelve feet of water at the landing. The main prison building is 484 feet in length, north and south, and 44 feet in width, fronting westerly on the Hudson, being five stories in height, and containing 1,000 cells; in front and rear are located workshops of different kinds, which, together with the keeper's house, are all built of rough dress marble. Attached to the prison building, on the south, is a chapel, hospital, kitchen, storehouses, etc. A new prison for female convicts stands on elevated ground, and is built of marble in the Ionic order.

CROTON, or TELLER's POINT, about a mile north of Sing Sing, separates Tappan from Haverstraw Bay. It projects southerly into the river more than a mile, immediately above the confluence of the Croton River with the Hudson. On the opposite side of the river rises *Verdreitje's Hook*, a bold headland 668 feet high, forming a beautiful feature in the landscape.

HAVERSTRAW BAY is another expansion of the Hudson River, 2 to 3 miles wide and 6 miles long, terminating on the north at Verplank's and Stony Points.

HAVERSTRAW, or WARREN, lies on the west side of the bay or river, 35 miles from New York, to which city a steamboat runs daily.

GRASSY POINT, 2 miles above, on the same side of the river, is a convenient steamboat landing.

VERPLANK's POINT, on the east side of the river, 40 miles north of the city of New York, is an excellent landing-place, and memorable from its connection, in the Revolutionary war, with STONY POINT, on the opposite side. On the latter point is now a light-house, erected on the site of the old fortification, which completely commanded the channel of the river. These points, where the river contracts to about half a mile in width, were the first important positions north of the city of New

York at which the American forces attempted to defend the passage of the Hudson against the British, in the struggle for independence. (*See Engraving.*)

CALDWELL'S LANDING, on the west side of the river, 44 miles from New York and 101 miles from Albany, is the first place at which steam passage-boats of the large class touch on their upward trip, to land and receive passengers. This landing is situated at the south entrance of the "Highlands," and is connected by a steam ferry with

The village of PEEKSKILL, 43 miles from New York, a large and thriving village, from which two or three steamboats run directly to the city of New York, carrying large quantities of produce, manufactured articles, and passengers. It was incorporated in 1827, and now contains 4,500 inhabitants, 8 churches, 6 public houses, 30 stores, and about 600 dwellings, besides many large manufacturing establishments.

On *Oak Hill*, where is now situated the Peekskill Academy, is a venerable oak tree, on which was hung, during the Revolutionary war, two noted spies, Strang and Palmer. Peekskill was then the head-quarters of the American army under General Putnam, who here dated his laconic reply to Sir Henry Clinton, commander of the British forces in the city of New York, who sent up a flag of truce, demanding the release of Edmund Palmer, a lieutenant of a Tory regiment, who had been detected in the American camp. The following was the reply sent back by Putnam:

"HEAD-QUARTERS, 7*th Aug.*, 1777.

' Edmund Palmer. an officer in the enemy's service. was taken as a spy, lurking within the American lines; he has been tried as a spy condemned as a spy, and shall be executed as a spy, and the flag is ordered to depart immediately. ISRAEL PUTNAM.

'' P. S. He has been accordingly executed."

During summer, a stage leaves Peekskill every day for Mahopac Lake, and in the hottest of the season, when the lake is most visited, twice a day, leaving Peekskill morning and evening.

MAHOPAC LAKE is a beautiful sheet of water in the town of Carmel, Putnam County, and is one of the chief sources of the Croton River. It is about one mile in diameter, and embosoms two or three small islands. The waters abound with various kinds of fish of a fine flavor. It is a place of considerable resort, with good accommodations for visitors. Here is a good public house for the accommodation of strangers.

Old FORT INDEPENDENCE lies opposite Caldwell's Landing, on the northeast, near the mouth of the Peekskill. The situation is delightful, facing down the river, with an unobstructed view for many miles, while immediately in the rear rise the "Highlands" in majestic grandeur.

On leaving Caldwell's Landing, the river takes a sudden turn to the west for about a mile, this reach having the local designation of the "*Horse Race*," and then resumes its northern course, passing between the bold, wooded, and overshadowing hills known as the "*Highlands*," or "Matteawan Mountains." This latter name, meaning "the country for good fur," was given by the aborigines, and is a fine, distinctive, and appropriate name for the whole group

The "HIGHLANDS," the grandest, and next to the Palisades, the most remarkable feature of the scenery of the Hudson, are about 16 miles in width, and extend in a southwest and northeast direction for some 20 or 30 miles, covering a part of the counties of Rockland and Orange on the west side of the river, and Putnam and Dutchess on the east. Several of their summits reach an elevation of 1,000 to 1,685 feet. This may be considered classic ground, as many of the points or eminences in view from the river are celebrated in history for being the scene of stirring events during the struggle for American Independence, 1776 to 1783.

The sites of old *Fort Clinton* and *Montgomery*, of Revolutionary memory, are on the west side of the river, opposite the lower *Anthony's Nose*, 6 miles below West Point. These forts, deemed almost impregnable, were erected at this point for the defense of the river, which was also obstructed by chevaux-defrise, boom, and chains. On the 6th of October, 1777, they were attacked by a superior British force under Sir Henry Clinton, and captured after a sharp resistance, the garrison of 600 men being overpowered by a disciplined army of 3,000 strong. The works were resolutely defended until dark, when the enemy effected an entrance at several places, there not being a sufficient number of soldiers in the fort to man the lines.

WEST POINT is romantically situated on the west bank of the Hudson River, 52 miles from New York and 93 miles from Albany. It is the seat of the United States Military Academy, established by an act of Congress in March, 1802, and the land ceded to the United States Government by the State of New York, 1826. Here are now erected two stone barracks, one of three and the other four stories in height, occupied by 250 cadets, which is the number authorized by law; an academic hall, a large three-story stone building, 275 feet in length, by 75 feet in width, used for military exercises in winter, and as a depository of the chemical apparatus, models of fortification, artillery, architecture, and machines, and as recitation and drawing rooms; a new and beautiful two-story stone building, to be used for the library and philosophical apparatus, constructed in the Elizabethan style of architecture, and is 150 feet in length by 60 feet in width; the north front has three towers suited for the astronomical apparatus; the center tower is surmounted by a dome of 28 feet 10 inches in diameter, the whole of which revolves on its vertical axis, adapting it to the use of a large equatorial telescope; a chapel, an hospital, a mess hall, two cavalry stables, several workshops and store-rooms, and seventeen separate dwellings occupied by the officers of the institution. In addition to the above, here are located a magazine, a laboratory, soldiers' barracks, a store, and about 25 dwelling-houses, occupied by families connected with the military school—in all containing a population of about 1,000 souls. Here, also, is a well-kept hotel, calculated to accommodate about 150 visitors.

No place in the Union, probably, exceeds West Point in beauty of location and the stirring incidents connected with its early history, being "hallowed by the footsteps of Washington and Kosciusko," during the Revolutionary struggle, the interest in which is continued to the present time by its being the residence and school of the future defenders of the Union. In 1777, immediately after the capture of Forts Clinton and Montgomery by the British army, West Point was first occupied by the American army, and fortified at the instance of Gov. George Clinton, of Revolutionary memory. At the present time are to be seen the remains of Forts Putnam and Arnold (after the treason of the latter, called Fort Clinton), which is situated on the extreme eastern point of this military position, 160 feet above tide-water, while Fort Putnam is situated on Mount Independence, 1,000 yards southwest, elevated about 500 feet above the river; there are also numerous other redoubts and batteries crowning the various eminences in the vicinity, built under the direction of the celebrated Kosciusko as engineer. In August, 1780, General Arnold was assigned to the command of this important military station, extending from Fishkill to Verplank's Point. On the 25th of September he precipitately made his escape from his head-quarters, the *Robinson House*, situated two miles below West Point, on the opposite side of the river, his treason having been discovered by the fortunate capture of Major Andre. From this period to the close of the Revolutionary war in 1783, West Point was garrisoned by a strong division of the American army; after which the garrison was reduced, and this location made a depôt for the Revolutionary armament and other military stores. In 1794, at the recommendation of General Washington, a military school was commenced in a building which was burned down two years thereafter, and the school suspended until 1802.

There are now connected with the West Point Academy thirty-four officers and professors, a company of artillery, and a detachment of dragoons, besides the cadets, who generally remain here for a period of four years, in which time they are qualified to become subaltern officers of the several corps of the army.

No stranger should leave this place without visiting the public buildings, Kosciusko's Monument, and a wild and romantic retreat near the water's edge called " Kosciusko's Garden." the ruins of old Fort Putnam, which commands a view of West Point, the Hudson River, and the surrounding mountain scenery. The Cemetery, about half a mile north of the hotel, is also well worthy of a visit.

On the south, toward Buttermilk Falls, about a mile distant, there is a pleasant road running near the river, and most of the way through a beautiful grove of trees. In this vicinity, and most agreeably located, is situated Cozzens' Hotel, under the superintendence of a favorite publican.

If the visitor tarries through the day at this attractive place, any time during the summer months, when the hotels are usually thronged with fashionable people from every section of the Union, he will have an opportunity to view West Point in all its loveliness

The village of COLD SPRING, 54 miles from New York, a mile or more above West Point, on the opposite side of the river, is a thriving manufacturing village. Here are situated the extensive iron works commonly known as the " West Point Foundry," and supposed to be on as broad a scale as any in the Union, and a machine shop, giving constant employment to about 500 workmen. The largest kind of machinery, for steamboat and other purposes, and warlike implements, are here constructed. The ore on which the works depend is found in the immediate vicinity; and there is also a quarry of granite of a very superior quality, easy of access, and inexhaustible.

BEACON HILL and BREAKNECK, both on the east side of the river, are situated immediately above Cold Spring. The former, sometimes called the " *Grand Sachem*," is the highest peak of the Highlands, being elevated 1,685 feet above the river. The latter presents the rocky projection called the " *Upper Anthony's Nose.*"

CROW'S NEST and BUTTER HILL are situated on the west side of the river. They rise abruptly from the water's edge. The latter, which is the more northerly peak, lifts its summit 1,520 feet above the Hudson, and the other is nearly as high.

POLLOPEL'S ISLAND is a mass of rock lying in the Hudson River, near its east shore, at the northern entrance into the Highlands, 6 miles above West Point. Here the river begins to widen and expand to the width of more than a mile for some 5 or 6 miles, for which distance it is sometimes called *Newburgh Bay*.

CORNWALL, CANTERBURY, and NEW WINDSOR are small villages situated on the west side of the river, immediately above the Highlands, the last-named village being distinguished as the birth-place of De Witt Clinton.

NEWBURGH, 61 miles north of New York and 84 south of Albany, is pleasantly situated on rising ground, on the west bank of the river. It was incorporated in 1800, and now contains about 12000 inhabitants, 1,500 dwelling-houses, a court-house, and jail, this being a half-shire of Orange County; a Theological Seminary under the direction of the Associate Reformed Presbyterian denomination; an incorporated academy; a high school, two female seminaries, and a number of select schools, all in a flourishing condition; two large public libraries; eleven churches of different denominations; three banking-houses; fourteen hotels and taverns; 150 stores of different kinds; nine storehouses; five freighting establishments; four steamboats and two barges, running to and from the city of New York, besides a number of sloops trading to different places on the Hudson River, and schooners and other craft running to Southern and Eastern ports, altogether transporting an immense amount of lumber, coal, plaster, and agricultural and manufactured products; two good steamboats, also, are attached to the ferry between this place and Fishkill, on the opposite side of the river, which is here about one mile in width. The location of Newburgh, in addition to its romantic beauty and healthiness, is peculiarly favorable as a place of business, being surrounded by a rich grazing and agricultural region, celebrated for butter and livestock. The *Newburgh Branch* of the New York and Erie Railroad extends from this place to Chester, 20 miles.

Newburgh was for a period the head-quarters of Gen. Washington, and at the close of the Revolutionary war the army was here disbanded, June 23, 1783. The celebrated *Newburgh Letters*, addressed to the officers and men of the army, were here dated, supposed to have been written by the late General John Armstrong.

It is proposed to erect a suitable column to the memory of Washington, in front of the old stone house, in the south part of this village, where his family resided; it is to be from 80 to 100 feet high, constructed of white marble or granite, at an estimated cost of $50,000. It will be in plain sight from the water, commanding one of the finest prospects on the Hudson.

FISHKILL LANDING, 60 miles from New York by railroad route, lies on the east side of the river, directly opposite Newburgh, with which it is connected by a steam ferry, is a thriving village, containing about 1,500 inhabitants, and surrounded by delightful country residences.

MATTEAWAN, an extensive and celebrated manufacturing village, is situated on the Fishkill, a mile and a half east of Fishkill Landing.

GLENHAM, 3 miles from the landing, is also a celebrated manufacturing village, celebrated for its superior woolen cloths.

The village of FISHKILL is pleasantly situated on a plain, 5 miles east of Fishkill Landing, and 65 miles north of the city of New York, on the great post-road to Albany. This road, from Peckskill to Fishkill, a distance of 19 miles, traverses the Highlands, and is remarkable for its formidable hills and the wild scenery of this mountain route. As you approach Fishkill from the south, the character of the scenery suddenly changes to that of a fertile and cultivated farming district.

During the Revolutionary war, this village was for a period

the head-quarters of the American army. The church is still standing here in which Enoch Crosby, the spy of Revolutionary memory, was confined for a time, his escape being admirably described in Cooper's romance of the "SPY," under the assumed name of *Harvey Birch.*

NEW HAMBURGH, 6 miles north of Newburgh, is a steamboat landing on the east side of the river, where Wappinger's Creek, an important mill-stream, empties into the Hudson.

HAMPTON is another landing nearly opposite, being connected with New Hamburgh by a ferry. One or two miles north is the village of MARLBOROUGH.

BARNEGAT, a few miles above, on the east side of the river, is celebrated for the manufacture of large quantities of lime.

MILTON, 9 miles above Newburgh, and 4 miles below Poughkeepsie, is a convenient steamboat landing; the village stands about half a mile back from the river.

The City of POUGHKEEPSIE is handsomely situated on the east side of the Hudson, about equi-distant between the cities of New York and Albany, being 75 miles from the former, and 71 from the latter by water. It was incorporated in 1801 as a village, and chartered as a city in 1854; it now contains about 15,000 inhabitants; 1,600 dwelling-houses, many of them tasty edifices; a court-house, and jail and county poor-house; a splendid collegiate building; the Dutchess Academy; two female seminaries, besides several select schools; a lyceum and reading-room; two public markets; one Presbyterian, one Congregational, two Episcopal, one Baptist, two Methodist, one Dutch Reformed, one Universalist, one Roman Catholic, and one African Church, and two Friends' meeting-houses; three banking-houses, and a savings' institution. Poughkeepsie contains several well-kept hotels and taverns; 30 dry good stores, 60 groceries, besides a large number of other different kinds of stores and shops; also two breweries, one of which is very extensive, perhaps the largest in the State, being capable of making 30.000 barrels of beer annually, and an extensive pin manufactory. Here are owned three steamboats, three freight barges, and eight sloops, engaged in transporting produce and merchandize to and from the New York market, and other places on the river. No place on the Hudson exceeds this city for beauty of location; it is surrounded by one of the richest agricultural districts in the Union, and may justly be ranked as the queen of cities in the Empire State. Population in 1855, 12,763.

The Poughkeepsie Collegiate School, situated on *College Hill*, about half a mile northeast of the compact part of the village, is unrivaled in its location, commanding an extensive prospect of the river and surrounding country, which can not fail to excite the admiration of every lover of picturesque scenery; in addition to the collegiate building, which is a splendid edifice, here has been erected an extensive gymnasium. This is a well-established and flourishing institution, conducted on philosophical principles.

Poughkeepsie is a corruption of the Indian word *Apokeepsing*, signifying *safe harbor*. It was early settled, and in 1788 the State convention met here to ratify the federal Constitution of the United States; previous to that date the State legislature frequently convened in this city, which has long been considered a favorite place of residence.

The *Hudson River Railroad* affords a speedy communication with the city of New York on the south, and Albany on the north. Cars arrive and depart almost hourly.

The *Landing* opposite Poughkeepsie is in the town of NEW PALTZ, by which name it is called. A ferry here crosses the Hudson; a short distance from the river is a scattered settlement. Three or four miles above Poughkeepsie, is a turn in the river called *Crum-Elbow*.

HYDE PARK, 80 miles from New York and 65 from Albany, is pleasantly situated on the east side of the Hudson. The principal settlement is about half a mile from the landing. It contains three churches, two public houses, several stores and shops, about 140 dwelling-houses, and 900 inhabitants. No section of the country between New York and Albany excels this part of Dutchess County for the beauty of its country residences.

At STAATSBURGH, 5 miles north of the village of Hyde Park, are situated several fine country residences.

ESOPUS MEADOWS, as they are called, 6 or 7 miles above Hyde Park, are extensive marshes, covered with water during high tide; they lie opposite the town of Esopus, on the west side of the river. PELHAM is a small landing on the same side, a little south of the meadows.

RONDOUT, 89 miles north of the city of New York, is situated at the mouth of a large stream of the same name, where there is a light-house built by the United States government. This is an important place of considerable trade, containing an active population of about 8,000 inhabitants; many of whom are engaged in navigation, and others are furnished employment by the *Delaware and Hudson Canal*, which terminates at EDDYVILLE, 2 miles above Rondout. The canal is 108 miles in length, extending in connection with a railroad of 16 miles, to the coal mines of Pennsylvania. From the mouth of Rondout Creek a number of steamboats, freight barges, and sloops are regularly employed in carrying an immense quantity of Lackawaxen coal, lumber, lime, and produce of different kinds. Stages run from this place to the village of Kingston, and to the Landing opposite Rhinebeck, where the line boats land and receive passengers several times daily.

KINGSTON LANDING is situated on the west side of the Hudson River, 90 miles north of the city of New York; this Landing was formerly called *Columbus Point*. A steam ferry-boat here plies across the river.

The village of KINGSTON is handsomely situated on a plain, through which flows the Esopus Creek, 3 miles west of the landing on the river. It was incorporated in 1805, and now contains about 7,000 inhabitants, 800 dwelling-houses, a court-house and jail; six churches; two banking-houses, an incorporated academy in a flourishing condition, and a female seminary; also several well-kept public houses. Stages leave this place three times a week for Dehli, Delaware County; a tri-weekly line also leaves for Ellenville, and accommodation stages are in constant attendance, and run to the several steamboats that land and receive passengers at Rondout and Kingston Landing. Kingston, anciently called *Esopus*, was early settled by the Dutch, many of whose descendants now reside in this vicinity.

In April, 1777, the first convention of the Representatives of the State of New York met in the village of Kingston, and formed the Old Constitution of the State; and on the 16th day of October following it was taken and burnt by the British army, under the command of Gen. Vaughan, while marching to the relief of Gen. Burgoyne, who was obliged to surrender to the American army on the following day at Schuylerville. Immediately after destroying the village, the British troops precipitately retreated to their vessels lying in the Hudson River, and returned to the city of New York. Some of the ruins of the stone buildings were standing as late as 1836, when the last of the walls were taken down, and the Kingston banking-house erected on the same spot.

RHINEBECK LANDING, 90 miles from New York and 55 from Albany, is situated on the east side of the river. In this vicinity are located a number of beautiful country residences overlooking the Hudson.

The village of RHINEBECK is handsomely situated on a plain, 2 miles east of the landing. It is incorporated, and now contains about 1,600 inhabitants. This vicinity was early settled by Dutch families, many of whose descendants still retain the habits and language of their forefathers, and are a frugal and prosperous class of citizens.

BARRYTOWN, or *Redhook Lower Landing*, also on the east side of the Hudson, is 97 miles from New York, and is surrounded by several delightful country residences. The *Catskill Mountains*, in the west, at a distance of some 12 or 15 miles, may now be seen from the river to great advantage; and the *Catskill Mountain House*, elevated nearly 3,000 feet above the Hudson, is distinctly visible in clear weather. It stands near the precipitous front of a rocky *plateau*, of a few acres in extent, called *Pine Orchard*, from the scattered pines which formerly grew out from the fissures of the rock. It commands a vast and noble prospect, and is a most refreshing retreat from the heats of summer.

TIVOLI, or *Upper Redhook Landing*, 100 miles from New York and 45 miles from Albany, is a regular steamboat landing. In this vicinity are also a great number of beautiful country residences. In the Hudson, near Tivoli, are annually taken, during the months of May and June, large quantities of shad and herring. A steam ferry-boat here plies across the river, landing on the west side near the iron-works at Saugerties.

SAUGERTIES is a large manufacturing village by the chartered name of *Ulster*, situated on the Esopus Creek, near its entrance into the Hudson, where is a water-fall affording an immense hydraulic power, much of which is advantageously used in driving different kinds of machinery. The village contains about 4,500 inhabitants, 600 dwelling-houses, 6 churches, and 3 or 4 public houses. A steamboat and several sloops run from the mouth of the creek, although the usual steamboat landing for the passage-boats is at

BRISTOL, or MALDEN, 2 miles above Redhook and 1½ miles from Saugerties. A stage runs to and from the landing to the village, on the arrival and departure of the steam passage-boats.

EAST and WEST CAMP, a few miles above Bristol, are old Dutch settlements on both sides of the river.

The village of CATSKILL, 111 miles from New York and 34 miles from Albany, is situated on both sides of Catskill Creek, near its junction with the Hudson; the principal street being about half a mile back from the steamboat landing. It was incorporated in 1806, and now contains about 3,800 inhabitants, 500 dwelling-houses, a court-house and jail, 2 banking-houses, 5 churches, and several public houses. Here is owned a steam

NEW YORK TO ALBANY, TROY, ETC. 39

boat and 4 barges, besides several sloops employed in transporting produce and merchandise to and from the city of New York and different places on the river. A ferry-boat plies across the river from the landing at that place, to Oak Hill, Columbia County A stage runs from Catskill to Hudson, *via* Athens, twice daily, and a stage runs semi-weekly to Prattsville, *via* Hunter and Lexington. Stages also run daily during the warm weather from the steamboat landing to the

CATSKILL MOUNTAIN HOUSE, at the *Pine Orchard*, distant about 12 miles from Catskill. The following is a glowing description of this well-known and charming summer retreat :

"PINE ORCHARD, forming a part of the Catskill Mountain range, is situated about 12 miles from Catskill, Greene County. It is elevated 3,000 feet above the tide-waters of the Hudson, which noble stream, and the surrounding country, it overlooks for a great distance, affording a varied and extensive view of the greatest interest. On the summit is erected a large and commodious public house, called the *Mountain House*, for the accommodation of visitors, who resort here in great numbers during the summer months. In this vicinity are other mountain peaks of still greater elevation, and water-falls of the most wild and romantic character, altogether forming unrivaled attractions, which are well worthy of a visit. From this lofty eminence all inequalities of surface are overlooked. A seemingly endless succession of woods and waters, farms and villages, towns and cities, are spread out as upon a boundless map. Far in the east rise the Taghkanic Mountains, and the highlands of Connecticut and Massachusetts. To the left, and at a still greater distance, the Green Mountains of Vermont stretch away to the north, and their blue summits and the blue sky mingle together. The beautiful Hudson, studded with islands, appears narrowed in the distance, with steamboats almost constantly in sight; while vessels of every description spreading their white canvas to the breeze, are moving rapidly over its surface, or idly loitering in the calm. These may be traced to the distance of nearly seventy miles with the naked eye; and again at times all below is enveloped in dark clouds and rolling mist, which, driven about by the wind, is constantly assuming new, wild, and fantastic forms. From Pine Orchard, a ride or walk of a mile or two brings you to the Kaaterskill falls. Here the outlet of two small lakes leaps down a perpendicular fall of 130 feet, then glides away through a channel worn in the rock, to a second fall of 80 feet. Below this it is lost in the dark ravine, through which it finds its way to the valley of the Catskill."

The City of HUDSON, situate on the east side of the river, 116 miles from New York and 29 miles from Albany, is a place of much trade and importance. It lies near the head of ship navigation, and was formerly celebrated for being largely engaged in the West India trade, and more recently in the whale fishery. Hudson was first settled in 1783, by Thomas Jenkins and others, most of whom were Quakers, from Massachusetts and Rhode Island. The city was chartered in 1785, and is divided into 2 wards; in 1860 it contained 7,187 inhabitants, about 900 dwelling-houses, a court-house and jail, with a beautiful white marble front, surmounted by a dome; 8 churches of different denominations, including 2 Friends' meeting-houses; 2 banks, 2 public markets, and 5 hotels. The Hudson Academy at this place is an old chartered institution, and the Hudson Female Seminary is a new and flourishing boarding-school for young ladies; besides which there are several schools, both male and female. The Franklin Library Association is a young and popular institution, to which is attached a large library and philosophical apparatus. The *Hudson Lunatic Asylum* is situated on State Street, on the north side of the city, facing the court-house on the south. The city is supplied by pure and wholesome water by a chartered aqueduct company, who bring the water in iron pipes from a spring about 2 miles distant. The *Hudson and Boston Railroad* commences at this place, and extends to West Stockbridge, Mass., a distance of 34 miles; running within 7 miles of *Lebanon Springs*, which are much resorted to during the summer. The New

York and Albany steamboats also land and receive passengers, in addition to the passage-boats which run to and from New York direct, thus affording a speedy communication between the cities of New York and Boston, a total distance by this route of about 300 miles, extending through an interesting country.

The *Hudson River Railroad* passes through the city, near the water's edge. A steam ferry-boat crosses the river from Hudson to *Athens*, a chartered village on the west shore, containing about 1,700 inhabitants.

FOUR MILE POINT, 120 miles above New York, is considered the *head of ship navigation* on the Hudson. Kinderhook Creek here enters the river on the east side, and near its mouth is situated the manufacturing village of COLUMBIAVILLE.

COLUMBIA SPRINGS.—These Springs are situated about 4 miles north of the city of Hudson, in the town of Stockport, Columbia County, N. Y., and although but little known to the public, they may be ranked among the most valuable of any in the State for the peculiar medicinal and curative qualities of the water.

The scenery in the vicinity is not only beautiful, but highly romantic, and well calculated to attract and please the visitor. In the immediate vicinity flows a fine stream of water, where those who are fond of sailing, or delight in the sports of fishing, can wile away their time in a pleasant and agreeable manner. Here, too, those who love to ramble o'er hill and dale, or follow the windings of the rivulet as it flows along, now smooth and placid, and anon lashing itself into a foam as it dashes from rock to rock, in its wild and majestic course, can find enough to gratify their curiosity.

The proprietor of these Springs, in addition to the erection of a large and commodious house, is engaged in laying out and fixing up the grounds—erecting bathing, spring, and summer houses, necessary for the convenience and comfort of those who may desire to avail themselves of the full benefits to be derived from the use of the water.

New Lebanon Springs.—This justly celebrated Spa is delightfully situated near the division line between the States of New York and Massachusetts, 25 miles from Albany. There are fine accommodations at the Springs, which are situated on the side of a hill, overlooking one of the most lovely valleys of our country. The cavity from which the water gushes is 10 feet in diameter, and the quantity is sufficient to drive a mill. Its temperature is uniformly 72°. It is tasteless, inodorous, and soft, admirably adapted to bathing, and excellent in cutaneous affections, rheumatism, internal obstructions, liver complaint, nervous debility, etc.

A person standing on the side of the hill, in the rear of Columbia Hall, will find he can produce a fine echo, at pleasure. In the neighborhood are small lakes and streams filled with trout, and there are beautiful roads and beautiful villages within a few hours' ride, in all directions.

About two miles from the hotel is the celebrated *Shaker Settlement*, which is much visited by strangers, particularly on Sunday, when their very remarkable forms of worship are practiced.

Lebanon Springs are now upon the line of railways, and are reached without difficulty either from Hudson, Albany, New York, or Boston.

Coxsackie Landing, 8 miles above Hudson, is situated on the west side of the Hudson, 22 miles below the city of Albany Here are three separate landings within the distance of a mile, altogether containing about 1.800 inhabitants, 250 dwelling-houses, 4 churches, an academy, 4 public houses, 20 stores of different kinds, and 15 warehouses, 1 steam plaster mill and 1 furnace, 1 ship-yard and 2 dry docks for building and repairing vessels; 19 extensive brick yards, where are manufactured yearly about 30,000,000 bricks. This is also a convenient steamboat landing, at which steamboats touch several times daily during the season of navigation.

The village of COXSACKIE, 1 mile west of the landing, contains about 600 inhabitants, and is surrounded by fertile lands, extending to the base of the Helderberg Mountains.

STUYVESANT, 4 miles farther on the east side of the river, is a flourishing place of business, from which large quantities of produce are annually sent to the New York market, the country in the interior being justly celebrated for its fertility.

A short distance north is the steamboat landing for the above place, and for the village of KINDERHOOK, situated about 5 miles east of the river, and noted for the beauty of its location. It is the birth-place of ex-President Van Buren, and his present residence is a pleasant seat about 2 miles south of the village.

NEW BALTIMORE, 4 miles above, on the west side of the Hudson, and 14 miles from Albany, is a village of about 900 inhabitants. Here is a convenient steamboat landing, where the passage-boats usually land and receive passengers.

COEYMANS, on the west side of the river, 12 miles below Albany, is the last landing the boats make on their upward trips. The village contains about 900 inhabitants, and here are owned several sloops trading with the New York market. *Barren Island,* lying immediately below the village of Coeymans, is on the south bounds of the old colony of Rensselaerwyck, and was fortified and garrisoned by one of the early Patroons in 1644. All foreign traders were here obliged to come to, and learn the terms on which the port of the colony might be entered. It now presents a rocky and sterile appearance, being well adapted for the purposes for which it was originally occupied, as it completely commands the channel of the river.

CASTLETON, 4 miles above Coeymans and 8 miles from Albany, is on the east side of the river. Here is forming a bar in the channel of the river, which is very injurious to navigation.

The OVERSLAUGH, 3 miles below the city of Albany, has

heretofore formed the principal obstruction to the free navigation of the Hudson on its tide-waters. Here were several bars or flats, with narrow channels, affording at low tides but a small depth of water—this obstruction, however, has of late been mostly removed by an expenditure by the United States Government, the depth of the water being materially increased, the channel made straight, and the navigation much improved.

GREENBUSH, opposite the south part of the city of Albany, with which it is connected by a steam ferry-boat, contains about 3,000 inhabitants. Immediately above may be seen the depôt and buildings attached to the Hudson River Railroad.

EAST ALBANY, 144 miles from New York and 6 miles below Troy, is the terminus of the Hudson River Railroad and Albany and West Stockbridge Railroad, a link of the *Western Railroad* of Massachusetts. Here also terminates the *Troy and Greenbush Railroad.*

ALBANY, the capital of the State, and one of the oldest cities in the Union, is eligibly situated on the west side of the Hudson River, 145 miles north of the city of New York; 298 miles by railroad, east of Buffalo; 200 west of Boston, and 250 south of Montreal. It was originally called "Beaver Wyck" (*i. e.*, Beaver Town), and afterward "Williamstadt." It received its present name in 1664, in honor of James, duke of York and Albany, afterward James II., in whose reign the original city charter was granted by Governor Dongan, July 22, 1686, and the government vested in "The Mayor, Aldermen, and Commonalty of the city of Albany," consisting of the Mayor, Recorder, ten Aldermen, and ten Assistants. The charter has been materially altered by recent enactments of the Legislature; the assistant aldermen are merged in ten aldermen, but the corporate name is still preserved. It is now divided into ten wards. In 1860 its population was 62,367.

It is indebted for its prosperity to the enterprise of its inhabitants, and the impulse given to its trade by the Erie and Champlain canals, which unite about 8 miles to the north, and enter the Hudson River at the north end of the city. A basin has been formed in front of the city, protected from the river by a pier one mile and a quarter in length, furnishing a safe harbor for vessels, and securing them from injury by the ice, which in the spring freshets comes down the river in immense quantities, sometimes causing great damage. The city is commanding in its situation, and appears to great advantage from the river. There are three ravines running from east to west, known as the Foxes Kill, the Rutten Kill, and the Beaver Kill, on each side of which the land is high, being at an elevation of from 140 to 160 feet above, and gradually ascending from the river The view from either of the heights is picturesque in the highest degree. To the north may be seen the city of Troy and the adjacent villages, and in the distance the hills of Vermont. To the east the beautiful extent of country lying beyond the Hudson River, and to the south the Helderbergs and Catskill Mountains. The public buildings are of the most beautiful and tasteful character. The Capitol, occupied by the Legislature and the State courts; the State Hall, for the accommodation of the public offices; the City Hall, occupied for city and county purposes, and by the United States courts; and the Albany Academy, having 300 pupils, face the public square at the head of State Street. This square is formed by the Capitol and Academy parks, which are inclosed with substantial iron fences, erected on stone bases, and are laid out with walks lined with ornamental trees of choicest species. A more delightful spot in the summer is not to be found in any inland city in the Union. A few rods south of the square, on Eagle Street, is the County Jail and the Medical College. This college was incorporated in 1839, and occupies a building granted to it by the corporation of the city, admirably adapted for its purposes. The college already possesses one of the most valuable museums in the country, which has recently been greatly enlarged and enriched by specimens imported direct from Germany and France. The Albany Exchange, situated at the foot of State Street, is a large and commodious building, constructed of granite. It is occupied for stores, offices of professional men, and the post-office. The Young Men's Association, established for "Mutual Improvement," was the pioneer institution of its kind in this State, and embraces all ranks and professions, now numbering about 1,500 members. It has an extensive reading-room, supplied with the leading newspapers of this country and England; also a room, furnished with the most popular and standard periodicals and reviews, native and foreign; an excellent library of several thousand volumes, and a lecture-room capable of seating 300 persons, in which two lectures a week are delivered, from the first of December to the first of March. Strangers have free access to all except the lecture-room and library. There are four Presbyterian churches, one Associate do., three Dutch Reformed, one Unitarian, four Methodist Episcopal, one African do., three Baptist, one colored do., two Lutheran, five Episcopalian, one Universalist, three Roman Catholic, one Independent church, one Mission House, two Jewish Synagogues, one Bethel, and one Friends' meeting-house.

The Old State Hall, recently occupied for state offices, is converted into a museum for the reception of the geological cabinet formed under the direction of the State geological surveyors. The New York State Agricultural Society also here hold their meetings in a room reserved for that purpose. The other public institutions whose meetings are held at Albany are the New York State Temperance Society and the State Medical Society. There are also in the city, in addition to those mentioned, various benevolent, religious, and scientific institutions; among them the Albany Institute, with a valuable library and extensive museum, occupying a room in the Albany Academy.

The *Dudley Observatory* is a new and popular institution, being very liberally endowed by a lady whose name it bears.

PRINCIPAL HOTELS IN ALBANY.

American Hotel, H. B. Clark, 100 State Street.
Congress Hotel, James L. Mitchell, Park Place.
Delevan House, T. Roessle & Son, Broadway, near R. R. Depôt.
Stanwix Hall, Francis Rider, Broadway, op. Railroad Depôt.

NEW YORK TO ALBANY, TROY, ETC.

RAILROADS.

The *Hudson River Railroad*, 144 miles in length; the *Western Railroad* of Massachusetts, 200 miles in length; the *Albany Northern Railroad*, and the great *New York Central Railroad*, extending to Buffalo and Niagara Falls, all terminate at Albany, rendering it one of the greatest thoroughfares in the Union.

NEW YORK CENTRAL RAILROAD and its BRANCHES:

Albany to Buffalo—*Direct Route*	298 miles.
Troy and Schenectady Branch	21 "
Auburn and Rochester "	104 "
Rochester and Charlotte "	7 "
Lockport and Niagara Falls Branch	75 "
Lockport and Buffalo "	12 "
Buffalo, Niagara Falls, and Lewiston Branch	28 "
Batavia and Attica "	11 "
Total	556 miles.
Length of Double Track	398 miles.
Total Cost of Road and Equipment	$32,740,068

CANANDAIGUA AND NIAGARA FALLS RAILROAD, leased by the Central Railroad.................. 86 miles.
Making a total length of Railroad operated by the above Company of......................... 642 miles.
Fare for first-class passengers............. 2 cents per mile.
Average rate of speed adopted by Express Trains, including stops............... 30 miles per hour.

Albany and Susquehannah Railroad, when completed, will extend from Albany to Binghamton, 140 miles; finished to Schoharie Bridge, 35 miles, passing through an interesting section of country. ☞ To *Sharon Springs*, 10 miles by stage.

Two *City Railroads* are finished and in operation, running to different parts of the city.

DISTANCES FROM ALBANY TO MONTREAL, *via* Saratoga Springs and Lake Champlain:

To Troy, *by Hudson River or railroad* ..		6	Miles.
Ballston Spa, "	..	25	31 "
Saratoga Springs, "	..	7	38 "
Whitehall "	..	39	77 "
Burlington, *by steamboat*		76	153 "
Plattsburgh, *by steamboat*			178 "
Rouse's Point, *by steamboat*			203 "
St. John's, Canada, *by railroad*.........		23	226 "
Montreal, *by railroad*................		22	248 "

We copy the following Extract relating to the early history of Albany:

"The younger race of fashionables and semi-fashionables know Albany, or affect to know it, merely as a big, city-looking place, full of taverns and hotels, where they land from the steamboat, on their way to Saratoga, Niagara, or Quebec. Another set of less locomotive good folks, especially in New York and Philadelphia, have no notions about it, but those derived from the old traditionary jokes upon its ancient Schepens and Schoutens, its burly burgomasters, 'its lofty spires glittering with tin, and hospitable boards smoking with sturgeon.'

"But, in honest truth, there are few cities of the size anywhere which can exhibit a greater or a more agreeable variety of society and manners. In Albany may be found talent and learning, accomplishment and beauty. The towns of Europe of the same size and relative importance, can in this respect bear no sort of comparison with it. Then, too, its situation, the prospect from its higher grounds and streets, abound in scenes meet for romantic fiction. Albany is rich also in more sober but equally interesting recollections of our national history. There (to use the once familiar personification in which Indian oratory delighted to speak of the French and English governments), Corlaer and Ononthio were wont to meet and plant the tree of peace, or else extinguish their council fire and part in wrath. There, about the middle of the last century (1751), the governors of the several provinces met the chiefs of the Six Nations, and the ambassadors of the Catawbas and other Southern tribes, and buried the hatchet between the whole Indian race on this continent, and planted the tree of peace in Fort Orange.* There, three years after, was held that first General Congress, in which the earliest arrangements for national defense were made, and where, by one of those remarkable coincidences with which the hand of Providence has legibly inscribed the evidence of his own workings in every part of our national history, upon the 4th of July, 1754, Benjamin Franklin, and other patriots destined to the highest honors of their country, signed the first plan of American Union, and proclaimed to the colonies that they were one people, fit to govern and able to protect themselves Why need I speak of the events of the Revolution? At Albany, in the most eventful periods of that struggle, Montgomery, and Schuyler, and Gates, and the elder Clinton, in turns, planned or directed the operations of war, while the civil wisdom and moral courage of Jay gave new confidence to public spirit, and fresh vigor to our counsels."

ALBANY, NINETY YEARS SINCE.

The following description of Albany is taken from Mrs. Grant's interesting "Memoirs of an American Lady:"

"The city of Albany was stretched along the banks of the Hudson; one very wide and long street lay parallel to the river, the intermediate space between it and the shore being occupied by gardens. A small but steep hill rose above the center of the town, on which stood a fort, intended (but very ill adapted) for the defense of the place and of the neighboring country. From the foot of this hill another street was built [now State Street], sloping pretty rapidly down till it joined the one before mentioned that ran along the river. This street was still wider than the other; it was only paved on each side, the middle being occupied by public edifices. These consisted

---

* On the spot where now stands the house formerly occupied by the venerable Simeon De Witt, for many years Surveyor-General of the State, and at present known as the FORT ORANGE HOTEL, situated in Market Street, near Lydius Street.

of a market-place, or guard-house, town hall, and the English and Dutch churches. The English church stood at the upper end of the street; the Dutch church was situated at the bottom of the descent where the street terminated. The town, in proportion to its population, occupied a great space of ground. This city, in short, was a kind of semi-rural establishment; every house had its garden, a well, and a little green behind; before every door a tree was planted, rendered interesting by being coeval with some beloved member of the family."

The City of Troy, 150 miles north of New York by railroad route, is pleasantly situated on the east bank of the Hudson River, at the head of tide-water and steamboat navigation, 6 miles above Albany. It was incorporated as a city in 1816, when it contained nearly 5,000 inhabitants; it has recently been made a port of entry, and contained in 1860, 39.235 inhabitants, who are mostly engaged in commerce, navigation, and manufactures. Since the completion of the Erie and Champlain canals, in 1825, which, opposite this place, at the village of West Troy, unite the waters of the lakes with those of the Hudson, Troy has rapidly increased in wealth and population. Here are a fine court-house, built of marble, in the Grecian Doric order; a jail constructed of brick; a county poor-house, to which a farm containing about 200 acres is attached; the Troy Female Seminary, a flourishing chartered institution; the Troy University recently established, is a chartered institution largely endowed; there are besides several select schools for males and females. Troy contains two new finely-modeled and expensive market buildings; seven Presbyterian churches, three Episcopal, two Baptist, two Methodist, two Catholic, one Universalist, one Friends' meeting-house, and an African church; ten banks; four savings' banks; two insurance companies; one lyceum of natural history, with a choice scientific library, and an extensive collection of minerals, and collections in various branches of natural history; a Young Men's Association for mutual improvement, with a large library and extensive reading-room. The principal hotels are the American Hotel, Fourth, corner of Elbow Street; Mansion House, 4 Washington Square; Troy House, River, corner of First, Street.

Here are owned about 60 masted vessels, four large passage steamboats of the first class, two smaller steam passage-boats, and five steam tow-boats, with 22 barges, which ply between Troy and New York, transporting annually an immense amount of produce and merchandise. Four lines of passage and freight boats run on the Champlain Canal from Troy; a line of packet schooners run from this place to Boston and other Eastern ports; a line of canal packets to Whitehall, and lines of daily stages run to Whitehall, and Bennington, Vt., and to Brattleboro, Vt., and Boston. The water-power at Troy is immense, and a large portion of it still unoccupied. Within the limits of the city, and about a mile east of the Hudson, a tunnel has been excavated by Mr. Benjamin Marshall, extending from the Peekskill, a distance of about 800 feet, and gives a fall of 180 feet. Several large mills and factories, to be supplied with water from this fall, are now in the progress of erection. Near the northern boundary of the city a dam has been built across the Hudson, by the State, which here makes a fall of 11½ feet, and creates an incalculable amount of hydraulic power. This place is abundantly supplied with wholesome water, brought from the Piscawin Creek through large iron pipes, with hydrants at the corners of the streets.

The *Rensselaer and Saratoga Railroad* commences at this place, crossing the Hudson River by a substantial bridge, 1,650 feet in length, to Green Island; thence it continues north across several branches of the Mohawk River to Waterford; following the valley of the Hudson until it reaches Mechanicsville, where it diverges to the west and continues to the village of Ballston Spa, a distance of 25 miles, and unites with the Saratoga and Schenectady Railroad. The *Schenectady and Troy Railroad*, 21 miles in length, was completed in 1842; it now forms part of the New York Central Railroad. The *Troy and Greenbush Railroad*, 6 miles in length, connects with the Hudson River Railroad; and the *Troy and Boston Railroad*, when completed, will make a direct railroad communication from Troy to Boston, and furnish a continuous line of railroads from Boston to Buffalo.

The city of Troy has long been celebrated for its beauty and healthiness. The streets are laid out at right angles, are generally wide, remarkable for their cleanliness, and planted with beautiful and, in the hot season, most grateful forest and shade trees. From Mounts Ida on the east and Olympus on the north, an extensive and charming prospect is presented, embracing a view of the valley of the Hudson for miles, the city of Albany, the villages of West Troy, Lansingburgh, Waterford, and Cohoes, and the Cohoes Falls; a landscape presenting more beauty and a greater variety of scenery can hardly be imagined. From the elevations just mentioned, the eye rests at once, as on a map spread out before it, on city and village teeming with life and activity—the broad Hudson rolling on in majesty to the ocean, and bearing on its bosom fleets of boats and vessels—a long extent of the Erie Canal, itself no common stream, floating to market the products of the West—railroads, over which are passing with lightning speed multitudes in pursuit of business or pleasure—on woodlands and cultivated fields harmoniously blended—and on a western horizon of undulating highlands, which toward the south blend with the famed Catskill Mountains, lifting their giant heads to the clouds.

WEST TROY, situated on the west bank of the Hudson River, 6 miles above the city of Albany, is a place of growing importance. It was incorporated as a village in 1836, and now contains about 10,000 inhabitants, 1,200 dwelling-houses, 10 churches, six public houses, a large number of stores, and mechanics' shops. The *Erie Canal*, which passes through the center of the village, communicates with the Hudson by two commodious side-cuts. It is a convenient depôt for vast quantities of produce, lumber, and merchandise, being on the Junction

Canal, and at the head of sloop navigation. The southern mouth of the Mohawk here unites with the Hudson.

The *Watervliet Arsenal*, situated in West Troy, near the river, was established by the United States Government in 1813. This is the largest arsenal of construction in the Union, having great facilities for the manufacture and transportation of warlike implements, and is well worthy of a visit. The grounds attached to the arsenal consist of about 100 acres, inclosed in front by an iron fence, and in the rear by a stone wall. Here are located 33 buildings, comprising storehouses for small arms, gun sheds for cannon carriages, timber sheds, magazines, sawmill. paint, carriage, machine, casting, and blacksmith shops; offices, barracks, hospitals, and officers' quarters. About 200 officers, soldiers, and hired workmen are constantly employed at this post. which number could be greatly increased if found necessary. Here are now manufactured munitions of war amounting to an estimated value of $500,000 annually.

LANSINGBURGH, 3 miles above Troy, on the east side of the Hudson, is one of the oldest villages in the State, being incorporated as early as 1787. It now contains about 4,500 inhabitants. During the Revolutionary war it was a place of considerable importance. It has since increased but slowly, owing to obstructions in the channel of the Hudson, and the consequent growth of Troy.

WATERFORD, situated 1 mile above Lansingburgh, on the opposite side of the river, and 155 miles north of the city of New York, is at the very head of sloop navigation on the Hudson, with which the northern mouth of the Mohawk here unites. Navigation is kept up to this place by means of a *dam* and *sloop lock* at the upper part of the city of Troy. Waterford was incorporated in 1805, and now contains a population of about 8,000 inhabitants.

The village of COHOES, 2 miles west of Waterford, is situated on the southwest bank of the Mohawk River, a short distance below the Cohoes Falls, and near the junction of the Erie and

Champlain canals. Here is afforded by the Mohawk an immense amount of hydraulic power. If found necessary, the whole volume of water in the river can be used for propelling machinery to almost any extent, having a total fall of about 140 feet. Here are several extensive cotton and other manufacturing establishments; six churches, two or three hotels, and a population of 7,000 inhabitants, mostly employed in the above manufactories. The *Schenectady and Troy Railroad* passes near the village, also the *Albany Northern Railroad* crossing the Mohawk a short distance below the falls, affording a speedy conveyance to and from this interesting locality.

COHOES FALLS, situated in the immediate vicinity of Cohoes village, is an object of great attraction. It is much resorted to during the summer months by visitors from all parts of the Union. The water of the Mohawk here has a perpendicular fall of 70 feet, besides a rapid descent above and below. The banks of the river present a grand and romantic appearance, varying in almost perpendicular height of from 50 to 120 feet, for a distance of half a mile below the falls, where a substantial bridge, about 800 feet long, spans the stream.

For a distance of 70 miles above these falls, the Mohawk winds through a romantic valley, formerly affording batteaux navigation. At Little Falls occurs a descent of about 40 feet in the distance of half a mile. Above this point the stream again resumes its original character to its head, near the village of Rome, Oneida County—the whole valley being celebrated for its fertility and historic reminiscences.

NEW YORK TO ALBANY, TROY, ETC. 55

HUDSON RIVER STEAMBOATS.

THE following list embraces all the PASSAGE BOATS built and running on the Hudson River, between New York, Albany, and Troy, since their first introduction by Robert Fulton, in the fall of 1807:

Built.	Name.	Tons.	Commanders.	Remarks.
1807	Clermont		James Winans	Name changed
1808	North River	160	Samuel Wiswall	Broken up.
1809	Car of Neptune	295	A. H. Roorbach	Broken up.
1811	Hope	280	E. S. Bunker	Broken up.
1811	Perseverance	280	J. Sherman	Broken up.
1811	Paragon	331	Andrew Bartholomew	Sunk 1825.
1813	Richmond	370	Joab Center	Broken up.
1815	Olive Branch	265	James Moore	Broken up.
1816	Ch. Livingston	494	Samuel Wiswall	Coal barge.
1823	James Kent	346	Thomas Wiswall	Coal barge.
1824	Hudson	170	M. Bartholomew	Broken up.
1825	Sandusky	289	James Penoyer	Tow-boat.
1825	Constitution*	276	Wm. J. Wiswall	Now Indiana
1825	Constellation	276	Robert G. Cruttenden	Tow-barge.
1825	Ch. Jus. Marshall†	300	Richard W. Sherman	Lost in L. I. Sound.
1825	Saratoga	250	James Benson	Tow-barge.
1826	Sun ‡	280	H. Drake	Burnt, 1831.
1826	New Philadelphia	300	George E. Seymour	Delaware River.
1827	Albany	398	J. G. Jenkins	Broken up.
1827	Independence	368	Wm. J. Wiswall	Broken up.
1827	North America	497	Gideon Lathrop	Destr'd by ice, 1839.
1827	Victory	290	Sanford Cobb	Sunk in 1845.
1827	Emerald	300	Capt. Ketchum	Tow-boat.
1828	De Witt Clinton	571	J. Sherman & S. R. Roe	Eng. in Knick.
1829	Ohio §	412	M. Bartholomew	Tow-barge.
1830	Novelty	477	Daniel Peck	Broken up.
1832	Champlain	471	Adolphus Gorham	Tow-barge.
1832	Erie	471	James Benson	Tow-barge.
1833	Helen		Henry Burden	Destroyed, 1834.
1835	Robert L. Stevens	298	Joseph P. Dean	Tow-boat.
1836	Rochester	491	A. Houghton	Laid up.
1836	Swallow	426	Alex. McLean	Wrecked, Ap., 1845.
1837	Utica	340	A. H. Shultz	Laid up.
	Belle	430	G. B. Riggs	Tow-boat.
	Express	283	A. Hitchcock	Sent South.
1838	Diamond	398	A. Flower	Laid up.
1838	Kosciusko		D. Haywood	Tow-boat.
1838	Arrow		Capt. Smith	Burnt, 1849.
1839	Balloon	204	David Hitchcock	Runs on Delaware
1839	North America	494	R. G. Cruttenden	Tow-boat.
1840	South America	638	M. H. Truesdell	Runs to Rondout.
1840	Troy	724	Adolphus Gorham	Laid up.

* Exploded her boilers in 1825, killing three persons.
† Exploded her boiler in 1830, killing 11 persons.
‡ Built to run as a day-boat between New York and Albany.
§ Exploded her chimney, or flue, in 1832, killing five persons.

NEW YORK TO ALBANY, TROY, ETC.

Built	Name	Tons	Commanders	Remarks
1841	Columbia	391	T. P. Newbury	Runs to Hudson.
1841	Rainbow	230	Capt. Fury	Delaware River.
1842	Curtis Peck		Wm. Peck	James River.
1843	Empire	936	R. B. Macy	Broken up.
1843	Knickerbocker	858	W. B. Nelson	Runs to Albany.
1845	Hero	469	J. W. Hancox	N. York to Albany.
1845	Niagara	730	A. Degroot	Tow-boat.
1845	Rip Van Winkle	510	D. Haywood	New York to Troy.
1845	Oregon	1000	Capt. St. John	Sunk in 1863.
1845	Hendrik Hudson	1170	Curtis Peck	N. York to Albany.
1846	Isaac Newton	1750	Wm. H. Peck	Burnt Dec. 5, 1868.
1848	Alida	700	Capt. Roe	Tow-boat.
1848	Commodore	985	C. W. Farnham	New York to Troy.
1850	Armenia		I. P. Smith	N. York to Albany.
1850	Henry Clay*		Capt. Tallman	Burnt, July 27, 1852.
185	Reindeert		C. W. Farnham	Burnt, Sept., 1852.
1850	Metamora		J. F. Tallman	
1851	Francis Skiddy	1100	Levi Smith	New York to Troy.
	Vanderbilt		Geo. H. Tupper	New York to Troy.
1851	New World	1750	A. P. St. John	Used as a hospital.
1859	Daniel Drew		John F. Tallman	N. York to Albany.
1864	Chauncey Vibbard		Captain Hitchcock	N. York to Albany.
1864	St. John	2300	Wm. H. Peck	N. York to Albany.

* Burnt to the water's edge near Yonkers, by which dreadful calamity about 70 lives were lost.

† Exploded her boiler at Bristol Landing, killing 36 persons; afterward destroyed by fire.

Copy of an Advertisement taken from the Albany Gazette, dated September, 1807.

"THE NORTH RIVER STEAMBOAT will leave Pauler's Hook Ferry [now Jersey City] on Friday, the 4th of September, at 9 in the morning, and arrive at Albany on Saturday, at 9 in the afternoon. Provisions, good berths, and accommodations are provided.

"The charge to each passenger is as follows:

  To Newburgh .... dols. 3.   Time, 14 hours.
  " Poughkeepsie ...... " 4.   " 17 "
  " Esopus .... " 5.   " 20 "
  " Hudson .... " 5½.   " 30 "
  " Albany .... " 7.   " 36 "

"For places, apply to Wm. Vandervoort, No. 48 Courtlandt Street, on the corner of Greenwich Street.

"*Sept.* 2, 1807."

NEW YORK TO ALBANY, TROY, ETC. 57

THE CLERMONT.

"The above is a correct drawing of *Fulton's first American Steamboat*, called the 'CLERMONT.' She was built at the shipyard of Charles Brown, at the Dry Dock, New York city, in the year 1807. Omitting every thing in regard to the difficulties with which Fulton had to contend, and the utter incredulity of almost every person until the boat left the wharf moved by steam, we will give a short account of her trial trip.

"Mr. Livingston and Mr. Fulton had invited many of their friends to witness the first trial, among whom were those learned men, Dr. Mitchell and Dr. McNeven, to whom we are indebted for some account of what passed on this occasion. Nothing could exceed the surprise and admiration of all who witnessed the experiment. The minds of the most incredulous were changed in a few minutes. Before the boat had made the distance of a quarter of a mile, the greatest unbeliever must have been converted. The man who, while he looked on the expensive machine, thanked his stars that he had more wisdom than to waste his money on such idle schemes, changed the expression of his features as the boat moved from the wharf and gained her speed, and his complacent expression gradually stiffened into wonder. The jeers of the ignorant, who had neither sense nor feeling enough to suppress their contemptuous ridicule and rude jokes, were silenced for a moment by a vulgar astonishment which deprived them of the power of utterance, till the triumph of genius extorted from the incredulous multitude which crowded the shore, shouts and acclamations of congratulations and applause. By reference to the engraving it will be seen that she labored under a great disadvantage in having the wheels hung on the shaft without any outward support. This is now supplied by what are called the wheel-guards."—*Sci. Am*

HUDSON RIVER.

This beautiful and celebrated stream was first discovered by HENRY HUDSON, in 1609, while in the employ of the Dutch East India Company. It rises from numerous sources on the Adirondack Mountain region of Essex and Hamilton counties, west of Lakes George and Champlain. Its principal head branches are known as the Adirondack River, Boreas River, Indian River, Schroon River, and the Sacandaga River, while the Mohawk, rising in Oneida County, and flowing eastward, is its principal affluent. Its whole length is estimated at 320 miles; the tide flowing up for nearly half that distance, to the city of Troy. On the upper part of this river, justly celebrated for its varied and romantic beauties, are several picturesque falls, of which Baker's Falls, Glen's Falls, and Hadley, or Great Falls, are the most noted. In the head waters of the Hudson, surrounded by mountain peaks of Alpine grandeur, are to be found trout, and other fish of a fine flavor, in great abundance, and in its tide waters are taken annually large quantities of shad, herring, bass, sturgeon, and many other kinds of fish. From its mouth to the city of Hudson, a distance of 116 miles, it is navigable for ships of a large burthen, and to Albany and Troy, 150 miles, for steamboats of a large class. By means of a lock and dam, vessels can ascend 4 miles farther to the village of Waterford. When we reflect that this important river receives the tributary waters of the great western and northern lakes, by means of the Erie and Champlain canals, and then commingles with the Atlantic Ocean, after passing the "Highlands," the Palisades, and through the secure and spacious bay of New York, well may we give it the appellation of the NOBLE HUDSON.

The *Adirondack Group of Mountains*, rising in Essex County to an altitude of 5,467 feet above the ocean, are much frequented by tourists fond of hunting and fishing.

TOUR TO SARATOGA SPRINGS, LAKE GEORGE, ETC.

THERE are now two or three Railroad Routes from Albany and Troy to Ballston Spa and Saratoga Springs.

1st. From Albany *via* Schenectady, 17 miles; from thence by the *Saratoga and Schenectady Railroad*, terminating at the village of Saratoga Springs; total distance, 39 miles.

2d. From Albany *via Albany Northern Railroad*, connecting with the *Rensselaer and Saratoga Railroad* at the *Junction*, 2 miles above Waterford; from thence proceeding northward a farther distance of 26 miles to Saratoga Springs; making a total distance from Albany, 38 miles.

3d. From Troy *via Saratoga and Rensselaer Railroad*, terminating at Ballston Spa, 25 miles, there uniting with the railroad extending from Schenectady to Saratoga Springs, a farther distance of 7 miles.

The above railroads afford the traveler a choice of several interesting routes. There being little difference of time or expense, it is well for the tourist to *go* by one route and *return* by another, thus changing the scenery.

MECHANICSVILLE, 12 miles north of Troy, is the station where the cars running on the Rensselaer and Saratoga Railroad leave the valley of the Hudson, diverging westward to Ballston Spa, a farther distance of 13 miles.

BALLSTON SPA, the county seat for Saratoga County, is an old and somewhat celebrated watering-place. It is situated in a valley near the Kayaderosseras Creek, 31 miles north of the city of Albany, and 7 miles south of Saratoga Springs, by railroad route. It was incorporated in 1807, and now contains about 2,500 inhabitants; a court-house and jail, one Presbyterian, one Episcopal, one Baptist, one Methodist, and one Roman Catholic church; one banking-house, five hotels and taverns. The *Sans Souci Hotel* at this place, erected by the late Nicholas Low, Esq., in 1803, is an old and popular boarding-house, delightfully situated near the center of the village.

The oldest and still the most esteemed mineral fountain is known as the "Public Well," on the flat west of the center of the village. It is said to have been first discovered by the whites in 1769, during the survey and partition of the Kayaderosseras Patent. It issues from a bed of stiff blue clay and gravel. Besides the above there are several other springs of less note, possessing medicinal properties of a similar character. The *New Spring*, also on the flat, is of similar properties, and evidently belongs to the same class with those of Saratoga Springs, now so justly celebrated.

Within a few miles of Ballston Spa are situated two or three lakes, the largest of which are *Ballston*, or *Long Lake*, on the south, and *Saratoga Lake* on the east; the latter abounds with fish of different kinds.

The village of SARATOGA SPRINGS, 38 miles north of Albany and 40 miles south of Whitehall, by railroad route, is pleasantly situated on a plain, surrounded in part by a beautiful grove of pine trees. This is the most noted watering-place in the Union, or on the continent of America; the mineral springs, possessing great medicinal properties, vary somewhat in their analyses, although all lying in a valley contiguous to each other within one mile. The village is built chiefly on one broad street, intersected by cross streets: and the numerous large hotels and boarding-houses for the accommodation of visitors give it a lively and imposing appearance, particularly when thronged with fashionable company, as it usually is during the summer months Population about 6,000.

The principal hotels are the United States Hotel, Union Hall, Congress Hall, Columbian Hotel, American Hotel, and Marvin House, all being situated on the main street or avenue running north and south. Other hotels and private boarding-houses are to be found in every direction. There are also several public bathing-houses near the Springs, where cold and warm water and shower baths can at all times be obtained.

The railroads afford a speedy communication between the Springs and the cities of Albany Schenectady, and Troy on the south, while the *Saratoga and Whitehall Railroad* affords a direct and speedy route to Whitehall, Lake George, and Lake Champlain on the north.

SARATOGA MINERAL SPRINGS.—These are so well known to tourists, and so thoroughly described in our guides for travelers, that it is almost a work of supererogation to repeat what is said of them. They are, without doubt, the most remarkable chalybeates in the world; grateful and refreshing to the palate, and remedial to invalids beyond all others. In Germany alone have they any rivals

They become every year the resort of the most wealthy, educated, and refined Americans and foreigners; and, unfortunately, as a consequence, attract also those chevaliers who prey upon society, wherever it is accessible, lavish in its expenditure, and free in its amusements.

The accommodations at Saratoga are very extensive and very elegant. Thousands of people are entertained at the same time, without inconvenience.

The drives in the vicinity are beautiful, extending on the east to Saratoga Lake and the Hudson River.

The following *History and Analyses* of the principal springs are mostly copied from " *Allen's Analyses of the Mineral Fountains at Saratoga Springs.*"

" HIGH ROCK SPRING.—This spring was, beyond a question, the primeval fountain, and the one mainly used by the aborigines. The other springs, if they existed during the early savage settlements about them, would have been less pure, have contained more fresh water, have been more incorporated with the vegetable mold and decaying foliage of the forest than this; for it is so admirably secured by Nature against every thing foreign to it. This fountain receives its name from the peculiar stone which incloses its mouth.

" To this fountain the Indian resorted for relief, when laboring under disease. Here he brought his sick friends, and by the use of the water relieved them from disease.

"For many years after its introduction to the white man, it was the great source of health to the afflicted among them, even as much as it had before been to their savage neighbors; and it still retains its strength and early purity.

"Perhaps there is no mineral fountain, either here or at Ballston Spa, which has been so uniform in every particular as this. Nature did for it what man from necessity has been compelled to do for the other fountains here, viz., carefully to tube it. And while the artificial tubes, and various other improvements which from time to time have been made about the other fountains, have uniformly been subject to decay, and were almost annually to be renovated, or the several springs would have been lost, this spring, having had Nature for its architect, has needed no repairs.

"It is an excellent tonic water, and as an alterative, to be taken during the day in small quantities, it is a very valuable spring; and many invalids. every year since it was first visited by Sir William Johnson, can bear testimony to its remedial powers.

"The temperature of this spring was 48°, the surrounding atmosphere at 0, and its specific gravity 1.007; and one cubic gallon of the water, in January, 1844, gave the following ingredients on analysis:

Chloride of Sodium......................	190.233 grs
Carbonate of Magnesia	62.100
Carbonate of Lime	71.533
Carbonate of Soda	18.421
Carbonate of Iron	4.233
Hydriodate of Soda.....................	2.177
Silex and Alumina	2.500
Hydro-Bromate of Potash	"
"Solid contents in one cubic gallon...........	351.197
Carbonic Acid	331.666
Atmospheric Air	2.
"Gaseous contents in a gallon	333.666

"The circumference of the High Rock at the surface of the ground is twenty-five feet.

"Circumference at the top, two feet eight inches.

"Diameter of the opening in its top, ten inches.

"Distance from the top of the rock to the water within, is two feet eleven inches.

"Height of the column of water within the rock above the surface of the ground, one foot.

"Depth of the fountain, ten feet.

"One hundred grains furnished the following on analysis:

Carbonate of Lime .... 41.000 grs.
Carbonate of Magnesia 30.166
Carbonate of Iron......................... 13.501
Silex and Alumina 15.333
                                          ———
                                          100.000

"These substances vary very materially in different parts of the rock.

"CONGRESS SPRING.—This fountain was first discovered by a hunting party, in the summer of 1792. One of this party was *John Taylor Gilman*, who then was or had been a member of the United States Congress. Gilman had a brother who was also one of the party at the time of the discovery; and the credit of first discovering this valuable spring has been awarded to them. But which of the brothers noticed it first can not be decided at the present time, neither is it important. It was then issuing from an aperture in a calcareous rock, which faced the small stream of fresh water passing by it to the main brook of the valley. This little rivulet receives the surplus water of our Saratoga mineral springs, and passes *via* Owl Pond, Saratoga Lake, and Fish Creek, to the Hudson River.

"The novel appearance of the spring, as it flowed from the rock, attracted their attention, and induced them to apply such tests of its qualities as were within their reach. After their examination, they came to the conclusion that it was a very extraordinary fountain, containing all the constituents of the other mineral springs here, and perhaps other qualities besides; or at least the same of the other fountains in larger or different proportions; and in either case. it was in all probability a very extraordinary fountain. And as they believed it possessed more or less of every constituent which enters into the composition of the other mineral fountains here, they very appropriately made selection of that name which it now bears, viz., CONGRESS SPRING.

"The temperature of the water of this spring, as shown by Fahrenheit's thermometer, when immersed at the bottom of the well, is 50 degrees, and it does not appear to suffer any sensible variation either during the summer or winter months.

"The specific gravity of the water at the temperature of 60 deg., the barometer ranging at 29.5 inches, is 1009.7, pure water being one thousand. Excessively wet, or long seasons of dry weather, seem to produce a slight variation from this result; but repeated experiments, made at different periods, and under various circumstances of season, etc., for the space of more than twenty years, have in no instance produced a deviation of more than the 0.5 of a grain."

One gallon, or 231 cubic inches, of the water of the Congress Spring contains the following substances, viz.:

Chloride of Sodium	385.000 grs.
Hydriodate of Soda	3.500
Bi-carbonate of Soda	8.982
Bi-carbonate of Magnesia	95.788
Carbonate of Lime	98.098
Carbonate of Iron	5.075
Silex	1.500
Hydro-bromate of Potash, a trace	.000
Solid contents in a gallon	597.943 grs.
Carbonic Acid Gas	311
Atmospheric Air	7
Gaseous contents in a gallon	318 cubic inches.

The EMPIRE SPRING, situated in the north part of the village, a few rods above the High Rock Spring, is a highly valuable fountain, possessing all the curative qualities of these most celebrated mineral waters.

The grounds in the vicinity of the Empire Spring are susceptible of great improvement, which is about being effected by the Saratoga Empire Spring Company. (See *Advertisement.*)

It was analyzed by Prof. E. Emmons in 1846, and found to be highly medicinal in its properties.

The analysis of the Empire Water, by Prof. E. Emmons, is as follows:

Chloride of Sodium...................... 269.696 grs.
Bi-carbonate of Lime.................... 141.824
Bi-carbonate of Magnesia................ 41.984
Bi-carbonate of Soda.................... 30.848
Hydriodate of Soda or Iodine............ 12 000
Bi-carbonate of Iron, a trace........... .000

Solid contents in a gallon............... 496 352
Specific gravity................. 1.039

The following remarks are copied from the *American Journa. of Agriculture and Science*, and the facts as stated in 1846 have been fully corroborated by observation and experience:

" The most remarkable fact brought out by this analysis is the presence of a large quantity of Iodine. We were able to detect it in one ounce of the water. This water, too, is mainly free from iron, as tincture of nutgalls, after standing twenty-four hours, produced merely a green tinge or color, and the salt, when evaporated, is white, or slightly yellowish white The spring, it seems to us, is quite an accession to the waters of Saratoga. It has a remarkably pleasant saline taste, with a pungency and liveliness which makes it agreeable as a beverage.

PAVILION FOUNTAIN.—This truly beautiful fountain is situate in the rear of the Columbian Hotel, and a few rods southeast of the Flat Rock Spring. It was long since discovered, and experiments made upon the water by the late Dr. J. H. Steed. Its remoteness, however, from the bank which gave egress to the other mineral fountains in the valley, places it in the midst of a deep morass, where it makes its appearance through an alluvial deposit of some forty feet in depth.

This water has been much used, both at home and abroad, since 1840. The free acid of the spring is most abundant, and passes off in great quantities from the mouth of the fountain. Its water is not so heavy as that of the Congress Spring; but the liberal quantities of free gas which is present impart to it, when drank, a very smart, pungent taste, and induce many to think it the strongest water of the valley. They form their opinion from the effects it produces on the palate while drinking it. This smart, pungent, and grateful taste, which is so characteristic of all our mineral waters here, would be enhanced by drinking them from metallic cups, instead of the glass tumblers so generally used. The reason is obvious to those who have studied the principles of galvanism.

Analysis of the Pavilion Fountain.

Chloride of Sodium	226.58 grs.
Carbonate of Magnesia	62.50
Carbonate of Lime	60.24
Carbonate of Soda	4.70
Oxide of Iron	3.10
Iodine of Sodium } Bromide of Potassium }	2.75
Silica	.62
Alumina	.25
	361.74
Carbonic Acid Gas, cubic inches	480.01 } 488.10
Atmospheric air	8.09 }

PUTNAM'S CONGRESS.—This fountain is situated midway between Broadway and Putnam Street, and nearly opposite the United States Hotel. It was discovered a long time since by Mr. Lewis Putnam, who, in 1835, excavated, tubed, and carefully secured it from the fresh water, and all other foreign substances about it.

It is justly a popular fountain, and is much used by both citizens and strangers, many of whom are particularly attached to it, and use it instead of the Congress, for cathartic purposes, with good success.

The water has been vended in considerable quantities every year since it has been in complete operation.

In connection with the spring is a bathing establishment, second to no other in the place for commodious baths, large rooms, and proper attendants. This, as well as the spring, is owned by Messrs. Putnam & Son, and always subject to their personal superintendence.

Temperature of this spring, 48°.

Analysis.

One gallon of the water furnished the following constituents, on analysis:

Chloride of Sodium	220.000 grs.
Carbonate of Soda	15.431
Carbonate of Magnesia	45.500
Carbonate of Lime	70.433
Carbonate of Iron	7.833
Hydriodate of Soda	2.500
Bromide of Potash	"
Silex and Alumina	1.500
Solid contents in one gallon	362.697
Carbonic Acid	317.753
Atmospheric Air	3.080
Gaseous contents in a gallon	320.833

THE SARATOGA SPRING.

This new mineral fountain is situated a few rods north of the curious High Rock Spring. It was dug down to, and tubed from, the rock in April, 1862. The water is composed of five distinct veins or jets, issuing out of five separate crevices in the rock; one of these veins undoubtedly formed the old and well-known IODINE SPRING—the other veins being new. The quality of the water as a beverage, and its virtues of a medicinal character, are conceded by all who have tested its merits. The verdict of the thousands of visitors and citizens who have used it has been so uniform in its favor, that the proprietors feel not the least hesitation in claiming, that as a CATHARTIC, a DIURETIC, and a TONIC, it is *unequaled;* while in other respects it is not excelled by the most popular and celebrated mineral waters of the world.

SOUTHERN DEPOT for the sale of the above mineral water, 68 Barclay Street, New York.

Saratoga Lake, four miles east of Saratoga Springs, is a place of great resort during the summer months. A large public house is situated at the north end of the lake, from whence a small steamer runs to the WHITE SULPHUR SPRING, some seven or eight miles, affording a delightful excursion. Boating and fishing parties are also accommodated with facilities for aquatic sports.

PRINCIPAL HOTELS IN SARATOGA SPRINGS.

AMERICAN HOTEL	Richard McMichael	Broadway.
CLARENDON HOTEL	Samuel L. White	Broadway.
COLUMBIAN HOTEL	U. N. Benedict	Broadway.
CONGRESS HALL	Hathorn & McOmber	Broadway.
CONTINENTAL HOTEL		Washington St.
MARVIN HOUSE	A. & D. Snyder	Broadway.
UNION HALL	W. W. Leland & Co.	Broadway.
UNITED STATES HOTEL	J. M. Marvin & Co.	Broadway.

SARATOGA SPRINGS. 69

TEN SPRINGS.—About a mile from the High Rock Spring, in an eastern direction, are situated the *Ten Springs*, so called from the circumstance of there being that number located near together. They never have acquired much celebrity, and it is probable, from their proximity to others so distinguished, that they will never rise into much consequence.

WHITE SULPHUR SPRING.—This spring is situated on the east side of Saratoga Lake, about half a mile south of Snake Hill. Its location is in a beautiful ravine, in the middle of which runs a fine little stream of fresh water, and a few rods east of the fountain it falls into the lake. As the ravine approximates the shore of the lake it widens a little, and the south bank particularly rises very abruptly to the height of some 35 or 40 feet above the surface of the brook.

Within some twenty rods of the lake shore a deep niche is formed in the south bank, somewhat in the form of a horseshoe. The bank here is almost perpendicular with its base, but a little elevated above the brook, which is within a few feet of the main bank of the ravine. At the base of this high bank, and at the center of the horse-shoe, passes out this sulphur spring, and its course to the brook is marked by the white sulphur which is deposited.

The temperature of this spring is 48°, barometer at 30°, and the temperature of the atmosphere at zero.

Its specific gravity is 1000.5.

 Sulphureted Hydrogen........................ 0.5
 Atmospheric Air 4.0
  Silex and Alumina, three grains to the gallon.

The QUAKER SPRINGS, situated about 10 miles in a southeast direction from Saratoga Springs, in the town of Saratoga, are of some celebrity. They contain lime, magnesia, and iron, held in solution by carbonic acid, and, like the others in the county they likewise contain a portion of common salt and soda.

The other springs of less note are the *Flat Rock, Hamilton, Columbian,* and *Washington Spring.*

On leaving Saratoga Springs for Whitehall, 40 miles, or Lake George, 29 miles, the northern route is continued by the *Saratoga and Whitehall Railroad*. If the traveler is destined for Lake George, the cars are left at *Moreau Station*, 15 miles above Saratoga Springs, where stages will be found in readiness to transport passengers over a good plank road to *Glen's Falls*, 5 miles, and from thence to *Caldwell*, 9 miles farther. Here are situated two large and popular hotels, affording every accommodation that may be desired; also, other luxuries that money alone can not purchase, viz., good mountain air, pure, wholesome water, and delicious fish of different kinds, such as ought to satisfy any "gourmand or faster" who has long been waiting to enjoy the luxury of partaking of the finely-flavored trout of *Lake Horicon* or its tributaries.

Passengers bound for Whitehall, Rutland, Burlington, Plattsburgh, or Montreal, proceed north from Moreau Station or Fort Edward, situated on the Hudson River, direct to the former place. At Whitehall the railroad route diverges east toward Rutland and Boston, while steamers of a large class run twice daily on Lake Champlain, leaving Whitehall morning and evening.

For a further description of Lake George and Lake Champlain, see pages 197 and 201.

WESTERN TOUR.

ROUTES FROM ALBANY AND TROY TO BUFFALO, NIAGARA FALLS, ETC.

THE first link of the great chain of railroads connecting the navigable waters of the Hudson with Lake Erie is the *Albany and Schenectady Railroad*, now forming a part of the great *New York Central Railroad*. It was one of the first constructed railroads in this State, the company having been chartered in 1826. It extends from Albany to Schenectady, 17 miles, and passes over a tract of sandy land, covered nearly the whole distance with a thick growth of stunted pines.

The *Schenectady and Troy Railroad*, also forming part of the New York Central, extends from the city of Troy to the city of Schenectady, on a line of 20 miles in length, and making, with the other road, two lines of travel diverging from the tide waters of the Hudson, in addition to the *Erie Canal*. This road from Troy inclines to the north, running parallel with the Mohawk River, and is remarkable for the variety and beauty of its scenery. This road also now forms a part of the *New York Central Railroad*.

The City of SCHENECTADY, 16 miles west of Albany, is handsomely situated on the south bank of the Mohawk, at the true commencement of the celebrated valley of that river. This is an ancient place, having been settled as early as 1620, by the Dutch, many of whose living descendants reside in the dwellings of their ancestors, and retain many of their primitive habits. This place was called by the Indians *Schagh-nac-tua-da*, signifying, in their language, "*beyond the pine plains.*" During the old French and Indian wars, Feb. 9, 1690, it was taken by surprise in the dead of night, was sacked and burned by the Indians; a great number of its inhabitants were massacred, and others carried away into captivity. It was chartered as a city in 1798, and in 1860 contained 9,579 inhabitants. Few inland towns present a more thronged thoroughfare than Schenectady. In addition to the *Erie Canal*, which passes through the center of the city, here diverge three important railroads. Besides those already mentioned, there is the *Saratoga and Schenectady Railroad*, running to Ballston Spa and to Saratoga Springs, 21½ miles.

The public buildings, dwellings, and stores in Schenectady present a plain appearance, perfectly in keeping with the general character of the place. There are several well-kept hotels, affording every desirable accommodation for the traveler, if inclined to tarry for business or pleasure. The place derives its most extended celebrity from being the seat of *Union College*, situated on the elevated ground about half a mile east of the compact part of the city. This institution was incorporated in 1795, and derived its name from the fact that its founders were members of different denominations, and proffered its advantages indiscriminately to the followers of every faith. The buildings consist of one stone and two brick edifices, containing accommodations for the president and professors and their families; two chapels, lecture and library rooms, four halls for the meeting of literary societies, and dormitories for students, of whom there are usually from 200 to 300, from every section of the country. Attached to the institution are about 250 acres of land, appropriated in part to groves for recreation and health. These are distinguished for beauty of feature and situation, and present great capability for improvement. The annual commencement takes place on the fourth Wednesday of July, after which there is a vacation of six weeks.

On leaving Schenectady for Saratoga Springs and for Utica, the railroad tracks cross the Erie Canal and Mohawk River by substantial bridges. If bound for the Springs, you proceed northward through an interesting region, passing on the way the village of Ballston Spa, an old and celebrated place of resort, and the terminus of the *Rensselaer and Saratoga Railroad*, which comes up from Troy. If bound to the West, your route is on the north side of the Mohawk, and your first halt is at the village of

AMSTERDAM, 15 miles from Schenectady, and connected by a toll-bridge with PORT JACKSON, on the opposite side of the river. Amsterdam contains about 2,500 inhabitants, and in the immediate vicinity are annually quarried large quantities of a fine quality of limestone, much used for the construction of locks and other public works.

Stages leave Amsterdam daily for the FISH HOUSE, on the Sacondaga River, and for other places to the north in Fulton County. One or two miles west of Amsterdam, on the line of the railroad, are situated two of the old stone mansions of the Johnson family, who figured largely in the early history of this part of the country.

FONDA, a pleasant village of recent date, and the county seat of Montgomery County, is 42 miles by railroad from Albany. It stands on the north side of the Mohawk, and opposite the village of FULTONVILLE, on the Erie Canal.

JOHNSTOWN, the county seat of Fulton County, lies 4 miles north of the Mohawk River, and 45 miles from Albany. This is an old and interesting place, containing about 1,700 inhabitants. It was originally founded by Sir William Johnson, whose residence, built of limestone, is still standing about one mile west of the village. A daily line of stages runs from Johnstown to Fonda, connecting with the cars on the New York Central Railroad.

SPRAKER'S BASIN, on the line of the Erie Canal, is 36 miles from Schenectady. Here is located a thriving settlement, containing a church and some 30 or 40 dwellings.

PALATINE BRIDGE, 54 miles from Albany, connects with the village of CANAJOHARIE, on the south bank of the Mohawk River. Canajoharie was incorporated in 1829, and now contains about 1,500 inhabitants. The Erie Canal passes through the center of the village. Stages leave this place daily, during the summer season, for Sharon Sulphur Springs and Cooperstown.

SHARON SPRINGS, some 8 or 10 miles south of Canajoharie, and 45 miles west of Albany, *via* the Cherry Valley turnpike, being 55 miles by railroad, *via* Palatine Bridge, has become a place of great resort for health and pleasure. The rides in the vicinity; the numerous villages; extensive views; neighboring caves, and romantic scenery, together with the delightful fishing in Otsego Lake, are among the many attractions offered to those seeking in the heat of summer either health or pleasure. Here are 5 or 6 first-class Hotels for the accommodation of visitors, being usually thronged with guests during the summer months.

These healthful fountains possess powerful attractions for the seekers of health, of pure air, and of splendid natural scenery. The springs are highly medicinal, and exceedingly pleasant and grateful, because the water is very cold when first taken from the fountain. Magnesia is the prevailing medicinal ingredient in one spring, and sulphur in the other.

The country around the Springs, and the Springs themselves, are elevated 900 feet above the Mohawk River, from which they are distant about eight miles. The elevation is achieved by a gradual ascent throughout the whole of this distance. A traveler who leaves the city of New York in the evening boat for Albany, may take breakfast in that city the next morning, and then place himself in a railroad car, which will convey him to Schenectady, and up the romantic valley of the Mohawk, to Palatine Bridge. There he takes a post-coach, and, availing himself of a plank road most of the way, is set down at the Springs before 1 o'clock, P. M. Fare from Albany, $1 10 in car, and $1 in post-coach.

Arrived at the Springs, he will find a number of houses for the temporary, and always very agreeable, accommodation of travelers or boarders. The oldest and most conspicuous of these is the "*Pavilion*," kept by Mr. Gardiner. This house being very large, will accommodate some three hundred persons, and it is kept in a style of elegance and luxury unsurpassed at any watering-place in the country. The site of the house, and piazza in front, command a most extensive and variegated prospect of the country for many miles around in the vicinity. The house next in importance is kept by Mr. S. Eldridge, and called the "Eldridge House." It is nearer to the Springs than the "Pavilion," and the charges for board are more moderate, although the house is extremely well provided.

The pure, clear waters of these springs, greatly resembling those of the White Sulphur Springs of Virginia, have been proved to be highly efficacious in rheumatic, cutaneous, and dyspeptic complaints, and, in some respects, possess medicinal and healing properties unsurpassed, and believed to be unequaled, in the United States or Canada.

COOPERSTOWN, although off from the great line of travel, east and west, is well worthy of a visit. It is 66 miles west of the city of Albany, by stage route, and most delightfully situated on a plain at the outlet of Otsego Lake, this being the chief source of the Susquehanna River. No inland village in the Union probably excels Cooperstown in elegance of situation and beauty of surrounding scenery. *Otsego Lake*, in the immediate vicinity, is a most beautiful sheet of water, abounding in trout and bass, celebrated for their peculiar flavor.

RICHFIELD SPRINGS, 69 miles from Albany, is situated near the head of Canaderaga Lake. There are also three or four well-kept hotels for the accommodation of visitors.

Richfield Sulphur Springs are some 1,800 feet above tide water, in a valley south of the Mohawk, amidst surrounding mountains, about 70 miles west of Albany, 13 south of Herkimer, in the immediate vicinity of the beautiful lakes of Otsego and Schuyler; in fact, there are five lakes, abounding with fish, within one hour's ride of the American Hotel, kept by Wm. P. Johnson.

Visitors will always find private conveyances at Herkimer Station, on the line of the N. Y. Central Railroad, or they can avail themselves of the daily stages which convey the mail to

Richfield Springs, so that parties visiting the Springs can leave the city of New York in the evening boats, and reach the Springs on the afternoon of the next day, and those leaving it by morning cars reach it on the same day.

FORT PLAIN, 57 miles from Albany by railroad route, on the south side of the Mohawk River, is situated on the line of the Erie Canal. It was incorporated in 1834, and now contains about 1,500 inhabitants. A daily line of stages runs from this place to Cherry Valley, Cooperstown, and Sharon Springs, in Schoharie County.

SAINT JOHNSVILLE, 63 miles from Albany, and 31 from Utica, is situated on the north side of the Mohawk, on the line of the New York Central Railroad; it contains about 300 inhabitants. The railroad cars usually stop here a sufficient time to enable passengers to obtain refreshments.

EAST CANADA CREEK enters the Mohawk River 3 miles west of St. Johnsville. This stream, for a considerable distance, forms the boundary line between the counties of Montgomery and Herkimer.

LITTLE FALLS, Herkimer County, is situated on both sides of the Mohawk, 73 miles west of the city of Albany. It was first incorporated in 1811, and amended in 1827; it now contains about 4,000 inhabitants and 400 dwelling-houses. The Mohawk River here falls, in the distance of half a mile, about 42 feet, affording hydraulic power to a large extent, only a small portion of which is at present occupied for manufacturing purposes.

This place and vicinity is justly celebrated for its wild and romantic scenery, and is much resorted to by the admirers of nature and art. The gap between the mountains, through which the river has apparently worn for itself a passage, though confined, is still of breadth sufficient to afford room for a large town. The rock at the river bed is primitive granitic gneiss, very hard, but is readily quarried and broken into building stone. Above this, on the mountain sides, lies the sand rock, and still higher, at the top, are extensive beds of blue limestone, great quantities of which have been used in constructing the locks, and for building, for coping, and for flagging. Through this gorge passes the Erie Canal, on the south side of the river, and the Utica and Schenectady Railroad and the Mohawk turnpike on the north. It is the gateway through which the product and travel of the vast West must, of necessity, pass to tide water. An aqueduct crosses the Mohawk at this place, communicating with a feeder on the north side of the river, and is a fine specimen of masonry. A daily line of stages runs between Little Falls and Trenton Falls, and several mail routes north and south branch off at this place.

WEST CANADA CREEK enters the Mohawk River 5 miles west of Little Falls. Its whole length is about 60 miles from its sources, in the wilds of Hamilton County. It is a romantic and lovely stream, and abounds with fine trout. About 20 miles from its mouth are situated *Trenton Falls*, being on the border of the town of the same name in Oneida County.

The village of HERKIMER, 79 miles from Albany, is handsomely situated in the valley of the Mohawk, on the north side of the river. It was incorporated in 1807, and now contains about 1,200 inhabitants, 150 dwelling-houses, a new brick court-house, and stone jail, built on an improved model, combining security and comfort to the prisoners. Here is a flouring mill, containing four run of stone, situated on a *hydraulic canal*, which is fed by the waters of the West Canada Creek. It is about three miles in length, and has two falls, one of 22 feet, and another of 15 feet, affording water-power sufficient to propel upward of 100 run of stone, most of which is unoccupied.

The village of MOHAWK, situated on the south side of the river, one mile west of Herkimer, is a thriving place of business, through which passes the Erie Canal.

The village of FRANKFORT, 9 miles east of Utica, is also situated on the line of the Erie Canal, and contains about 500 inhabitants.

The City of UTICA, situated on the south side of the Mohawk River, is on the site of old *Fort Schuyler*, 95 miles west of the city of Albany. It was chartered in 1832, and is now divided into seven wards, and governed by a common council, consisting of a mayor and 14 aldermen. In 1860 it contained 22,529 inhabitants, about 2,500 dwelling-houses, 4 Presbyterian churches, 1 Reformed Dutch, 4 Episcopal, 4 Baptist, 3 Methodist, 2 Roman Catholic, and 1 African church, and 1 Friends' meeting-house; 1 Protestant and 1 Catholic orphan asylum; 5 banking houses and 2 savings' banks; 1 mutual insurance company; 2 incorporated academies, one for males and the other for females; a museum located in the Exchange building; 10 hotels and taverns, besides several private boarding-houses; 2 extensive steam woolen factories; 1 large steam cotton factory, and 1 screw factory—all recently erected.

The *New York State Lunatic Asylum*, situated on somewhat elevated ground, about one mile west of the center of Utica, is a noble and imposing structure. The finished building can accommodate upward of 600 patients This humane establishment is calculated for the reception of all insane persons in the State, whose friends or county authorities may apply in their behalf.

In addition to the Erie Canal, which passes through the center of the city, the Chenango Canal commences at this place, and terminates at Binghamton, in Broome County.

UTICA AND BLACK RIVER RAILROAD.—This road is now finished from the city of Utica to Booneville, 35 miles. When completed it will extend to Philadelphia, Jefferson Co., a distance of 86 miles, connecting at the latter place with the *Rome, Watertown, and Ogdensburgh Railroad*. Passenger cars leave Utica twice daily for Booneville, passing near Trenton Falls, situated 16 miles north of Utica. Stages run from Booneville to Carthage and Watertown on the arrival of the trains.

The UTICA AND CLINTON RAILROAD extends from Utica to Clinton, 9 miles southward.

The principal hotels in Utica are chiefly situated on Genesee Street, of which the following are the most noted: Baggs' Hotel or Bleecker House, American Hotel, and Central Hotel.

TRENTON FALLS, 15 miles northeast from Utica by railroad and stage, situated on the West Canada Creek, in the town of Trenton, are among the most remarkable scenes in our coun try. The wild, secluded, and primeval aspect of the place serves greatly to heighten the effect of the striking spectacle presented by the stream; and the whole is so deeply embosomed in the primitive forest that no token of the long and deep gorge through which the waters rush is visible till you are on its very brink. Within a distance of about two miles there are no less than six distinct cascades, interchanging with rapids as picturesque as the falls themselves.

The first fall, beginning up stream, is called the *Upper Falls*, and has a descent of about 20 feet. The river then dashes along its rocky bed about a mile, with a descent, in that distance, of about 20 feet more, to the second falls, called *The Cascades*. A little farther down you come to the third fall, called the *Mill-dam*, from the regularity and smoothness of the ledge of rock, about 20 feet high, over which the waters pour. About 40 rods more bring you to the *High Falls*. At this place the volume of the stream is separated, by rifts in the rock, into three distinct cataracts, having a perpendicular pitch of more than 100 feet. Here the chasm has become very deep, and the high wooded banks and cliffs of bare rock on each side combine with the cataracts to make a spectacle of wild and savage grandeur. About 70 rods farther down you come to the fifth, or *Sherman's Falls*, having a descent of nearly 40 feet, from the foot of which the stream pours along a less rapidly descending bed to the sixth, or *Conrad's Falls*, a pitch of some 15 or 20 feet, and soon after the river, escaping from the deep and dark ravine, flows onward between more sunny banks and through a softer landscape.

HIGH FALLS—Trenton, N. Y.

The chasm, for the whole distance, is cut through a vast mass of lime-rock, which abounds with organic remains; and the path which the tourist *must* take, if he would obtain any adequate conceptions of the scene, is along a narrow shelf of rock near the foot of the high and in some places overhanging precipice, and on the immediate verge of rushing waters. This shelf is so narrow in several places, and so perilous, that it has been found necessary to guard it with a chain supported by iron standards let into the rock; though, sad to say, this safe-guard was not furnished till two interesting young females had been lost in the terrible flood. The entire descent of the stream, from the top of the *Upper Falls* to the foot of *Conrad's Falls*, is stated at 312 feet.

Trenton Falls Hotel, kept by Mr. Moore, is a place of great and fashionable resort.

The village of WHITESBOROUGH, 4 miles west of Utica, is situated on the south side of the Mohawk River. This is one of the oldest white settlements in this section of country, and has long been celebrated as a pleasant and attractive place of residence, being surrounded by fertile lands settled by an intelligent and wealthy community. It was incorporated in 1813, and now contains about 1,200 inhabitants, many of whom are engaged in manufacturing pursuits.

ORISKANY, 7 miles west of Utica, is a large manufacturing place, situated on the Oriskany Creek, near its junction with the Mohawk River. It contains about 1,000 inhabitants, 200 dwelling-houses, 2 churches, 4 public houses, 4 stores, and 2 large factory buildings, belonging to the "Oriskany Manufacturing Company," which annually manufacture into broad cloths and cassimeres about 200.000 pounds of wool, giving employment to about 150 men, women, and children. The buildings, grounds, and machinery of this establishment cost about $200,000.

It was here that the battle of Oriskany was fought, one of the bloodiest, in proportion to the numbers engaged, during the whole war of our Revolution, and in which Gen. Herkimer, of German Flats, lost his life. He was on his way, with about 800 of the militia of the Mohawk Valley, to the relief of the garrison at Fort Stanwix, when at Oriskany a deadly fire was opened on him and his corps, by a body of British regulars, tories, and Indians, from an ambuscade in a narrow ravine. The Americans were completely surrounded, but the gallant Herkimer and his brave compatriots maintained the fight for near six hours. Herkimer received his mortal wounds early in the fight, but he kept the field, seated on his saddle placed on a hillock, which gave him a view of the contest, and from which he calmly issued his orders to the last. This was on the 6th of August, 1777.

The village of ROME, 14 miles west of Utica, is situated near the head waters of the Mohawk, and on the line of the Erie Canal, where it is intersected by the *Black River Canal*. Here commences the *Watertown and Rome Railroad*, extending to Cape Vincent, 97 miles. The village was incorporated in 1819, and is a half-shire town with Whitesborough for Oneida County; it contains about 8,000 inhabitants, 800 dwelling-houses, a court-house and jail, and other public buildings. This place stands on the site of old *Fort Stanwix*, which was an important military post during the Revolutionary and French wars. Owing to its natural and artificial advantages, this village is fast increasing in wealth and numbers.

ONEIDA DEPÔT, 27 miles west of Utica, and 26 from Syracuse, is a new and thriving settlement, where the train of passenger cars usually stops some 10 or 15 minutes. One or two miles south of the depôt is the incorporated village of ONEIDA CASTLE, near which resides a remnant of the Oneida tribe of Indians, numbering about 300 souls.

WAMPSVILLE, 3 miles farther west, is a small settlement, through which passes the Syracuse and Utica Railroad.

CANASTOTA, 32½ miles west of Utica, by railroad, and on

the Erie Canal, was incorporated in 1835, and now contains about 1,000 inhabitants.

CHITTENANGO, 39 miles west of Utica, by railroad, is situated one mile south of the Erie Canal, with which it is connected by a side-cut. It contains about 1,000 inhabitants, 180 dwelling-houses, 3 churches, 3 taverns, 10 stores, 1 woolen factory, 1 flouring mill, and 2 large factories for the manufacture of water-lime, which is found in this vicinity, and is extensively used on the different public works of the State and for other purposes. There is a *sulphur spring* one mile south of the village of Chittenango, of some celebrity

The village of CAZENOVIA is situated on the Cherry Valley turnpike, about 10 miles south of the Erie Canal, 118 miles from Albany. It was incorporated in 1810, and now contains about 1,400 inhabitants, 250 dwelling-houses, and 4 churches of different denominations. Here is situated the Oneida Seminary, a theological institution sustained by the Methodist denomination of this and the neighboring States.

CAZENOVIA LAKE is a small but beautiful sheet of water, in the town of the same name. It is 4 miles long by 1 mile in width, abounding in different kinds of fish.

The City of SYRACUSE, 148 miles from Albany and 150 miles from Buffalo, by railroad route, is advantageously situated on the line of the Erie Canal, where it unites with the Oswego Canal, near the south end of Onondaga Lake. This aspiring city was chartered in 1848, and is divided into eight wards. In 1860 it contained 28,119 inhabitants. Here are located a new court-house and jail, built of Onondaga limestone, in the Anglo-Norman style of architecture; a city hall, county clerk's building, State Idiot Asylum, 8 banks, 2 savings' banks, 1 insurance company, an orphan asylum, and the Franklin Institute, organized in 1837; 25 churches of different denominations, and several large and well-kept hotels. The city is lighted with gas, and furnished with pure water. The *Oakwood Cemetery*, situated in the south part of the city, is well worthy of a visit.

PRINCIPAL HOTELS IN SYRACUSE.

Globe Hotel.....Ira Garrison......Opposite Railroad Depôt.
Syracuse House..Wm. D. Stewart..Adjoining Railroad Depôt.
Voorhees House .Sprague & Gage...North Salina Street.

The *Salt Springs*, in Syracuse and its immediate vicinity, are of great importance to this place and surrounding country. They are owned by the State, from which a handsome yearly revenue is derived. There are within the city alone ten coarse and fine salt companies, manufacturing in the aggregate a very large amount of pure salt, of a superior quality. Besides the above works, there are a number of iron founderies and other large manufacturing establishments.

The railroad facilities are also a very important feature to the prosperity of Syracuse. In addition to the *New York Central Railroad*, passing through the center of the city, here commences the *Syracuse Binghamton. and New York Railroad*, and the *Syracuse and Oswego Railroad*, the latter communicating with Lake Ontario, 35 miles distant. in a northerly direction. There are also three city railroads.

The traveler, on going west from Syracuse to Rochester, Buffalo. or Niagara Falls, has the choice of three routes or modes of conveyance, viz. : by railroad, *via* Auburn, Geneva, Canandaigua, etc , 104 miles to Rochester ; or proceed by *direct route*, 81 miles ; or still another route, by proceeding to Oswego, 35 miles, by railroad, and then taking a steamer for Rochester or Lewiston, and thence to Niagara Falls, passing over Lake Ontario.

GEDDES is an incorporated village, 2 miles west of Syracuse, on the Erie Canal, and within the bounds of the Onondaga Salt Springs Reservation. The most considerable business of the place is the manufacture of salt.

LIVERPOOL is another village principally engaged in the manufacture of salt. It stands near the northeasterly shore of Onondaga Lake, and on the line of the Oswego Canal, about 5 miles from Syracuse. It contains about 1,000 inhabitants.

Liverpool and Geddes are all included in the town of Salina, and within the limits of the Onondaga Salt Springs Reservation; and though the *original* Reservation included a much larger extent of surface than is occupied by these villages, yet these are the only portions of it within which the making of salt is carried on, the State having sold to private citizens the whole of the Reservation not included within these villages, as well as a very large part of what is included within their bounds.

Salt was first made on this tract at Salt Point, near the margin of Onondaga Lake, and within the bounds of Salina village. The manufacture, in very trifling quantities, at that point, was carried on by the Indians prior to the appearance of any white man among them, as it was by the white men also, at a very early period of their settlement in that vicinity. The earliest systematic arrangements, so far as records show, for making salt, to any important extent, at that place, date as far back as 1787, when works were erected which produced 10 bushels daily—a very insignificant quantity when compared with the present extent and productiveness of the works on the Reservation.

The *fine* salt, which is so called from the small size of its crystals, is produced by the agency chiefly of artificial heat, and the process of evaporation is carried on by boiling the brine in large iron kettles. The *coarse* salt is produced exclusively by evaporation in the open air. It is sometimes termed *solar* salt, and the crystals are large. This salt is the *purest* muriate of soda known to commerce. The *dairy* salt is so called from the particularly neat and convenient manner in which it is prepared and boxed for use in *dairies*.

The State of New York, as the proprietor of these salines, receives a duty of one cent a bushel on all the salt inspected on the Reservation, and the works are erected under written *leases* of the ground for specific terms of years, for making the *fine* salt; and under licenses, somewhat of the character of conditional grants, for making the *coarse* salt; but both are gratuitous, the *duty* being substituted for rent.

FROM SYRACUSE TO ROCHESTER AND BUFFALO.

CAMILLUS, 8 miles west of Syracuse, is situated on the line of the New York Central Railroad. It contains about 600 inhabitants.

. The village of JORDAN is situated on the Erie' Canal, 19 miles west of Syracuse. It was incorporated in 1835, and now contains about 1,300 inhabitants. A railroad is contemplated from this place to Skaneateles, from which a branch road, already constructed to the Auburn and Syracuse Railroad, is a part of the contemplated work.

SKANEATELES, 5 miles south of the line of the New York Central Railroad, is delightfully situated at the foot of Skaneateles Lake. It was incorporated in 1833, and now contains about 1,500 inhabitants. The lake, 15 miles long, and from half a mile to a mile wide, is a beautiful sheet of water, surrounded by well-cultivated farms and country residences, and celebrated for its fine trout, which are taken in great abundance, weighing from 5 to 10 pounds.

The City of AUBURN is situated on the outlet of Owasco Lake, 26 miles west of Syracuse and 8 miles south of the Erie Canal. It was chartered in 1848, and contained in 1860 10,986 inhabitants, 1,200 dwelling-houses, a court-house, jail, and county clerk's office. The *Auburn State Prison*, on the north side of the Owasco outlet, a splendid edifice of the kind, was founded in 1816, and cost over half a million of dollars. Here are inclosed 10 acres of land, surrounded by a solid stone wall, from 16 to 40 feet in height and 3 feet thick. The main building. facing the east, is 3 stories high, besides the basement, surmounted by a turreted cupola, in which is an alarm bell. The wings are of two stories, the whole front being 276 feet long, and the wings 242 deep by 45 feet wide, inclosing on three sides a court in the rear, about 190 feet square. The cells in the interior are built within the exterior front, are 5 stories high, surrounded by galleries. There are 770 of these separate cells, each cell being 7 feet long, 3½ feet wide, 7½ feet high, and calculated to accommodate one prisoner during his relaxation from labor. In addition to the cells, the main building contains a chapel, a hospital, dining-room for the prisoners, cooking apartments, and store rooms; besides apartments in the main front building, used as offices for the clerk and agent, and for the residence of the principal keeper. Here are now about 700 convicts, mostly engaged in different kinds of mechanical pursuits, carried on in workshops and under large sheds within the outside prison walls.

The *Auburn Theological Seminary* is a large stone edifice, 4 stories high above the basement, and will be 200 feet front, when fully completed as designed.

OWASCO LAKE, a few miles southeast of Auburn, is 12 miles long and about 1 mile wide, being celebrated for its picturesque scenery. The water is very transparent, abounding in fish, and the banks rather rugged.

WEEDSPORT, 21 miles west of Syracuse, and 8 miles north of Auburn, is on the Erie Canal. It was incorporated in 1831, and now contains about 1,200 inhabitants.

PORT BYRON, 3 miles west of the above place, and on the line of the New York Central Railroad (*direct route*), was incorporated in 1837, and now contains about 1,700 inhabitants. Here is an extensive flouring mill, with 12 run of stones, and other manufacturing establishments.

MONTEZUMA, 205 miles from Albany, by canal route, is situated at the junction of the Cayuga and Seneca Canal with the Erie Canal. It contains about 700 inhabitants, 1 church, 3 taverns, and 5 stores. Here are a number of *saline springs*, from which salt has been manufactured ever since the earliest settlement of this part of the country, and the salt is of the best and purest quality. "The specific gravity of this brine is 1.09767; and 1,000 parts of it contain 129.33 parts of dry solid matter, or 12.93, in 100 parts of brine. This is within one per cent. of the strength of much of the brine now worked in Onondaga County."

The village of CAYUGA, 10 miles west of Auburn, is situated on the east bank of Cayuga Lake; it contains about 400 inhabitants, 50 dwelling-houses, 1 church, 2 taverns, and 3 stores. Here the celebrated "Cayuga Bridge" crosses the lake, which is upward of a mile wide; a new bridge has also been here erected for the New York Central Railroad, still longer. A steamboat runs from this place to Ithaca, a distance of 40 miles.

Tourists traveling for pleasure are recommended to deviate south on their arrival at the foot of Cayuga Lake, and make the pleasant

TOUR OF THE CAYUGA LAKE.

CAYUGA LAKE, which constitutes one of the Central Lakes of New York, is 40 miles long and from 1 to 4 miles wide. It lies between the counties of Cayuga and Seneca, extending some 10 or 12 miles into Tompkins County. This lake, which is very deep, is navigated by steamboats from Cayuga Bridge to the village of Ithaca, stopping at the intermediate landings. It is a most beautiful sheet of water, surrounded by well-cultivated farms and thriving villages, and abounds with salmon trout, white fish, pike, pickerel, perch, and catfish. On several of the inlets to this lake, toward the south, are most beautiful and picturesque *water-falls*, well worthy the attention of the lovers of natural scenery. The outlet flows north into Seneca River, and thence into Lake Ontario.

The traveler has now one of the pleasantest paths of journeying before him. He finds at the wharf, at East Cayuga—or, as the station is known on all the routes, *Cayuga Bridge*—a beautiful steamboat, the "Kate Morgan," and in this his transit over the clear and healthful waters of this lake is to be made. The old bridge, cotemporaneous with the century, is almost among the relics of another day; and yet it was a famous thoroughfare in its time. It was memorable as a dividing barrier in old political times, opposing majorities frequently testing the strength of numbers on these lines.

Cayuga village is mostly upon the hill. The station-house has clustered a group of buildings around it, but the traffic of the country around finds its way to the upper street. A neat church, lately renovated, gives a pleasant appearance to the height, its steeple being conspicuous far up the lake. Here was in the days of coach and wagon a wonderful gathering of travelers, and many hours have passed away here, while team and men gathered strength to go into the *plunge* on bad roads.

The Old Bridge is a mile and some rods in length. It is now a solitude compared to its former activity. The Central Railroad crosses on a separate bridge, and has in part protected its way by luxuriant willows.

The boat now proceeds on its way to Ithaca. It takes a course near the east shore, as its first landing is at the village of Springport. For the first six miles the Cayuga is not deep. The depth in some spots is considerable, but not over 15 or 20 feet. In approaching Springport, at the right hand, is seen

FRONTENAC ISLAND,

the only island in the lake, and a beautiful locality it is. It was ceded by the State in 1856 to the village of Springport, as a pleasure-ground, and the citizens, under the intelligent lead of Mr. John J. Thomas, have improved and tastefully arranged its surface. Mr. Street, the State Librarian, one of the most original and delightful poets of this land, has written some beautiful stanzas on the theme of this island. It was the mention of this locality by A. B. Street, in his poem of " Frontenac," published by Bentley, of London, which induced this name to be given.

SPRINGPORT is a neat village, of about 1,100 inhabitants, active and industrious. The houses are tasteful, and some of the upper streets deserve special notice. Its chief feature is the celebrated spring which issues out of the earth on the very margin of the lake; but at just height enough to give a sufficient and enduring water-power. There are also abundant quarries of limestone, of excellent material for building or for plaster. The traveler can notice on the hill-side, immediately at the north of the island, a superb stone mansion, of unusual beauty and value, the property of Robert W. Howland, formerly of New Bedford. This house is worthy of a visit, as among the first class of rural residences This village is the residence of Mr. J. J. Thomas, a celebrated agricultural writer.

After making its landing here, the boat proceeds, skirting the eastern shore, and passing a part of the lake where the variety of points and little indentations give peculiar picturesqueness to the sail. The boat next lands at

Levanna, a small post-hamlet, 10 miles from the bridge. Just before reaching this, the tourist will see on the east bank the residence of William R. Grinnell. Ingleside is one of the most agreeable farms in the State, and, as it slopes from its ample and handsome dwelling to the water, gives at a glance a rural picture scarcely surpassed. From Levanna the boat sails onward beneath cliffs that, by their abrupt vine-covered steeps, break the line of the shore. till, in a distance of 2 miles (12 from Cayuga Bridge), Aurora is the next reached.

Aurora has tasteful dwellings and well-cultivated gardens to an extent which would repay the tourist to remain there a few hours. Its one long street is directly on the water side, and heavy, dark stone sea walls are the protection of the soil against its storms. These gardens have tasteful appendages of summer houses, and hedges, and floral cultivation, so that a sail along the shore furnishes many pretty incidents. The dwellings of Henry Morgan and of Henry Wells, by their situation and their value, attract notice at once. The gardens of many of the citizens have been planned and cultivated with unusual nicety and attention to good taste.

The village terminates at the south in the valuable farm of Richard Hale, of the New York *Journal of Commerce.* The center of the view in the village is the Academy and Library Hall. The latter contains, besides its thousands of volumes, a capital full-length portrait of Governor Seward, by Elliot, one of the most distinguished of limners.

Leaving Aurora, the boat passes by two picturesque points, ROCKY and OSBORNE'S POINTS, and after this the boat pursues its way to the western side of the lake.

At SHELDRAKE POINT the tourist will see a very pretty hamlet, the superb farm directly south of which was one of the localities which received much support as the proper site for the State Agricultural College. At this landing travelers destined for Ovid and the Agricultural College are landed.

Then follows in succession Kidder's Ferry and Trumansburgh Landing. This latter is the point for a large and enterprising village, a mile to the westward, whose citizen. Herman Camp, is so well known in the annals of benevolent effort.

GOODWIN'S POINT is the landing for those who would visit the Taghanic Fall, the fairest, loveliest fall in all the country. Its crystal vail, as it wreathes itself in that vast gorge, is a picture of beauty worth all the journey. The eulogy here given to this fall all who visit it will affirm. It has no equal in its blending of the lovely water with the gloomy gorge

At the east side of the lake there is a landing for the Ridge road, and a very convenient one it is. Then the boat, after making a landing for the village of Ludlowville, proceeds to Ithaca, the end of its route.

ITHACA is a large, prosperous town, whose beauty and enterprise gratifies the good sense of the *Dewitt's,* who originated it. It has all the accessories of a large population, and is just such a home as those who enjoy life there may felicitate themselves on possessing. Here will be found several well-kept hotels, and much beautiful scenery.

THE LAKES OF WESTERN NEW YORK.

ONEIDA LAKE is a large and important sheet of water, surrounded by the counties of Oneida, Madison, Onondaga, and Oswego. It is 22 miles long, and from 4 to 6 miles wide. It receives Wood Creek and its tributaries on the east, Oneida Creek and Chittenango Creek on the south, besides some smaller streams. On the east end of the lake there is a beautiful shelving beach, which is much resorted to for fishing with seines. White fish, pike, pickerel, perch, and catfish are caught in great abundance. The north shore is remarkable for its bold and picturesque beauty. This lake, in connection with its outlet into Oswego River, forms an important channel of trade, there being a branch canal of 6 miles in length at its east end, connecting with the Erie Canal, thus forming a connection with the Oswego Canal, which runs from Syracuse to Oswego, along the east bank of Oswego River.

Oneida Lake, in connection with Wood Creek and Seneca River, in early days formed an important channel of water communication from east to west, being navigated by a small class of vessels or boats running through to Seneca Lake.

SKANEATELES LAKE lies partly between the counties of Cayuga and Onondaga. It is 15 miles long, and from half a mile to one mile wide. This is a beautiful and romantic sheet of water; on the north it is surrounded by highly cultivated farms and country residences, while on the south the banks are more rugged and the scenery very picturesque and romantic. It is also highly celebrated for its fine trout, which are taken in great abundance, weighing from 5 to 10 pounds.

ONONDAGA LAKE is situated in the northern part of this county. It is about 7 miles long, and from 2 to 3 miles wide. This lake abounds in pike, pickerel. bass, and catfish. On its banks are the city of Syracuse and the villages of Geddes and Liverpool. Many have supposed that the water at the bottom of this lake was salt, from the fact that the salt springs are located on its borders; but, from experiments made some two or three years since, it has been ascertained that such is not the fact

Oтisco Lake lies in the western part of Onondaga County, and is about 5 miles long by 2 miles wide. This is a beautiful sheet of water, and the scenery about it in many places truly romantic. Its outlet flows south into Onondaga Lake.

Cazenovia Lake is a small but beautiful sheet of water, situated in the town of the same name. It is 4 miles long by 1 mile in width, abounding with different kinds of fish.

Owasco Lake, situated in Cayuga County, is 12 miles long and about 1 mile wide, abounding with trout and other fish of fine flavor. The water is very transparent, and the banks rather rugged, being celebrated for its picturesque scenery.

Cayuga Lake, which constitutes one of the central lakes of New York. is 40 miles long and from 1 to 3½ miles wide. It lies between the counties of Cayuga and Seneca, extending some 10 or 12 miles into Tompkins County. This lake, which is very deep, is navigated by steamboats from Cayuga Bridge to the village of Ithaca, stopping at the intermediate landings. It is a most beautiful sheet of water, surrounded by highly cultivated farms and thriving villages, abounding in salmon trout, white fish, pike, pickerel, perch, and catfish. On several of the inlets to this lake, toward the south, are most beautiful and picturesque water-falls, well worthy the attention of the lovers of natural scenery. The outlet flows north into Seneca River, near where it is crossed by two bridges, each upward of a mile in length—one being a toll-bridge, known as the *Cayuga Bridge*, and the other a new bridge, erected by the old Auburn and Rochester Railroad Company. (See page 88.)

Seneca Lake is one of the largest, as well as the most beautiful, of the numerous lakes which so much adorn Western New York. It extends from south to north 40 miles, and varies in width from 2 to 4 miles. It is very deep, and. in consequence. is never frozen. The depth is not accurately known, but was found a year or two ago to be about 560 feet about 12 miles above the outlet. The water is very clear, and at a considerable depth below the surface of course cool; it is sometimes brought up for drinking by letting down a corked bottle, till it reaches a depth at which the pressure of the water forces in the cork, and fills it. The lands about the southern or upper extremity of the lake are high and picturesque; about the northern less elevated, but undulating, and covered with the richest crops, with here and there remains of the magnificent primitive forest. The outlet of the lake is at the northeastern angle, and the discharge of water furnishes an ample supply of power to the manufactories of Waterloo and Seneca Falls, which flourishing villages are situated, the former about 6, and the latter 10 miles from the lake. Seneca Lake receives the waters of Crooked Lake at Dresden, about 12 miles above Geneva. The outlet of Crooked Lake is about 6 miles in length, and the descent to Seneca Lake about 270 feet. A canal constructed along this outlet connects the two lakes. Seneca Lake does not so much abound with fish as some of the other lakes, probably in consequence of the depth and coldness of its waters. There are found in it, however, white-fish, pike, pickerel, trout, perch, herring, rock-bass, striped bass, chub, sunfish, catfish, eels, shiners, mullet, etc.

A steamer runs on this lake, summer and winter, for the conveyance of passengers.

CANANDAIGUA LAKE is a most beautiful sheet of water, 14 miles long, and from 1 to 1½ miles wide, lying mostly in the county of Ontario, and a small part in Yates County. It is surrounded by highly cultivated lands, justly celebrated for their fertility, diversified by charming scenery. Its waters, which are deep and clear, abound with fish of different kinds, and are elevated 670 feet above the Atlantic Ocean. *Canandaigua Outlet* flows northeast into Flint Creek, then into Clyde and Seneca River, all of which are important mill-streams. The steamer "JOSEPH WOOD" runs from the village of Canandaigua to the head of the lake, landing at Cheshire, Gorham, Middlesex, and South Bristol. Stages run from the landing at the head of the lake to *Blood's*, on the Buffalo, Corning, and New York Railroad, connecting at Corning with the New York and Erie Railroad.

CROOKED LAKE, by the Indians called *Keuka*, lies partly in the county of Steuben and partly in Yates. It is 22 miles in length, averaging 1½ miles in width, running nearly north and south. The waters of this lake are 270 feet above Seneca Lake, with which it is connected by an outlet and canal. It abounds in salmon trout, white fish, pickerel, perch, sunfish, bass, and catfish. Its waters are cool and transparent, and from 3 to 500 feet in depth. At *Bluff Point*, 9 miles north of the head of the lake, it is divided by a high promontory, extending on the east to near the village of Penn-Yan, a farther distance of 13 miles, while the northern branch extends 9 miles to Branchport. A steamboat for the conveyance of passengers and towing plies daily from Hammondsport to Penn-Yan, affording a fine view of the lake and adjacent country.

CHAUTAUQUE LAKE, lying in the county of Chautauque, N. Y., its head being within 8 miles of Lake Erie, is a most remarkable and beautiful sheet of water, and deserves a notice, although its waters flow south into the Allegany River, and thence into the Gulf of Mexico. It is 18 miles in length, and in breadth varies from 2 to 3 miles, except near the middle, where it contracts to a few rods. It is navigable for steamboats from Mayville, at its head, to the foot of the lake, thence by its outlet to the Connewango Creek. This lake is elevated 726 feet above the surface of Lake Erie, and 1,291 feet above the Atlantic Ocean, being the highest body of water in the Union on which a steamer floats.

Extract from a New York paper, dated September, 1856.

The starting of a new steamboat on Chautauque Lake, between Jamestown and Mayville, the county seat, is quite an event with us. This lake is eighteen miles long and three miles wide. It is a beautiful sheet of water, directly in the center of the county, which it adorns as gracefully as any jewel its settings. It is seven hundred feet higher than Lake Erie, though the distance between the two lakes is only seven or eight miles. Chautauque Lake is the highest water navigated by steam in the State of New York. The little steamboat which plies daily between Jamestown and Mayville is called the "C. C. Dennis." The ride on this boat to Mayville, and thence over the ridge which divides the two lakes to Westfield, is one of the most interesting and romantic in the country. Jamestown is situated four miles from Chautauque Lake, and on its outlet. The outlet is a deep, sluggish stream, shaded on both sides by a heavy forest of tamaracks, and hedged in by an undergrowth of shrubbery, so dense that the view is completely intercepted. The ride through the graceful windings of the outlet, reposing so quietly in the bosom of such luxuriant vegetation, reminds one of the accounts we often read of the scenery of tropical regions. The shores of the lake present no bluffs, but they slope back gradually from the water's edge, and are covered with fine farms. You leave the steamer at Maysville, and take the stage for Westfield. A ride of about 2 miles brings you to the summit of the ridge which divides the lakes, and here a most magnificent panorama is opened to your view. A few miles distant, and 700 feet below you, Lake Erie stretches its blue expanse toward Canada and Buffalo, which you can almost see. It is dotted over with the whited canvas of sailing vessels, from which you may now and then distinguish a steamer by its long trail of smoke.

At the foot of the hill on which you stand lies the beautiful village of Westfield, in the midst of a rich and fertile country. Behind you lies Lake Chautauque, which looks like Lake Erie in miniature. There is a barn on the ridge, the water falling on the eaves of which run one way through Lake Chautauque and the Allegany and Ohio rivers to the Mississippi and the Gulf of Mexico, and on the other side to Lake Erie and the Gulf of St. Lawrence.

The village of SENECA FALLS, 16 miles west of Auburn, and 190 miles from Albany, by railroad route, is advantageously situated on both sides of the outlet of Seneca Lake. It was incorporated in 1831, and now contains about 7,000 inhabitants, 800 dwelling-houses, 7 churches of different denominations, 1 cotton factory, and 8 flouring mills. In this neighborhood are large quantities of gypsum, which is here ground and sent to different parts of the country. The Cayuga and Seneca Canal and the Auburn and Rochester Railroad pass through this village. The water-power afforded by the Seneca outlet is very great; the descent from Seneca to Cayuga Lake, a distance of 12 miles, being about 75 feet. The stream is abundant, and not subject to freshets, scarcely ever having a rise to exceed two feet; the hydraulic power is great, and is but partially employed. At Seneca Falls there is a descent of upward of 40 feet within the distance of one mile. Here are five locks in the Cayuga and Seneca Canal, which unites with the Erie Canal at Montezuma.

WATERLOO, 193 miles west of the city of Albany, is handsomely situated on both sides of the outlet of Seneca Lake, which is in part used as the Cayuga and Seneca Canal. It was incorporated in 1824, and now contains about 5,000 inhabitants, 600 dwelling-houses, a court-house and jail, being a half-shire town with Ovid; 1 Presbyterian, 1 Episcopal, 1 Baptist, and 1 Methodist church; an academy, 8 hotels and taverns, 1 banking house, 25 dry goods, grocery, and other stores; 1 large woolen factory, which manufactures over 200,000 pounds of wool annually, and 5 flouring mills. containing 18 run of stone. The fall of water at this place is about 16 feet. In the immediate vicinity are quarried large quantities of limestone, extensively used for building. In addition to the Cayuga and Seneca Canal, the New York Central, or Auburn and Rochester Railroad, passes through this village, which is about equidistant between Cayuga and Seneca lakes.

GENEVA. 52 miles west of Auburn, and 200 miles from Albany, *via* New York Central Railroad, is beautifully situated near the foot, or north end, of Seneca Lake, on the western side. The principal part of the village, which is devoted to the residences of the inhabitants, lies upon a ridge along the banks of the lake, and elevated about 100 feet above the surface, while the business part extends to the plain which lies at the foot of the lake, and but little elevated. The land west of the village is peculiarly formed, consisting of a succession of ridges parallel to the lake, and rising higher and higher for some distance, commanding a view of its waters, as if formed for choice residences in this region of beauty. The village was incorporated in 1812, and now contains about 5,000 inhabitants and 800 dwelling-houses. The Geneva College, attached to which are three buildings, and the Geneva Lyceum, are located here, and 8 churches of different denominations. The new Episcopal church is a splendid edifice, erected at a cost of about $30,000. The accommodation for strangers at Geneva is very good, there being several well-kept hotels; and carriages are always in readiness at the railroad depôt and steamboat landing, to convey passengers to any part of the village. Two or three steamboats ply regularly on the lake, running daily up and down between Geneva and the village of Jefferson at the head of the lake, connecting with stages to Elmira and Corning, and at the latter place with the railroad to the cities of New York and Philadelphia. A boat is employed in towing canal boats, which come to Geneva by the Cayuga and Seneca Canal, a branch of the Erie Canal, and thence to the villages on the lake, and to the canal which connects this lake with Crooked Lake, and the Chemung Canal, leading from Jefferson to the Chemung River at Elmira, and by the feeder to Corning. The meridian of the capital at Washington passes through the lake about half a mile east of Geneva.

Geneva, or *Hobart*, *College* received its charter in 1825, and is a flourishing institution. The college buildings, three in number, are beautifully situated on Main Street, overlooking Seneca Lake. A large and handsome building is about being erected on the same street for the use of the medical department.

CLYDE, 186 miles from Albany, *via* the New York Central Railroad, is a flourishing town, situated on the line of the Erie Canal, containing about 1,800 inhabitants. It is proposed to construct a canal from this place to Lake Ontario.

LYONS, 16 miles north of Geneva, is eligibly situated on the Erie Canal, 193 miles west of Albany by *direct route*. It was incorporated in 1831, and now contains about 3,200 inhabitants, 450 dwelling-houses, a court-house and jail, county clerk's and surrogate's office; 1 Presbyterian, 1 Episcopal, 1 Methodist, 1 Baptist, and 1 Lutheran church. Stages leave Lyons daily for Geneva on the south, and Sodus Point on the north, situated on the north shore of Lake Ontario.

NEWARK, 7 miles west of Lyons, on the Erie Canal, is an active place of business. and contains about 2,000 inhabitants.

PALMYRA, 15 miles west of Lyons, and 206 from Albany, was incorporated in 1828, and now contains about 2,400 inhabitants. It is situated on an elevated and dry piece of ground, in the midst of a delightful wheat-growing country. The main street is over one mile and a quarter in length, and at each end touches the canal; it is intersected by cross streets of ample width, many of which are ornamented by beautiful shade trees.

On leaving Geneva, going west by railroad, you incline to the north, passing through a fine section of country, for which the county of Ontario is justly celebrated.

VIENNA, 8 miles from Geneva, is a flourishing place, on the outlet of the Canandaigua Lake, at the junction of Flint Creek. There are two settlements about one mile apart, known as *East Vienna* and *West Vienna*.

CLIFTON SPRINGS, 3 miles west of Vienna, are resorted to for their medicinal properties, and have become somewhat celebrated. They are *sulphur springs*, of a similar character to many others to be found in Western New York. Here is a large and commodious public house, for the accommodation of visitors.

" This place is admirably situated, remote from the noise and dust of large villages or cities, embracing a beautiful grove of forest trees, as its pleasure-grounds, from the midst of which flow its *springs of pure and healthful water*, so disposed by nature as to please and interest the visitor, and render it a desirable retreat, whether for those seeking a restorative from disease, those who have a few leisure days or weeks to spend in recreation and pleasure, or for those who, with their families, are disposed to leave the heated walls of a city residence to enjoy the refreshing breezes and pure atmosphere of the country, during the warm season."

The waters, which are mainly of a sulphurous character, charged somewhat with soda, magnesia, and carbonic gas, stand unsurpassed in their medicinal character, as a remedy for the various skin diseases, rheumatic affections, dyspepsia, general debility of the system, etc., and have effected cures in cases where the waters of other springs have failed.

CANANDAIGUA is delightfully situated near the foot of Canandaigua Lake, 223 miles west of Albany by railroad. It was incorporated in 1815, and now contains about 5,000 inhabitants, 800 dwelling-houses, a court-house, jail, surrogate's office, county clerk's office, and town-house; 1 Presbyterian, 1 Episcopal, 1 Baptist, 1 Methodist, and 1 African church; 2 banking houses and a savings' bank. No place in the State probably exceeds this village as a desirable place of residence, being surrounded by a rich agricultural district, abounding in almost every luxury for which *Western New York* is so justly celebrated. On the south, at a short distance, lies Canandaigua Lake, with its cultivated shores, in full view of this abode of taste and opulence.

The village of VICTOR is 9 miles west of Canandaigua, and a little to the north of the railroad.

PITTSFORD, 12 miles farther, is on the line of the Erie Canal, near its intersection with the railroad. It was incorporated in 1827, and now contains about 700 inhabitants.

BRIGHTON, 4 miles east of Rochester, is also on the line of the Erie Canal.

The City of ROCHESTER, 230 miles west from Albany, and 68 miles east of Buffalo, by railroad route, is advantageously situated on both sides of the Genesee River, and on the line of the Erie Canal, 7 miles south of Lake Ontario, with which the

Genesee River affords good water communication for steamboats and schooners from the landing, 2 miles below the center of the city. It was chartered in 1834, and is now divided into 9 wards, being governed by a mayor, recorder, and board of aldermen. It contained in 1860 48,204 inhabitants, mostly engaged in mercantile and manufacturing pursuits; a new city hall and court-house; a jail and county clerk's office; a surrogate's office; 2 public markets; gas works; water works; 10 banking houses; 3 savings' banks; 1 mutual insurance company; 5 Presbyterian churches, 4 Episcopal, 3 Baptist, 4 Methodist, 6 Roman Catholic, 1 Unitarian, 1 Universalist, 1 Covenanters, 1 Lutheran, 2 Friends' meeting houses, and 2 African churches; 2 orphan asylums; a collegiate institute; 4 female seminaries, and 16 public schools. The hotels are numerous, and most of them well kept, affording every desirable luxury. The *Osburn House* is a new and extensive hotel edifice, situated on the corner of Main and St. Paul streets.

The *Rochester University* is a new institution of learning, under the charge of the Baptist denomination. Here also is situated, on the north part of the city, the *House of Refuge* for Western New York, now containing about 400 inmates. The building is a large and substantial brick edifice, surrounded by a high stone wall.

To the immense water-power which Rochester possesses, by means of a succession of falls in the Genesee River, may be justly ascribed her rapid growth and substantial wealth There are now within the limits of the city, and all using water-power, 21 flouring-mills, with 108 run of stones, capable of manufacturing 600,000 barrels of flour annually; 3 woolen factories, 2 cotton factories, 11 iron founderies and machine shops, 2 brass founderies, 3 paper-mills, 2 oil-mills, 7 saw-mills, 1 pail factory, 3 pump factories, 2 edge tool factories, 2 threshing-machine and fanning-mill factories, 1 chair factory, 2 case factories, 2 stair manufactories, 3 sash factories, 4 tanneries, 3 distilleries, 6 breweries, 4 tobacco and snuff factories, and 4 steam-planing and flooring mills. Within the limits of the city, a distance of 3 miles, the total fall of water in the river is about 250 feet, affording during most of the year an almost inexhaustible supply of water-power, which is as yet but partly used for manufacturing purposes.

Here are about 20 forwarding establishments connected with the trade of the Erie and Genesee Valley canals, the latter running south through the rich valley of the Genesee River. There is also a limited shipping interest on the Genesee River and Lake Ontario. A great number of canal boats have been built at Rochester, there being no less than 11 boat-yards for their construction. Railroad cars and carriage-making are also extensively carried on here to advantage.

American and British steamboats arrive and depart daily, during the season of navigation, from the landing on the north of the city, and from *Charlotte*, at the mouth of the river, 7 miles distant, to where a plank road is now constructed, affording a most delightful ride during pleasant weather. Railroad cars and canal packets arrive and depart almost hourly.

No traveler for pleasure should pass through Rochester without stopping over at least one day to see the city and visit the objects of interest in its vicinity, the natural and artificial curiosities being well worthy of notice. The most important of them are the *Genesee Falls*, which are seen to great advantage from the east side of the river, a short distance below the railroad bridge, where is a perpendicular descent of 96 feet; 2 miles below is another fall of 75 feet. The noble aqueduct for the enlarged Erie Canal is a splendid specimen of mason work, well worthy of examination. The above, together with *Mount Hope Cemetery*, most beautifully situated on the east side of the River, about 2 miles south of the city, afford many points of attraction, well worthy the attention of the traveler.

The *Genesee Valley Canal* commences at Rochester, and ascends the rich valley of the Genesee, being now completed a distance of 88 miles, with a branch to Dansville, of 12 miles.

The *Rochester and Genesee Valley Railroad* is now completed to Mount Morris, 36 miles, passing through the village of Avon, connecting with a line of travel to Buffalo on the west and the city of New York on the east.

The most noted place of resort in the valley of the Genesee is AVON SPRINGS, 18 miles south of Rochester. The village is delightfully situated about half a mile east of the right bank of the Genesee River, and 2 miles from the Genesee Valley Canal, on an elevated terrace, about one hundred feet above the river, commanding an extensive prospect of the rich Genesee Valley and surrounding country.

Connected with the village, on the southwest, are the justly famed medicinal springs, giving celebrity to the place. The two principal springs are distinguished as the Upper and Lower Springs, distant from each other about 80 rods. They possess similar properties, differing only in the relative quantities of the same mineral ingredients. Analysis and experience have fully tested the sanative properties of these waters. They are found peculiarly efficacious in disorders of the digestive organs, rheumatic complaints, and gout, in all sorts of cutaneous affections, and in every kind of obstructions.

There are several well-kept hotels, both at the village and near the Springs. The most noted are the Avon Eagle Hotel, the Avon Hotel or Hosmer House, the Knickerbocker Hall, and the Spring Hotel. The two latter are situated near the Springs, the two former in the village. The accommodations for bathing are also extensive and handsomely arranged, there being three establishments, altogether affording great attractions not only for the invalid but for the seeker of pleasure.

RAILROAD ROUTE FROM ROCHESTER TO BUFFALO.

The *New York Central Railroad* extends west from Rochester, through the villages of CHURCHVILLE and BERGEN, forming the great eastern and western thoroughfare from the Atlantic Ocean to the *Great Lakes* of America.

BATAVIA, 32 miles west of Rochester, 36 east from Buffalo, and 262 from Albany, by railroad route, is pleasantly situated on a plain, through which flows the Tonawanda Creek. It was incorporated in 1823, and now contains about 3,000 inhabitants, 400 dwelling-houses, a court-house, jail, and county clerk's office, a State arsenal, and the general land office of the Holland Land Company. In addition to the New York Central Railroad, the Canandaigua and Niagara Falls Railroad, and the Buffalo, New York, and Erie Railroad, also pass through Batavia, affording great facilities to reach Albany, New York, Philadelphia, etc. Stages run from Batavia south to Warsaw; and north to Albion and Lockport.

The village of ATTICA, 11 miles from Batavia, and on the Tonawanda Creek, is pleasantly situated. It is an active place of business, containing about 1,000 inhabitants. The *Buffalo and New York City Railroad* passes through this village, connecting with the New York and Erie Railroad at Hornellsville.

RAILROAD ROUTE FROM ROCHESTER TO NIAGARA FALLS

BROCKPORT, 17 miles west of Rochester, and 246 by railroad from Albany, is handsomely situated on the Erie Canal. It was incorporated in 1829, and now contains about 2,200 inhabitants and 300 dwelling-houses.

The village of HOLLEY, 5 miles west of Brockport, contains about 700 inhabitants. Sandy Creek flows through this place, over which the canal passes by means of an embankment, 75 feet above the bed of the stream, which is conveyed under it by a culvert.

ALBION, on the Erie Canal, 30 miles from Rochester, and 250 miles from Albany, by railroad route, was incorporated in 1829, and now contains about 3,800 inhabitants, 500 dwelling-houses, a court-house, jail, and county clerk's office; 2 banking houses; an incorporated academy, and Phipps' Female Seminary, both in a flourishing condition, to each of which are attached large brick edifices.

The village of GAINES, 1 or 2 miles north of Albion, and on the *Ridge Road*, was incorporated in 1832, and now contains 600 or 700 inhabitants.

The ALLUVIAL WAY, or RIDGE ROAD, is a work of nature, extending from the Genesee River, near Rochester, to the Niagara River, near Lewiston. It is a gently curving ridge, composed of beach-sand and gravel-stones. apparently worn smooth by the action of water. Its general width is from 6 to 8 rods, raised in the middle, and the top presents an excellent road, called the "Ridge Road," extending upward of 80 miles, being from 6 to 10 miles south of the present shore of Lake Ontario, of which it once no doubt formed the beach. This same remarkable feature extends west to Hamilton, C. W., situated at the head of Lake Ontario.

KNOWLESVILLE, 7 miles west of Albion. is an incorporated village on the line of the Erie Canal, and contains about 500 inhabitants.

MEDINA, 4 miles farther west, on the Erie Canal, was incorporated in 1832, and now contains about 2,800 inhabitants, 250 dwelling-houses, and several mills and manufacturing establishments.

MIDDLEPORT, 17 miles west of Albion, contains about 400 inhabitants.

GASPORT, 5 miles farther west, takes its name from several mineral burning springs of some celebrity. situated near the line of the canal. The gas is used for domestic purposes.

The village of LOCKPORT is on the Erie Canal, 25 miles

northeast of Buffalo, and from Albany, by railroad route, 285 miles. It was incorporated in 1827, and now contains about 11000 inhabitants, 1,200 dwelling-houses, a court-house, jail, and county clerk's office.

The hydraulic power derived from the surplus waters of the Erie Canal at this place is sufficient to propel at least 300 run of mill-stones, and is admirably located for an extensive manufacturing town. In addition to the Erie Canal, which passes through the center of the village, the *Rochester, Lockport, and Niagara Falls Railroad* passes through this place, and runs to Niagara Falls, 20 miles; the *Lockport and Buffalo Railroad* extends a distance of 25 miles to the city of Buffalo, affording a speedy communication for travelers visiting the Falls and Buffalo. Here are ten combined locks, constructed of limerock, in the most finished style of masonry, to accommodate the enlarged Erie Canal.

On leaving Lockport for the West, passengers can proceed by railroad, direct to Buffalo, 25 miles, passing through Tonawanda, or continue on by direct route to the *Suspension Bridge*, 20 miles.

At the Suspension Bridge, or Niagara City, the New York Central Railroad cars connect with the trains running on the *Buffalo, Niagara Falls, and Lewiston Railroad*, forming a through line of travel from Lake Erie to Lake Ontario, on the American side of the Niagara River, length 28 miles, connecting with steamers running on Lake Ontario.

The *Erie and Ontario Railroad*, on the Canada side of the river, extends from Chippewa to Niagara, C. W., length 17 miles; also connecting with steamers running to Toronto and other ports on Lake Ontario and the St. Lawrence River.

The *Great Western Railway*, of Canada, commencing at the Suspension Bridge, also connects with the New York Central Railroad, forming the great line of travel to Hamilton, Toronto, Detroit, the Upper Lakes, and the *Far West*

BUFFALO.

This city possesses commanding advantages, being 22 miles above Niagara Falls, is distant from Albany 298 miles by railroad, and about 350 miles by the line of the Erie Canal; in N lat. 42° 53′, W. long. 78° 55′ from Greenwich. It is favorably situated for commerce at the head of Niagara River, the outlet of Lake Erie, and at the foot of the great chain of Upper Lakes, and is the point where the vast trade of these inland seas is concentrated. The harbor, formed of Buffalo Creek, lies nearly east and west across the southern part of the city, and is separated from the waters of Lake Erie by a peninsula between the creek and lake. This harbor is a very secure one, and is of such capacity, that although steamboats, ships, and other lake craft, and canal-boats, to the number, in all, of from three to four hundred, have sometimes been assembled there for the transaction of the business of the lakes, yet not one-half part of the water accommodations has ever yet been occupied by the vast business of the great and growing West. This is a great center for railroads running east, west, and south.

Buffalo was first settled by the whites in 1801. In 1832 it was chartered as a city, being now governed by a mayor, recorder, and board of twenty-six aldermen. Its population in 1830, according to the United States Census, was 8,668; in 1840, 12,213; and in 1850, 42,261. Since the latter period the limits of the city have been enlarged by taking in the town of Black Rock; it is now divided into thirteen wards, and, according to the census of 1860, contained 81,130 inhabitants, being now the third city in point of size in the State of New York.

The principal public buildings are a U. States custom-house and post-office; city hall; court-house and jail; two theaters, and fifty churches of different denominations. Here are also eight banking-houses, four savings banks, and several fire and marine insurance companies. The principal Hotels are the *American*, and *St. James Hotel*, and the *Mansion House*, on Main Street.

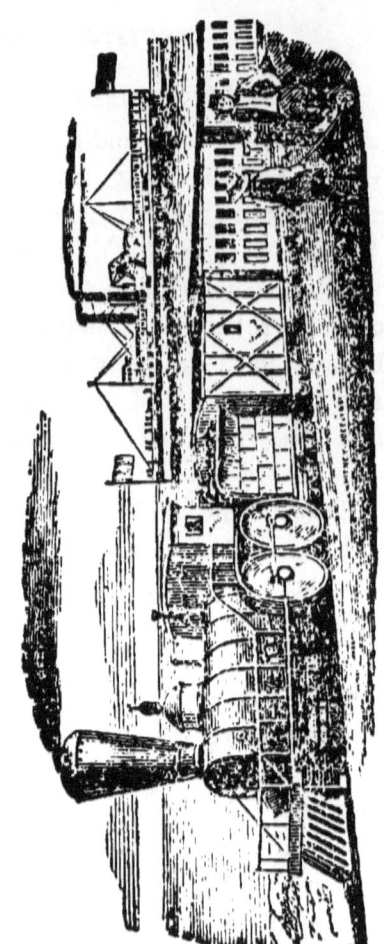

RAILROAD AND STEAMBOAT ROUTES FROM BUFFALO TO NIAGARA FALLS, TORONTO, ETC.

THE most usual mode of conveyance from Buffalo to the Falls of Niagara, and thence to Lake Ontario, or into Canada, is by the *Buffalo, Niagara Falls and Lewiston Railroad*, 28 miles in length. It runs through Tonawanda, 11 miles; Niagara Falls, 22 miles; Suspension Bridge, 24 miles, connecting with the Great Western Railway of Canada, and terminates at Lewiston, the head of navigation on Niagara River, 28 miles.

American and Canadian steamers of a large class leave Lewiston several times daily, for different ports on Lake Ontario and the St. Lawrence River.

There is also another very desirable mode of conveyance, by Steamboat, descending the Niagara River, from Buffalo to Chippewa, C. W., thence by the *Erie and Ontario Railroad*, 17 miles in length; passing in full view of the Falls, to the Clifton House, three miles below Chippewa; Suspension Bridge, five miles; Queenston, eleven miles, terminating at Niagara, C. W., thirty-five miles from Buffalo.

As the Steamboat leaves Buffalo on the latter route, a fine view may be obtained of Lake Erie and both shores of Niagara River. On the Canada side, the first object of interest are the ruins of old FORT ERIE, captured by the Americans July 3d, 1814. It is situated at the foot of the lake, opposite the site of a strong fortress which the United States government have recently erected for the protection of the river and the city of Buffalo.

WATERLOO, C. W., three miles below Buffalo and opposite Black Rock (now a part of Buffalo), with which it is connected by a steam-ferry, is handsomely situated on the west side of Niagara River, which is here about half a mile wide. The *Buffalo and Lake Huron Railroad* runs from Fort Erie. near Waterloo, to Paris, C. W., where it connects with the Great Western Railway of Canada. It is now completed to Stratford, 116 miles, will soon be finished to Goderich, lying on L. Huron.

GRAND ISLAND, belonging to the United States, is passed on the right in descending the river. It is a large and valuable tract of good land, abounding with white oak of a superior quality

NAVY ISLAND, belonging to the British, is next passed, lying within gunshot of the mainland. This island obtained great notoriety in the fall and winter of 1837-8, when it was occupied by the "Patriots," as they were styled, during the troubles in Canada. The steamer Caroline was destroyed on the night of December 29th, 1837, while lying at Schlosser's Landing, on the American shore, having been engaged in transporting persons to and from the island, which was soon after evacuated.

Opposite Navy Island, on the Canada side, near Chippewa battle-ground, is the house in which Capt. Usher resided when murdered in 1838. It is supposed he fell by the hands of some of the deluded patriots, having been shot by a secret foe, while in his own house.

CHIPPEWA, 20 miles below Buffalo and two miles above the Falls, is on the west side of Niagara River, at the mouth of a creek of the same name, which is navigable to PORT ROBINSON, some eight or ten miles west; the latter place being on the line of the Welland Canal. The village of Chippewa contains a population of about 1,000 souls. Steamboats and lake craft of a large size are built at this place for the trade of Lake Erie and the Upper Lakes. It has obtained a place in history on account of the bloody battle which was fought near it in the war of 1812, between the United States and Great Britain. The battle was fought on the 5th of July, 1814, on the plains a short distance south of the steamboat landing. The American forces were commanded by Major Gen. Jacob Brown, and the British, by Major General Riall, who, after an obstinate and sanguinary fight, was defeated with considerable loss.

At Chippewa commences the railroad extending to Niagara, at the mouth of the river, a distance of 17 miles. Steamboats continue the line of travel from both ends of this road, thus furnishing an interesting and speedy conveyance between Lakes Erie and Ontario.

On arriving in the vicinity of the FALLS OF NIAGARA, the cars stop near the *Clifton House*, situated near the ferry, leading to the American side. The site of this house was chosen as giving the best view of both the American and Canadian or Horse-Shoe Falls, which are seen from the piazzas and frontwindows.

In addition to the Falls, there are other points of attraction on the Canada side of the river. The collection of curiosities at the Museum, and the Camera Obscura, which gives an exact and beautiful, though miniature image of the Falls, are well worthy of a visit. The *Burning Spring*, two miles above the Falls, is also much frequented; and the rides to the battle-grounds in this vicinity make an exhilarating and very pleasant excursion. For further description of Falls, see page 211.

DRUMMONDSVILLE, one mile west of the Falls, and situated on *Lundy's Lane*, is celebrated as the scene of another sanguinary engagement between the American and British forces, July 25, 1814.

The following is a brief, though correct account of the engagement. "On the afternoon of the above day, while the American army was on their march from *Fort George* toward *Fort Erie*, ascending the west bank of the river, their rear guard, under the immediate command of Gen. Scott, was attacked by the advanced guard of the British army under Gen. Riall, the British having been reinforced after their defeat at Chippewa, on the 5th of the same month. This brought on a general conflict of the most obstinate and deadly character. As soon as attacked, Gen. Scott advanced with his division, amounting to about 3,000 men, to the open ground facing the heights occupied by the main British army, where were planted several heavy pieces of cannon. Between eight and nine o'clock in the evening, on the arrival of reinforcements to both armies, the battle became general and raged for several hours, with alternate success on both sides; each army evincing the most determined bravery and resistance. The command of the respective forces was now assumed by Maj. Gen. Brown and Lieut. Gen. Drummond, each having under his command a well-disciplined army. The brave (American) Col. Miller was ordered to advance and seize the artillery of the British, which he effected at the point of the bayonet in the most gallant manner. Gen. Riall, of the English army, was captured, and the possession of the battle-ground contested until near midnight, when 1,700 men being either killed or wounded, the conflicting armies, amounting altogether to about 6,000 strong, ceased the deadly conflict, and for a time the bloody field was left unoccupied, except by the dead and wounded. When the British discovered that the Americans had encamped one or two miles distant, they returned and occupied their former position. Thus ended one of the most bloody conflicts that occurred during the last war: and while each party boasted a victory, altogether too dearly bought, neither was disposed to renew the conflict."

CLIFTON is a new and flourishing village, situated at the western termination of the Great Western Railway, where it connects with the *Suspension Bridge*.

QUEENSTON, situated seven miles below the Falls, and about the same distance above the entrance of Niagara River into Lake Ontario, lies directly opposite the village of Lewiston, with which it is connected by a suspension bridge 850 feet in length. It contains about 500 inhabitants, 60 dwelling-houses, one Episcopal, one Scotch Presbyterian, and one Baptist church, four taverns, four stores, and three warehouses. This place is also celebrated as being the scene of a deadly strife between the American and British forces, Oct. 13, 1812. The American troops actually engaged in the fight were commanded by Gen. Solomon Van Rensselaer, and both the troops and their commander greatly distinguished themselves for their bravery, although ultimately overpowered by superior numbers. In attempting to regain their own side of the river many of the Americans perished, the whole loss in killed, wounded, and prisoners amounting to at least 1,000 men.

Major Gen. Brock, the British commander, was killed in the middle of the fight, while leading on his men. A new monument stands on the heights, near where he fell, erected to his memory. The first monument was nearly destroyed by gunpowder, April 17, 1840; an infamous act, said to have been perpetrated by a person concerned in the insurrection of 1837-8.

BROCK'S NEW MONUMENT was commenced in 1853, and finished in 1856; being 185 feet high, ascended on the inside by a spiral staircase of 235 stone steps. The base is 40 feet square and 35 feet in height, surmounted by a tablet 35 feet high, with historical devices on the four sides. The main shaft, about 100 feet, is fluted and surmounted by a Corinthian capital, on which is placed a colossal figure of Major General Brock, 18 feet in height. This beautiful structure cost £10,000 sterling, being entirely constructed of a cream-colored stone quarried in the

BROCK'S MONUMENT.—Queenston Heights.

vicinity. A massive stone wall, 80 feet square, adorned with military figures and trophies at the corners, 27 feet in height, surrounds the monument, leaving space for a grass-plot and walk on the inside of the inclosure.

The following is the inscription:

> Upper Canada has dedicated this Monument
> to the memory of the late
> Major-General Sir ISAAC BROCK, K.B.,
> Provisional Lieut.-Governor and Commander of the Forces in this Province,
> whose remains are deposited in the vault beneath.
> Opposing the invading enemy he fell in action, near the Heights,
> on the 13th October, 1812, in the 43d year of his age,
> Revered and lamented by the people whom he governed, and deplored by
> the sovereign to whose service his life had been devoted.

The last words of Major General Brock, when he fell mortally wounded by a musket-shot through the left breast, were, "Never mind, my boys, the death of one man—I have not long to live" Thus departed one of the many noble spirits that were sacrificed on this frontier during the war of 1812.

The village of NIAGARA is advantageously situated on the Canada side, at the entrance of the river into Lake Ontario, directly opposite *Fort Niagara*, on the American side. It contains about 3,000 inhabitants; a court-house and jail; one Episcopal, one Presbyterian, one Methodist, and one Roman Catholic church; ten hotels and taverns, and twenty stores of different kinds; also, an extensive locomotive and car factory. This is the most noted place in Canada West for building steamboats and other craft navigating Lake Ontario. Here is a dockyard with a marine railway and foundry attached, capable of making machinery of the largest description, and giving employment to a great number of men. It is owned by the "Niagara Dock Company." Steamers leave daily for Toronto, etc.

FORT GEORGE, situated a short distance south or up-stream from the mouth of the river, is now in ruins. This was the scene of a severe contest in 1813, in which the Americans were victorious. A new fort has been erected on the point of land at the mouth of the river, directly opposite old *Fort Niagara* on the American side. The new fortification is called *Fort Massasauga*.

The whole frontier on the Canada side, from Fort George to Fort Erie, opposite Buffalo, was occupied by the American army in 1814, when occurred a succession of battles of the most determined and brilliant character.

NIAGARA RIVER,

ITS RAPIDS, FALLS, ISLANDS, AND ROMANTIC SCENERY.

" Majestic stream ! what river rivals thee,
Thou child of many lakes, and sire of one—
Lakes that claim kindred with the all-circling sea—
Large at thy birth as when thy race is run !
Against what great obstructions hast thou won
Thine august way—the rock-formed mountain-plain
Has opened at thy bidding, and the steep
Bars not thy passage, for the ledge in vain
Stretches across the channel—thou dost leap
Sublimely down the height, and urge again
Thy rock-embattled course on to the distant main."

THIS most remarkable and romantic stream, the outlet of Lake Erie, through which flows all the accumulated waters of the Upper Lakes of North America, very appropriately forms the boundary between two great countries, the British province of Upper Canada on the one side, and the State of New York, the "Empire State" of the Union, on the opposite side. In its whole course, its peculiar character is quite in keeping with the stupendous Cataract from which its principal interest is derived.

The amount of water passing through this channel is immense; from a computation which has been made at the outlet of Lake Erie, the quantity thus discharged is about twenty millions of cubic feet, or upward of 600,000 tons per minute, all of which great volume of water, 20 miles below, plunges over the Falls of Niagara.

The Niagara River commences at Bird Island, nearly opposite the mouth of Buffalo harbor, and passes by the site of old Fort Erie and Waterloo on the Canada side. At the latter place a steam ferry-boat plies across the river to Black Rock, now forming a part of the city of Buffalo. It is here proposed to construct a railroad bridge across the stream, about 1,800 feet in width.

SQUAW ISLAND and STRAWBERRY ISLAND are both small islands lying on the American side of the stream, near the head of Grand Island The river is here used in part for the Erie Canal, a pier extending from Squaw Island to Bird Island, forming a large basin called Black Rock Harbor.

GRAND ISLAND, attached to Erie Co., N. Y., is a large and important body of land, about ten miles long from north to south, and seven miles wide. This island is partly cleared and cultivated, while the larger portion is covered with a large growth of oaks and other forest trees.

The ship or steamboat channel runs along the bank of Grand Island to nearly opposite Chippewa, where the whole stream unites before plunging over the Falls of Niagara, being again separated at the head of Goat Island. From this point the awe-struck traveler can scan the quiet waters above, and the raging rapids below, preparing to plunge over the cataract.

CAYUGA ISLAND and BUCKHORN ISLAND are small bodies of land belonging to the United States, situated immediately below Grand Island.

NAVY ISLAND, lying opposite the village of Chippewa, 18 miles below the head of the river, is a celebrated island belonging to the Canadians, having been taken possession of by the sympathizing patriots in 1837, when a partial rebellion occurred in Upper and Lower Canada.

TONAWANDA, 11 miles below Buffalo, is situated at the mouth of Tonawanda Creek, opposite Grand Island. The *Erie Canal* here enters the creek, which it follows for several miles on its course toward Lockport. A railroad also runs to Lockport, connecting with the *New York Central Railroad*, extending to Albany. A *ship canal* is proposed to be constructed from Tonawanda to some eligible point on Lake Ontario, thus forming a rival to the Welland Canal of Canada.

SCHLOSSER'S LANDING, two miles above Niagara Falls village, is a noted steamboat landing, opposite Chippewa, from whence the steamer *Caroline* was cut adrift by the British and destroyed, by being precipitated over the Falls during the Canadian rebellion, December 29th, 1837.

THE RAPIDS.—Below Navy Island, between Chippewa and Schlosser, the river is nearly three miles in width, but soon narrows to one mile, when the Rapids commence, and continue for about one mile before reaching the edge of the precipice at the Horse-Shoe Fall.

At the commencement of the Rapids " the bed of the river declines, the channel contracts, numerous large rocks heave up the rolling surges, and dispute the passage of the now raging and foaming floods. The mighty torrent leaping down successive ledges, dashing over opposing elevations, hurled back by ridges, and repelled from shores and islands—plunging, boiling, roaring—seems a mad wilderness of waters striving against its better fate, and hurried on to destruction by its own blind and reckless impetuosity. Were there no cataract, these Rapids would yet make Niagara the wonder of the world."

IRIS, or GOAT ISLAND, commences near the head of the Rapids, and extends to the precipice, of which it forms a part, separating the American Fall from the Canadian or Horse-Shoe Fall. It is about half a mile in length, eighty rods wide, and contains over sixty acres of arable land, being for the most part covered with a heavy growth of forest trees of a variety of species, and native plants and flowers. A portion of the island, however, has been cleared off, and a garden inclosed, in which are some excellent fruit trees, and a variety of native and foreign plants and flowers, and a fish-pond. The island is remarkably cool, shady, and pleasant, and is an object of unceasing admiration from year to year. Comfortable seats and arbors are placed at the most interesting points, where the visitor can sit at ease and enjoy the beautiful and sublime views presented to his sight—often entranced by a deafening roar of mighty waters in their descent, often accompanied by changing rainbows of the most gorgeous description.

NIAGARA.

WRITTEN BY LYDIA H. SIGOURNEY.

Flow on forever, in thy glorious robe
Of terror and of beauty; God hath set
His rainbow on thy forehead, and the cloud
Mantles around thy feet, and He doth give
Thy voice of thunder power to speak of Him
Eternally; bidding the lip of man
Keep silence, and upon thy rocky altar
Pour incense of awe-struck praise.

GOAT ISLAND BRIDGE.—The Niagara Falls *Gazette* gives the following description of this new structure:

"This bridge across the east branch of the Niagara River is situated in the Rapids, about sixty rods above the Cataract, on the site of the old wooden bridge. It is 360 feet long, and consists of four arches of ninety feet span each, supported between the abutments of three piers. The piers above water are built of heavy cut stone, and are twenty-two feet long and six feet wide, tapering one foot in the height. The foundations are formed of foot-square oak timber, strongly framed and bolted together in cribs, filled with stone, and covered with timber at the surface of the water. These timber-foundations are protected against wear and injury from ice by heavy plates of iron, and being always covered with water, will be as durable as the stone.

"The superstructure is of iron, on the plan of Whipple's iron-arched bridge. The whole width is twenty-seven feet, affording a double carriage-way of sixteen and a half feet, and two foot-ways of five and a fourth feet each, with iron railings. The arches are of cast iron, and the chords, suspenders, and braces of wrought iron. All the materials used in the construction are of the best quality, and the size and strength of all the parts far beyond what are deemed necessary in bridges exposed to the severest tests.

"This substantial and beautiful structure, spanning a branch of this majestic river in the midst of the rapids, and overlooking the cataract, is worthy of the site it occupies, and affords another instance of the triumph of human ingenuity over the obstacles of nature.

"The islands connected by this bridge with the American shore are the property of Messrs. Porter, and constitute the most interesting features in the scenery surrounding the cataract. This bridge has been erected by them to facilitate communication with these interesting localities not otherwise accessible."

This is a toll-bridge, every foot passenger being charged 25 cents for the season, or single crossing.

There are upward of thirty islands and islets in the Niagara River or Strait, above the cataract. Most of those not described are small, and scarcely worthy of enumeration, although those immediately contiguous to Goat Island form beautiful objects in connection with the rushing and mighty waters by which they are surrounded. *Bath Island, Brig Island, Chapin's Island*, and *Bird Island*, all situated immediately above the American Fall, are reached by bridges.

When on Goat Island, turning to the right toward the Falls, the first object of interest is *Hogg's Back*, a point of land facing the American Fall,—Bridge to Adington Island immediately above the Cave of the Winds, 160 feet below. Sam. Patch's Point is next passed on the right, from which he took a fearful leap some years since. Biddle's Stairs descend to the water's edge below and the Cave of the Winds, which are annually visited by thousands of visitors. Terrapin Bridge and Terrapin Tower afford a grand view of the Canadian or Horse-Shoe Fall and Rapids above the Falls. Three Sister Islands are contiguous to Goat Island, on the American side. Passing around Goat Island toward the south, a grand view is afforded of the river and rapids above the Canadian and American Falls.

CATARACT OF NIAGARA.

"Shrine of Omnipotence! how vast, how grand,
How awful, yet how beautiful thou art!
Pillar'd around thy everlasting hills,
Robed in the drapery of descending floods,
Crowned by the rainbow, canopied by clouds
That roll in incense up from thy dread base,
Hid by their mantling o'er the vast abyss
Upon whose verge thou standest, whence ascends
The mighty anthem of thy Maker's praise,
Hymn'd in eternal *thunders!*"

CATARACT OF NIAGARA.

NIAGARA is a word of Indian origin—the orthography, accentuation and meaning of which are variously given by different authors It is highly probable that this diversity might be accounted for and explained by tracing the appellation through the dialects of the several tribes of aborigines who formerly inhabited the neighboring country. There is reason to believe, however, that the etymon belongs to the language of the Iroquois, and signifies the "*Thunder of Waters.*"

"When the traveler first arrives at the cataract, he stands and gazes, and is lost in admiration. The mighty volume of water which forms the outlet of the great Lakes Superior, Michigan, Huron, and Erie, is here precipitated over a precipice 160 feet high, with a roar like that of thunder, which may be heard, in favorable circumstances, to the distance of fifteen miles, though, at times. the Falls may be nearly approached without perceiving much to indicate a tremendous cataract in the vicinity. In consequence of a bend in the river, the principal weight of water is thrown on the Canadian side, down what is called the *Horse-Shoe Fall*, which name has become inappropriate, as the edges of the precipice have ceased to be a curve, and forms a moderately acute angle. Near the middle of the fall, *Goat Island*, containing 75 acres, extends to the brow of the precipice, dividing the river into two parts; and a small projecting mass of rock at a little distance from·it, toward the American shore, again divides the cataract on that side. Goat Island, at the lower end, presents a perpendicular mass of rocks, extending from the bottom to the top of the precipice. A bridge has been constructed from the American shore to Bath Island, and another connects the latter with Goat Island, and a tower is erected on the brow of the Horse-Shoe Fall, approached from Goat Island by a short bridge, on which the spectator seems to stand over the edge of the mighty cataract, and which affords a fine view of this part of it. The distance at the fall from the American shore to Goat Island is 65 rods; across the front of Goat Island is 78 rods; around the Horse-Shoe Fall, on the Canadian side, 144 rods; directly across the Horse-Shoe, 74 rods. The height of the fall near the American shore is 163 feet; near Goat Island, on the same side, 158 feet; near Goat Island, on the Canada side, 154 feet. Table Rock, a shelving projection on the Canadian side, at the edge of the precipice, is 150 feet high. This place is generally thought to present the finest view of the Falls; though if the spectator will visit the tower on the opposite side on Goat Island, at sunrise, when the whole cavity is enlightened by the sun, and the gorgeous bow trembles in the rising spray, he can not elsewhere, the world over, enjoy such an incomparable scene. A covered stairway on the American side descends from the top to the bottom of the precipice.

"It has been computed that 100 million tons of water are discharged over the precipice every hour. The Rapids commence about a mile above the Falls, and the water descends 57 feet before it arrives at the cataract. The view from the bridge to Goat Island, of the troubled water dashing tumultuously over the rocks of the American fall, is terrific. While curiosity constitutes an attribute of the human character, these falls will be frequented by admiring and delighted visitors as one of the grandest exhibitions in nature.

"This stupendous cataract, situated in N. lat. 43° 6,' and W. long. 2° 6' from Washington, is twenty-two miles north from the efflux of the river at Lake Erie, and fourteen miles south of its outlet into Lake Ontario. The whole length of the river is therefore thirty-six miles, its general course is a few points to the west of north. Though commonly called a river, this portion of the St. Lawrence is, more properly speaking, a *strait*, connecting, as above mentioned, the Lakes Erie and Ontario, and conducting the superfluous waters of the great seas and streams above though a broad and divided, and afterward compressed, devious, and irregular channel to the latter lake, into which it empties—the point of union being about forty miles from the western extremity of Lake Ontario.

"The climate of the Niagara is in the highest degree healthful and invigorating. The atmosphere, constantly acted upon by the rushing water, the noise and the spray, is kept pure, refreshing, and salutary. There are no stagnant pools or marshes near to send abroad their foetid exhalations and noxious miasmas, poisoning the air and producing disease.

"Sweet-breathing herbs and beautiful wild flowers spring up spontaneously even on the sides, and in the crevices of the giant rocks; and luxuriant clusters of firs and other stately forest trees cover the islands, crown the cliffs, and overhang the banks of Niagara. Here are no mosquitoes to annoy, no reptiles to alarm, and no wild animals to intimidate, yet there is life and vivacity. The many-hued butterfly sips ambrosia from the fresh opened honey-cup—birds carol their lays of love among the spray-starred branches; and the lively squirrel skips chattering from tree to tree. Varieties of water-fowl, at

THE AMERICAN RAPIDS, FROM THE BRIDGE

THE AMERICAN FALLS BY MOONLIGHT.

certain seasons of the year, sport among the rapids, the sea-gull plays around the precipice, and the eagle—the banner bird of freedom—hovers above the cataract, plumes his gray pinions in its curling mists, and makes his home among the giant firs of its inaccessible islands.

"No place on the civilized earth offers such attractions and inducements to visitors as Niagara, and they can never be fully known except to those who see and study them, from the utter impossibility of describing such a scene as this wonderful cataract presents. When motion can be expressed by color, there will be some hope of imparting a faint idea of it; but until that can be done, Niagara must remain undescribed."

Below the Falls, the first objects of interest are the Ferry Stairs and Point View on the American side; while on the opposite side is a ferry and steamboat landing, where carriages are usually to be found to convey passengers to the Clifton House, Table Rock, and other places.

About 30 rods below the ferry stairs is the spot where the hermit Abbot was drowned. Half a mile below the latter point is Catlin's Cave, formerly much frequented.

The steamboat landing for the *Maid of the Mist* is situated on the American shore two miles below the Falls and about half a mile above the Suspension Bridge. This steamer, the second boat of the same name, first commenced running as an experiment boat in 1848; since then she has run annually without an accident of any kind. The first trip was made on September 18th, 1846, by Capt. H. Filkins, who with his small crew were the only persons on board, except an intrepid Canadian who was desirous of crossing the river with a horse, they both being safely landed on the Canadian shore.

The SUSPENSION BRIDGE, the greatest artificial curiosity in America, is situated two miles and a half below the Falls, where has recently sprung into existence *Niagara City*, or better known as the *Suspension Bridge*, on the American side, and *Clifton* on the Canadian side of the river, here being about 800 feet in width, with perpendicular banks of 325 feet.

The *Whirlpool* and *Rapids*, one mile below the Bridge, are terrific sights of great interest, and well worthy a visi'

The *Devil's Hole*, one mile farther down, is also a point of great attraction, together with the *Bloody Run*, a small stream where a detachment of English soldiers were precipitated in their flight from an attack by Indians during the old French war in 1759. An amphitheater of high ground spreads around and perfectly incloses the valley of the Devil's Hole, with the exception of a narrow ravine formed by Bloody Run—from which, against a large force, there is no escape, except over the precipice. The *Ice Cave* is another object of interest connected with the Devil's Hole.

The *Rapids* below the Whirlpool are the next object of attraction; then Queenston Heights and Brock's Monument on the Canadian side, and the *Suspension Bridge* at Lewiston; altogether forming objects of interest sufficient to fill a well-sized volume.

The Niagara River is navigable from Lewiston to its mouth at Fort Niagara, a farther distance of seven miles, or fourteen below the Falls of Niagara.

MONT-EAGLE HOUSE, AT THE SUSPENSION BRIDGE, NIAGARA, NEW YORK.

This Hotel, now open for the reception of guests, has been thoroughly refitted and improved, and will be found unequaled as a summer resort, for coolness, health, and comfort. Every window and piazza in the front and west side of the Hotel commands a full view of the great "Horse-Shoe" and "American Falls," "Goat Island," "Table Rock," and the "Railroad Suspension Bridge." On the Tower, 170 feet high, the scenery is most imposing, and from a grove in the garden you overlook the "Whirlpool" and the wildest portion of the lower "Rapids."

THE PROPOSED NIAGARA FALLS GUNBOAT CANAL.

GEN. STUART, in his report on the *Gunboat Canal* between tide water and the Lakes, estimates the cost of a Ship Canal around the Falls of Niagara, 105 wide on the surface, and 95 feet wide on the bottom, with twelve feet depth of water, having locks 275 feet long by 45 feet wide in the chamber, capable of passing a gunboat of 1,250 tons burden, at $5,958,947 25 with single locks, and $7,538,529 with double locks. This is the average cost of five lines surveyed last year. The average length of lines is 8 miles and 3,070 feet.

The village of NIAGARA FALLS, Niagara Co., N. Y., is situated on the east side of Niagara River, in the immediate vicinity of the grand Cataract, 22 miles from Buffalo and 303 miles from Albany by railroad route. No place in the Union exceeds this favored spot as a fashionable place of resort during the summer and fall months, when hundreds of visitors may be seen every day flocking to Goat Island, or points contiguous to the Rapids and Falls. The village contains several large hotels for the accommodation of visitors, the most noted of which are the Cataract House and the International Hotel; the Monteagle Hotel, situated two miles below the Falls, near the Suspension Bridge, and the Clifton House, on the Canada side, are all alike popular and well-kept hotels; there are five churches of different denominations; 15 stores, in many of which are kept for sale Indian curiosities and fancy work of different kinds. The water-power here afforded by the descending stream, east of Goat Island, is illimitable. A paper-mill, a flouring-mill, two saw-mills, a woolen factory, a furnace and machine shop, together with other manufacturing establishments, here use the water-power so bountifully supplied. The population is about 3,000.

The railroads centering at the Falls are the *Buffalo, Niagara Falls and Lewiston Railroad*, the *New York Central Railroad*, and the *Canandaigua and Niagara Falls Railroad*, the latter road connecting with the *New York and Erie Railroad*, and forming with other roads a direct route to Philadelphia, Baltimore, and Washington

An *omnibus line* runs hourly from the village of Niagara Falls to Niagara City, or Suspension Bridge, during the summer months, and thence to the Clifton House and Table Rock on the Canada side, affording a cheap mode of visiting both sides of Niagara River.

NIAGARA CITY, situated two miles below the Falls, at the *Suspension Bridge*, is a new and flourishing place. Here is located the Monteagle Hotel, and other public houses, together with several stores and manufacturing establishments.

DIMENSIONS OF SUSPENSION BRIDGE.

LENGTH of span from center to center of towers. 822 feet.
Height of railroad track above water.......... 250 "
Height of towers above rock on American side.. 88 "
Height of towers above rock on Canada side.... 78 "
Height of towers above floor of railway........ 60 "
Number of wire cables...................... 4
Diameter of each cable...................... 10 inches.
Number of wires in each cable...............3,659
Weight of superstructure.................... 750 tons.
Base of towers............................. 16 feet sq
Top of towers.............................. 8 "
Depth of anchor pits below surface of rocks.... 30 feet.

WEIGHT OF THE MATERIALS IN THE BRIDGE.

Timber of different kinds.................. 919,130 lbs
Wrought iron and suspenders............... 113,120 "
Castings................................... 44,322 "
Iron rails. .... 66.740 "
Cable between towers...................... 535,400 "

Total.............................1,678,722 "

The *Great Western Railway of Canada*, which unites with the New York Central Railroad, terminating on the American side of the river, here commences and extends westward through Hamilton, London, and Chatham to Windsor, opposite Detroit, Mich., forming one of the great through lines of travel from Boston and New York to Chicago and the Far West.

This road also furnishes a speedy route of travel to Toronto, Collingwood, etc.

RATE OF CHARGES AT NIAGARA FALLS.

The following are the rate of charges usually exacted from persons visiting Niagara Falls—but, unfortunately, impositions are often practiced by unprincipled individuals, at this, as well as other fashionable resorts:

AMERICAN SIDE.

Board, from one to two and a half dollars per day.
For services of guide, from one to three dollars
For guide behind the Central Fall, and visiting the Cave of the Winds, one dollar.
For crossing bridge to Goat Island, 25 cents.
Fare to and from Suspension Bridge, 12½ cents.
Fare for crossing Suspension Bridge, 25 cents
Fare to the Whirlpool, 50 cents.
For use of steps or cars on Inclined Plane, 10 cents.
Ferriage to Canada side, 18¾ cents.
Omnibus fare and steam ferriage to Canada side, 25 cents.

CANADA SIDE.

Board, from one to two and a half dollars per day.
Visiting Barnett's Museum, Camera Obscura, and Pleasure Grounds, 25 cents.
For guide and use of dress to pass behind the Fall at Table Rock, one dollar.
Carriage fare from ferry to Clifton House, 6¼ cents.
Carriage fare to Whirlpool, Lundy's Lane Battle Ground, Burning Spring, and back to Ferry, 50 to 75 cents.
Guide to Battle Ground and visiting Monument, 25 cents.
Carriage fare to Brock's Monument on Queenston Heights, one dollar.
Carriage fare per day, four dollars.
The drives in the vicinity of the Falls, on both sides of the river, are unrivaled, and no visitor should lose the opportunity to visit all the objects of attraction above and below the mighty Cataract.

LEWISTON, Niagara Co., N. Y., is delightfully situated on the east bank of the Niagara River, seven miles below the Falls, and seven miles above the mouth of the river where it falls into Lake Ontario. It is an incorporated village and contains about 1,000 inhabitants, four churches, an incorporated academy; a custom-house, it being the port of entry for the district of Niagara; three hotels, nine stores, and three storehouses. Here is a very convenient steamboat landing, from which steamers depart daily for Oswego, Ogdensburgh, etc., on the American side, and for Toronto, Kingston, etc., on the Canadian side. The Buffalo, Niagara Falls and Lewiston Railroad terminates at this place, where is a magnificent Suspension Bridge thrown across the Niagara connecting Lewiston with Queenston, Canada. The mountain ridge here rises about 300 feet above the river, forming many picturesque and romantic points of great interest. On the American side of the river stands the site of old Fort Gray, erected during the war of 1812, while on the Canadian side are situated Queenston Heights, surmounted by a beautiful monument erected to the memory of Gen. Brock, of the British army, who was here killed in a sanguinary conflict, October 13th, 1812. From this height a most extensive and grand view is obtained of Lake Ontario and the surrounding country.

YOUNGSTOWN, six miles below Lewiston, and one mile above old Fort Niagara at the mouth of the river, is a regular steamboat landing. The village contains about 800 inhabitants; three churches, two public houses, five stores, and two flouring-mills, besides other manufacturing establishments. A railroad is nearly completed, extending from this place to Niagara Falls, being a continuation of the Canandaigua and Niagara Falls Railroad, now completed to the Suspension Bridge. A ferry plies from Youngstown to the village of Niagara on the Canada side of the river, here about half a mile in width. This is the first landing, on the American side of the river, after leaving the broad waters of Lake Ontario

LAKE ONTARIO.

This Lake, the most eastern of the great chain of Lakes of North America, receives the surplus waters of Niagara River; it is 190 miles in length, and 60 miles in extreme breadth; being about 480 miles in circumference. The boundary line between the British Possessions and the United States runs through the middle of the lake, and so continues down the St. Lawrence to the 45th degree of north latitude, where the river enters Canada.

The lake is navigable throughout its whole extent for vessels of the largest size; and it is said to be in some places upward of 600 feet in depth. Its surface is elevated 234 feet above the Atlantic, and lies 330 feet lower than Lake Erie, with which it is connected by the Niagara River and by the Welland Canal in Canada. It has also been proposed to construct a ship canal on the American side. The trade of Lake Ontario, from the great extent of inhabited country surrounding it, is very considerable, and is rapidly increasing. Many sail vessels and splendid steamers are employed in navigating its waters, which, owing to its great depth, never freezes, except at the sides, where the water is shallow; so that its navigation is not so effectually interrupted by ice as some of the other large lakes. The most important places on the Canadian or British side of Lake Ontario are Kingston, Coburg, Port Hope, Toronto, Hamilton, and Niagara; on the American shore, Cape Vincent, Sacket's Harbor, Oswego, Charlotte or Port Genesee, and Lewiston on Niagara River. This lake is connected with the navigable waters of the Hudson River by means of the Oswego and Erie canals. It receives numerous streams, both from the Canadian and the American sides, and abounds with a great variety of fish of an excellent flavor. The bass and salmon, in particular, have a high reputation, and are taken in large quantities The principal Bays are Burlington, Irondequoit, Great and Little Sodus, Mexico, Black River, Chaumont, and the picturesque waters of the Bay of Quinte.

The passage across Lake Ontario in calm weather is most agreeable. At times both shores are hidden from view, when nothing can be seen from the deck of the vessel but an abyss of waters. The refractions which sometimes take place in summer, are exceedingly beautiful. Islands and trees appear turned upside down ; and the white surf of the beach, translated aloft, seems like the smoke of artillery blazing away from a fort.*

---

* BEAUTIFUL MIRAGE.—That grand phenomenon occasionally witnessed on the Lakes—mirage—was seen from the steamer Bay State, on a recent trip from Niagara to Genesee River (August, 1856), with more than ordinary splendor. The Lockport *Journal* says it occurred just as the sun was setting, at which time some twelve vessels were seen reflected on the horizon, in an inverted position, with a distinctness and vividness truly surprising. The atmosphere was overcast with a thick haze such as precedes a storm, and of a color favorable to represent upon the darkened background, vividly, the full outlines of the rigging, sails, etc., as perfect as if the ships themselves were actually transformed to the aerial canvas. The unusual phenomenon lasted until darkness put an end to the scene.

ROUTE AROUND LAKE ONTARIO.

	Miles.
Kingston, C. W., to Toronto, *via Grand Trunk Railway*.	160
Toronto to Hamilton, C. W., *Toronto and Hamilton R.R.*	38
Hamilton to Suspension Bridge, *via Great Western R.R.*.	43
Suspension Bridge to Rochester, N. Y., *via N. Y. Central Railway*	76
Rochester to Oswego, N. Y., by *stage*	70
Oswego to Richland, N. Y., "	35
Richland to Cape Vincent, *via Watertown and Rome R.R.*	55
Cape Vincent to Kingston, C. W., *via Wolfe Island*	12
Total Miles	489

NOTE.—The extreme length of L. Ontario is 190 miles, from Cape Vincent to Hamilton, C. W. ; being about four times as long as its greatest width. The circuit of the water is estimated at 480 miles. *See Lake Erie*, page 163.

AMERICAN STEAMBOAT ROUTE FROM LEWISTON TO OSWEGO, KINGSTON, AND OGDENSBURGH.

Ports, etc.	Miles.	Ports, etc.	Miles
LEWISTON	0	OGDENSBURGH	0
Youngstown	6	Morristown	11
Niagara, Can.	1-7	Brockville, Can.	1-12
Charlotte, or Port Genesee	80-87	Thousand Islands... Alexandria Bay	22-34
Pultneyville	20-107	Clayton, or French Creek	12-46
Sodus Point	10-117		
Oswego	30-147	Grand, or Wolfe Island	
Stoney Point and Island	33-180	KINGSTON, Can.	24-70
Sacket's Harbor	12-192	Sacket's Harbor	38-108
Grand, or Wolfe Island	28-220	Stoney Point and Island	12-120
KINGSTON, Can.	10-230	Oswego	33-153
Thousand Islands...		Sodus Point	30-183
Clayton, or French Creek	24-254	Pultneyville	10-193
Alexandria Bay	12-266	Charlotte, or Port Genesee	20-213
Brockville, Can.	22-288	Niagara, Can.	80-293
Morristown	1-289	Youngstown	1-294
OGDENSBURGH	11-300	LEWISTON	6-300

USUAL TIME from Lewiston to Ogdensburgh, *via* Oswego and Kingston, 28 hours.

USUAL TIME, *via* Toronto and Cape Vincent, 22 hours.

Cabin Fare, $5 50 (including meals). Deck Fare, $2 50.

STEAMBOAT ROUTE FROM LEWISTON TO TORONTO AND OGDENSBURGH, *via* EXPRESS LINE.

Ports, etc.	Miles.	Ports, etc.	Miles.
LEWISTON	0	OGDENSBURGH	0
NIAGARA	7	Brockville, Can,	11
TORONTO, Can.	42-49	Clayton, or French Creek	34-45
Point Peter and Light	128-177		
Duck Island	30-207	CAPE VINCENT	13-58
Tibbet's Point and L.	19-226	Tibbet's Point	3-61

STEAMBOAT ROUTES.

Ports, etc.	Miles.	Ports, etc.	Miles.
CAPE VINCENT	3–229	Duck Island	19–80
Clayton, or French Creek	13–242	Point Peter and Light	30–110
		TORONTO	128–238
Brockville, Can.	34–276	NIAGARA	42–280
OGDENSBURGH	11–297	LEWISTON	7–287

USUAL FARE, from Ogdensburgh to Montreal, $3 50
Through Fare, from Lewiston to Montreal, 9 00
" " from Buffalo to Montreal, 10 00

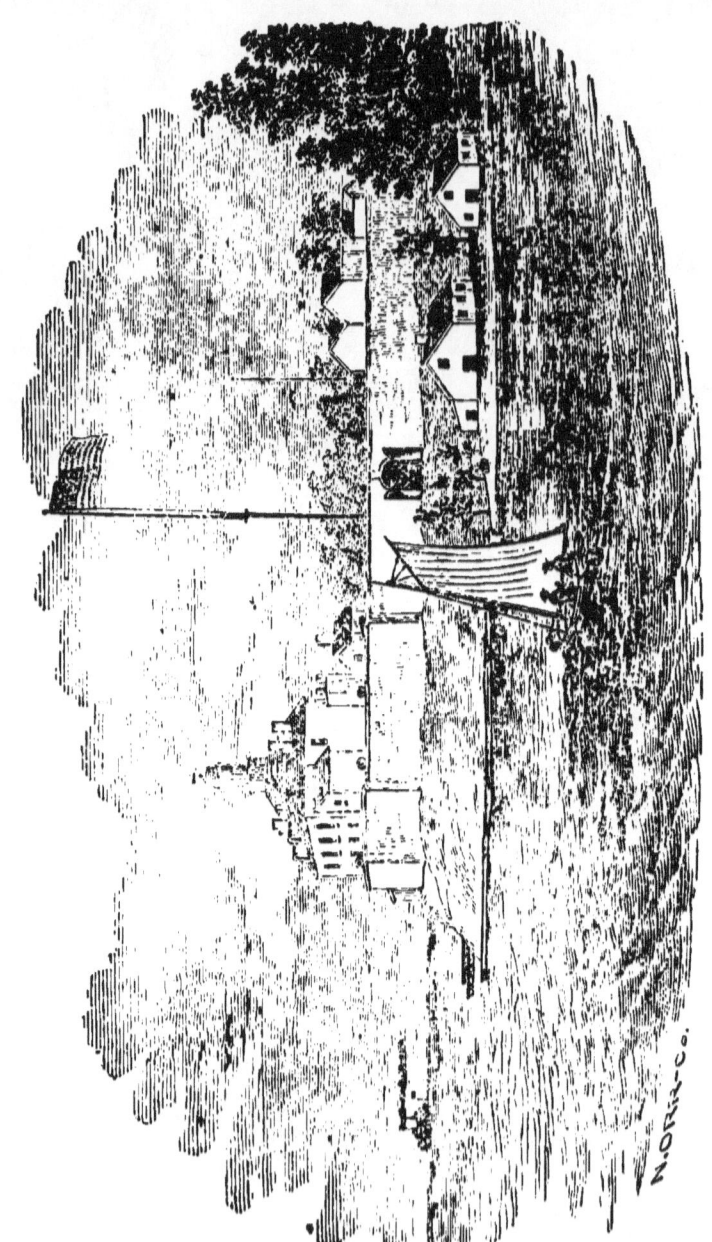

Fort Niagara — Mouth Niagara River.

TRIP FROM LEWISTON TO OSWEGO, KINGSTON, AND OGDENSBURGH.

During the season of navigation, steamers of a large class, belonging to the *Ontario and St. Lawrence Steamboat Company*, leave Lewiston daily, following the south or American shore to the foot of Lake Ontario, and thence to Ogdensburgh, on the St. Lawrence River.

On leaving the wharf at Lewiston, a most beautiful and extensive view is afforded of Niagara River, the lower Suspension Bridge, Brock's Monument on Queenston Heights, and the villages of Lewiston and Queenston, with the Mountain Ridge in the background. When are associated the stirring historical events connected with this vicinity, no spot exceeds it in interest. The banks of the river are here elevated from 40 to 50 feet, with bold shores, while the water rushes onward into Lake Ontario, the receptacle of all the waters of the Upper Lakes.

Fort Niagara, seven miles below Lewiston, lying on the American shore at the mouth of the Niagara River, is well worthy of a visit in connection with the ruins of *Fort George*, on the Canadian shore, near the village of Niagara. In 1679, M. De Salle, the explorer of the Mississippi, in the service of France, inclosed the spot on which the fort was here built in 1725, by palisades. In 1759 it was taken by the British, under Sir William Johnson, in whose hands it remained until 1796, when it was evacuated and given up to the United States. On the 19th of December, 1813, it was again taken by the British by surprise; and in March, 1815, again surrendered to the Americans. This old fort is as much noted for being the theater of tyranny and crime as for the scenes of military exploits. While in the hands of the French, there is no doubt of its having been at times used as a prison. In its close and impregnable dungeons, where light was not admitted, for many years there remained clear traces of the ready instruments for execution or for murder. During the war of the Revolution it was the head-quarters of all that was barbarous and unrelenting and cruel; this being the chief rendezvous of a savage horde that carried death and destruction into the remote American settlements. Of late years, the abduction of William Morgan, who was taken from the jail in Canandaigua, and conveyed more than 100 miles through a populous country, and lodged in the magazine at Fort Niagara, where he was kept three or four days, and then inhumanly drowned—has justly tended to continue its reputation for being the scene of tyranny and murder.

On passing out of the mouth of the Niagara River, and reaching the broad waters of Lake Ontario, a deeply interesting view is afforded of the town of Niagara and Fort Niagara, situated on opposite sides of the river, while in the distance may be seen Brock's Monument, rising nearly 500 feet above the waters of the lake, being eight or ten miles distant.

The steamer now pursues an easterly course in running for Charlotte, or Port Genesee, 80 miles from the mouth of Niagara River. The shores of the lake of a clear day are generally in sight, presenting an elevated and bold appearance for many miles. Eighteen Mile Creek, Thirty Mile Creek, and Oak Orchard River are passed in succession; at the mouth of each there are harbors and small settlements. *Braddock's Point* is a bold headland ten miles west of the mouth of the Genesee River.

CHARLOTTE, or PORT GENESEE, 80 miles from the mouth of Niagara River, and 60 miles west from Oswego, is situated at the mouth of Genesee River, seven miles by railroad below the city of Rochester, it being the outport for that place. It is a port of entry, possessing a safe harbor, being protected by two long government piers, on one of which is located a light; there is also a light-house on the mainland. The village contains about 400 inhabitants, two churches, three hotels, four stores, four warehouses, one steam elevator, one steam saw-mill, and an extensive brick-yard. American and British steamers run direct from Charlotte to Cobourg, Port Hope, Toronto, etc., on the Canada side of the lake; also to Oswego, Sacket's Harbor, etc., on the American side, all connecting at Charlotte with railroad cars for Rochester.

The FALLS of the Genesee, near Rochester, are well worthy attention. The banks of the river immediately above Charlotte rise from 50 to 150 feet in height, presenting a fine appearance. The river is navigable for five or six miles to the first fall at Carthage, within the city bounds of Rochester; then other falls occur, the principal and most interesting being near the center of the city, it extending on both sides of the stream. The water-power here afforded is very great, being used to a great extent in propelling flour-mills, saw-mills, etc.

GENESEE RIVER, a deeply interesting and romantic stream, rises in Potter Co., Pa., on the great table-land of Western Pennsylvania, interlocking with some of the head sources of the Alleghany and west branch of the Susquehanna River; it then pursues a north course to the New York State line, thence through the county of Allegany; then by many short turnings through the rich and fertile valley of the Genesee, which extends through Monroe County, where it falls into Lake Ontario, six miles below the city of Rochester. Its whole course is about 145 miles. Near its mouth, within the present city limits of Rochester, are two or three important falls, known as the *Genesee Falls;* within the distance of three miles there being an estimated descent of 226 feet; the great falls at Rochester are 96 feet, at Carthage 75, an intermediate one of 20, and the rest, rapids or small falls; altogether affording an immense amount of hydraulic power, which is used to a great extent, particularly at the Upper Falls, in propelling flouring-mills, and different kinds of manufacturing establishments. From the landing at Carthage, which constitutes a part of the city of Rochester, there is a steamboat navigation to Charlotte, or Port Genesee, a distance of four miles, where is a good harbor communicating with Lake Ontario. From the head of the rapids above Rochester it is navigable during high water for a considerable distance, passing through a rich and interesting region of country, celebrated for its fertility. This stream now constitutes the main feeder of the *Genesee Valley Canal*, which runs parallel to it for the greater part of its length through the State. There are also important falls on this river, both in Allegany and Livingston counties, where are to be found some of its most interesting features. In the town of Portage, Allegany Co., " there are three distinct falls on the river, respectively 60, 90, and 110 feet, within the space of two miles, each differing in character, and each having peculiar beauties. Although the cascades are highly admirable, they are almost disregarded in the wonder and fear caused by the stupendous, perpendicular walls of the river, rising to 400 feet in height, and extending along the stream for three miles, with almost as much regularity as if constructed by art. To this great depth the river has worn its bed in the solid rock, in turns as short and graceful as if winding through the softest meadow."

After leaving Charlotte for Oswego the steamer passes *Pultneyville* (occasionally stopping), Great Sodus Bay and Little Sodus Bay, running within sight of the south shore; the lake here presenting an irregular coast-line.

GREAT SODUS BAY is a fine sheet of water, affording a secure harbor for lake craft, being from one to three miles wide and five miles long. The fishing is here good, as well as in all the bays along the south shore of the lake.

SODUS POINT, Wayne Co., N. Y., situated at the entrance of Great Sodus Bay, is a port of entry, with a good harbor, and contains a church, a public house, two stores, a steam saw-mill, and about 300 inhabitants.

LITTLE SODUS BAY, 14 miles east of Great Sodus, is another important body of water. "At Little Sodus, in high winds, vessels can often come within the protection of Long Point on one side, and the protecting shores west, between it and Big Sodus, and ride out the storm in the indented shore of the lake, and can, when the improvements to Little Sodus harbor are completed, enter the bay with ease, and take refuge there. This fact gives great advantages to Little Sodus Bay, as it makes it accessible at all times."

The City of Oswego, 36 miles north of Syracuse by railroad, is advantageously situated on both sides of Oswego River, at its entrance into Lake Ontario. It is a port of entry, was chartered in 1848, being divided into four wards. In 1855 it contained 16,000 inhabitants, 1,500 dwelling-houses, two Presbyterian, two Episcopal, two Baptist, two Methodist, two Roman Catholic, one Universalist, and one African church, besides a Bethel congregation; a court-house and jail, a custom-house, four banking houses, two savings' banks; a gas company, a female seminary, and orphan asylum. There are several well-kept hotels; the Munger House and the Hamilton House on the east side of the river, and the Niagara House on the west side, are the most frequented by pleasure travelers. The Pardee House is a new and commodious hotel which is nearly completed, situated on the west side of the river, near the steamboat landing.

The *Oswego and Syracuse Railroad*, 36 miles in length, connects this place with the Central Railroad of New York, while another railroad is being constructed on the east side of the Oswego River, to run to Syracuse and connect with the Syracuse and Binghamton Railroad, thus forming another direct route to the cities of New York and Philadelphia, and the coal region of Pennsylvania. The *Oswego Canal* also connects with the Erie Canal at Syracuse, altogether affording great facilities for trade and commerce, in connection with the lake navigation and water privilege. Here are now in operation 15 flouring-mills, with 84 run of stones, making 8,400 barrels of flour per day when in full operation; ten elevators capable of elevating 38,000 bushels of grain per hour, with storage room for 2,000,000 bushels. These huge edifices are so arranged as to unload and load vessels with great dispatch.

The *Oswego Starch Factory*, owned by an incorporated body, was erected in 1848, since which large additions made. The entire front of the building is now 510 feet, five stories high, extending back over the river 250 feet; it is capable of manufacturing twelve millions pounds of corn starch per year, consuming some 600,000 bushels of corn for the purpose, and giving employment to 300 persons. In addition to the above are two steam-engine and machine works, two iron and brass foundries, one cotton-mill, besides several other mills and factories.

The quantity of water flowing in the Oswego River at ordinary high water is 700,000 cubic feet per minute, at low water 200,000. Fall at the two lower dams in the city, 86 feet, affording altogether an immense and reliable water-power.

The number of vessels which arrive and depart annually from this port is very large; there being here owned eight steamers and propellers and about 100 schooners, averaging over 100 tons burden, besides a large number of canal boats. The harbor is capacious and safe, being well protected by two large stone piers, constructed by the United States government. On the end of the west pier is situated a light-house; about half a mile above are two bridges extending across the river, 600 feet in length. An extensive forwarding business is done at this place by means of lake, river, and canal navigation; goods passing through from New York to Oswego, and thence over the Collingwood route, or through the Welland Canal to the Upper Lakes.

Oswego now ranks as one of the greatest grain markets in the world, and will no doubt continue to increase with the growth and production of the Western States and Canada. The lumber trade is also very great, immense quantities being shipped from Canada to this port, and re-shipped to Eastern markets.

The impulse imparted to the commerce of Oswego by the late Reciprocity Treaty, which went into force October, 1854, is very great, as will be seen by the following returns made from official figures:

	1854.	1855.
Value of Foreign Imports	$2,860,918	$6,139,743
" " Exports	3,734,168	5,870,920
Total	$6,595,086	$12,010,663

Here it will be seen that the trade with Canada nearly doubled in the first year under the operation of the above treaty. The domestic or coastwise trade is also constantly and rapidly increasing.

One of the Steamers of the Ontario and St. Lawrence Steamboat Company leaves Oswego daily for Sacket's Harbor, Kingston, C. W., and Ogdensburgh, connecting with steamers running to Montreal, and Rouse's Point, *via* the Northern Railroad of New York.

A steamer also leaves Oswego daily, for Rochester, Niagara, C. W., and Lewiston, connecting with steamers for Toronto, etc.

RAILROAD AND STEAMBOAT ROUTE FROM SYRACUSE TO NIAGARA FALLS, *via* OSWEGO AND LEWISTON.

This route, during the season of navigation on Lake Ontario, is a most interesting line of travel, affording the tourist a fine opportunity of viewing the scenery peculiar to Lake Ontario and Niagara River.

The *Oswego and Syracuse Railroad*, 35 miles in length, runs along the west side of Onondaga Lake to the Seneca River, which is passed near BALDWINSVILLE, the first stopping-place after leaving Syracuse. From thence the road runs north on the west side of Oswego River, passing opposite to the village of FULTON, 11 miles from the city of Oswego. Passenger cars usually leave Syracuse and Oswego three times daily.

American steamers leave Oswego daily for Sacket's Harbor, Kingston, Canada, Ogdensburgh, etc., in the morning, on the arrival of the cars from Syracuse; while in the afternoon a steamer leaves for Rochester, Lewiston, etc., running up the lake. Passengers passing through Oswego are afforded a hasty glance of the city, the harbor, and Fort Ontario, the latter being located on the east shore of the river at its entrance into Lake Ontario.

DISTANCES AND FARE BETWEEN SYRACUSE AND NIAGARA FALLS, *via* OSWEGO AND LEWISTON.

Stopping Places.	Miles.	Fare.	Stopping Places.	Miles.	Fare.
SYRACUSE	0		NIAGARA FALLS	0	
OSWEGO	35	$1 00	LEWISTON	6	$0 50
Pultneyville	75	—	NIAGARA, C.W.	14	—
CHARLOTTE, or Port Genesee	100	—	CHARLOTTE, or Port Genesee	88	—
NIAGARA, C. W.	174	—	Pultneyville	113	—
LEWISTON	182	—	OSWEGO	153	—
NIAGARA FALLS	188	4 00	SYRACUSE	188	4 00

On resuming the trip from Oswego to Sacket's Harbor, the steamer runs in a northerly direction off *Mexico Bay*, being a large expanse of water at the east end of Lake Ontario, where lies PORT ONTARIO, at the mouth of Salmon River. On this stream is situated one of the most romantic falls in the country.

SALMON RIVER rises in Lewis Co., and flows west through Oswego Co. into Lake Ontario; discharging its waters into Mexico Bay, at the village of Port Ontario. This is a fine and durable stream, having a tolerably good harbor at its mouth, and is boatable during high water to the Falls in Orwell, a distance of 14 miles. "The *Falls of Salmon River* may be classed among the principal natural curiosities of the country. The current is gentle above for six or more miles, then two miles of rapids, and at the falls drops almost perpendicular 107 feet. At high water the sheet is 250 feet in width, but at low water it is narrowed down to about half that extent. The rocky strata seem to be composed of slate stone and granite, or gneiss, and the height of the banks immediately above the fall is variously estimated at from 70 to 90 feet; below it is said that the walls, perpendicular rock, are about 200 feet. At the foot of the cataract there is very deep water, abounding in fine fish, such as salmon, trout, etc."

GREAT STONEY ISLAND and other islands are passed as the steamer approaches Black River Bay, which affords the most capacious and safe harbor on Lake Ontario. Here enters Black River, an important stream, which rises many miles to the eastward, interlocking with the waters of the Mohawk and other tributaries of the Hudson River.

SACKET'S HARBOR, 45 miles north of Oswego, and distant 38 miles from Kingston, Canada, possesses one of the best and most secure harbors on Lake Ontario, being situated on *Black River Bay*, ten miles below Watertown, with which place it is soon to be connected by a railroad. It was an important naval and military station during the war of 1812, with Great Britain; it being the rendezvous of the American fleet on Lake Ontario. Here now lies a large war vessel under cover, which was commenced at the above period. *Madison Barracks*, garrisoned by United States troops, is handsomely situated near the steamboat landing, being in full view from the water.

This place is an important port of entry, and no doubt destined to increase in wealth and numbers on the opening of railroad facilities. The village now contains four churches, two hotels, twenty stores, four storehouses, a ship-yard and rope-walk, three saw-mills, two furnaces, an iron foundry and machine-shop.

The *Sacket's Harbor and Ellisburgh Railroad*, 18 miles in length, connects with the Watertown and Rome Railroad.

BLACK RIVER, so called from the color of its water, is the third in magnitude that has its whole course in the State of New York. Its whole course is about 120 miles, and is navigable from the High Falls in Leyden, where it has a fall of 63 feet, to the Long Falls at Carthage, a distance of 40 miles; thence, by a succession of rapids and falls, it continues a circuitous route, until it empties into *Black River Bay*, near the foot of Lake Ontario. It is a deep, sluggish stream, but the navigation is much obstructed by falls; affording, however, fine water-power. The land on the borders of the lower part of the river is very fertile and thickly settled; Jefferson County—and the vicinity of Watertown in particular, where is a good water power—is justly celebrated for its agricultural products.

CHAUMONT BAY, situated north of Sacket's Harbor at Black River Bay, is a large body of water abounding in fish of several kinds and fine flavor; here being extensive fisheries, where are annually taken large quantities of fish.

The trip across the foot of Lake Ontario from Sacket's Harbor to Kingston, Can., 38 miles, is a very interesting excursion during pleasant weather. Here may be seen beautiful headlands and several picturesque islands; the Fox and Grenadier islands are passed before reaching *Grand* or *Wolfe Island*, attached to Canada. This latter island, situated in the St. Lawrence River, at the foot of Lake Ontario, is a large and fertile body of land, being settled by Canadians.

CAPE VINCENT, Jefferson Co., N. Y., is situated at the head of the St. Lawrence River, where terminates the *Watertown and Rome Railroad*, and is a port of entry. It contains about 1,100 inhabitants, four churches, five hotels and taverns, ten stores, and an extensive storehouse connected with the railroad; one steam grist-mill, one foundry and machine-shop, one steam planing-mill, and a ship-yard. Steamers arrive and depart daily for different ports on Lake Ontario and the St. Lawrence River. A steamer also leaves Cape Vincent twice daily for Kingston, Canada, during navigation; while in winter, stages run across the ice to Grand or Wolfe Island, and thence to Kingston, distant 12 miles by direct route. Cape Vincent is a healthy and pleasant location, being much resorted to in warm weather by fishing and pleasure parties, being contiguous to the "Thousand Islands."

CLAYTON, or FRENCH CREEK, 18 miles below Cape Vincent, lies opposite Grindstone Island, attached to the State of New York. The village contains three churches, two public houses, ten stores, and a foundry and machine-shop. Here is an extensive ship-yard for the construction of steamers and other lake craft.

The *Black River and Utica Railroad*, when completed, will extend to Clayton, a distance of 109 miles from Utica.

ALEXANDRIA BAY, 12 miles below Clayton, is favorably situated on the southeast shore of the St. Lawrence, in the immediate vicinity of the greatest cluster of the Thousand Islands. The village contains one Presbyterian church, two good hotels for the accommodation of summer visitors, three stores, a steam saw-mill, a ship-yard, and about 350 inhabitants. No place on the St. Lawrence River exceeds this vicinity for its salubrity of climate and picturesque water scenery. The islands here, almost innumerable, are annually resorted to by visitors from almost every section of the country for health, and to enjoy the pleasure of fishing and hunting.

WELL'S ISLAND is settled by some 20 or 30 families, and is, no doubt, destined to become a favorite resort, as a hotel is projected, to be located near the foot of this lovely island.

MORRISTOWN, N. Y., 11 miles above Ogdensburgh, lies nearly opposite Brockville, C. W., with which it is connected by a ferry. This is a regular landing-place for the American steamers. The village contains two churches, two taverns, three stores, and about 350 inhabitants.

OGDENSBURGH, St. Lawrence Co., N. Y., is advantageously situated at the mouth of the Oswegatchie River where it empties into the St. Lawrence. It was first incorporated as a village in 1817, and now contains about 8,000 inhabitants, 1,000 dwelling-houses; one each Episcopal, Presbyterian, Baptist, Methodist, and Roman Catholic church—and a Universalist congregation; an incorporated academy, three banks, two insurance offices, a custom-house, six public houses, 100 stores of different kinds. The Oswegatchie River here furnishes an abundance of water-power, where are situated one woolen factory, two flouring-mills, three grist-mills, three saw-mills, one paper-mill, two planing-mills and two furnaces, a ship-yard and marine railway. This place is situated near the foot of sloop navigation on the St. Lawrence, although steamers of a large class run the Rapids to Montreal, 120 miles, ascending through the St. Lawrence canals

Two daily lines of steamers leave Ogdensburgh for Cape Vincent, Kingston, Oswego Toronto, Lewiston, etc., while two daily lines leave Ogdensburgh or Prescott for Montreal, etc. Two steam ferry-boats run across the St. Lawrence, here one mile and a half wide, to Prescott, forming a close connection between the two shores. The *Northern Railroad* extends from Ogdensburgh easterly to Rouse's Point, N. Y., 118 miles, connecting with steamers and railroads extending to Boston and New York. A railroad is also finished, extending from Ogdensburgh and form a junction with the *Potsdam and Watertown Railroad*. Propellers and lake craft annually deposit an immense amount of Western produce, to be carried forward by railroads to Eastern markets. As a stopping-place for pleasure travelers, Ogdensburgh stands unrivaled, having the Thousand Islands above and the magnificent Rapids of the St. Lawrence below. Passengers are here usually transferred from the floating palaces of Lake Ontario to the equally safe but smaller steamers which run the Rapids to Montreal.

The *Northern Transportation Com.* has here its branch office for the trans-shipment of produce and merchandise going East and West. This company owns 15 propellers, of about 350 tons burden, running from Ogdensburgh and Oswego to Cleveland, Toledo, Detroit, Milwaukee, Chicago, etc. This line affords a cheap and speedy route of travel for travelers and emigrants.

The *Oswegatchie River*, which empties into the St. Lawrence at Ogdensburgh, is the outlet of *Black Lake*, lying in the county of St. Lawrence. The lake and river are navigable for about 25 miles, to within four miles of Ogdensburgh. At the mouth of this river, now a part of the village of Ogdensburgh, an early settlement was made by the French, and fortifications erected, all of which have gone to decay.

The Trip from Kingston to Ogdensburgh and Montreal is described in another part of this work, following the Canadian route from Hamilton and Toronto to Kingston, Prescott, and Montreal. For further information, see advertisements of **Lake Ontario and River St. Lawrence Steamers.**

TRIP FROM NIAGARA AND HAMILTON TO TORONTO AND KINGSTON, CANADA.

AMERICAN and CANADIAN steamers leave Lewiston, or Niagara, C. W., daily for Toronto, 40 miles from the mouth of Niagara River, connecting with railroad cars from Buffalo and Niagara Falls, running on both sides of the river.

A Canadian steamer also leaves Port Dalhousie daily for Toronto, connecting at St. Catherine's with cars on the Great Western Railway, altogether affording great facilities both in summer and winter to resort to the capital of Canada.

On leaving the mouth of Niagara River, the steamer pursues a N.W. course direct for Toronto, having, on a clear day, land constantly in sight from the deck of the steamer. Nothing can exceed the pleasure of this trip during pleasant weather. Usually may be seen propellers and sailing vessels on their way to or from Port Dalhousie, the mouth of the Welland Canal, a magnificent work, of which the Canadians are justly proud.

PORT DALHOUSIE, 12 miles west of the mouth of Niagara River, and distant 38 miles from Toronto, is a small village situated at the terminus of the Welland Canal, four miles below St. Catherine's, with which place it is connected by the *Port Dalhousie and Thorold Railroad,* five miles in length, connecting with the Great Western Railway.

The WELLAND CANAL, 28 miles in length, connecting Lake Erie with Lake Ontario, and overcoming the Falls of Niagara, is a work alike beneficial to the commercial interests of the United States and Canada, the former paying by far the greatest amount of tolls. The number of locks are 27, being 150 feet in length and $26\frac{1}{2}$ feet wide. The total rise is 330 feet. The depth of water is $8\frac{1}{2}$ feet, the canal being 45 feet wide at bottom and 81 feet at the surface. The feeder branch, from Junction to Dunnville, is 21 miles long. The Broad Creek branch from feeder to Port Maitland, the terminus on Lake Erie, is 1½ miles in length, with one lock each. The entire cost of the enlarged canal was about £1,000,000 Canadian currency, or $4,000,000.

St. Catherine's, 38 miles south of Toronto by water, 11 miles from Suspension Bridge, and 32 miles from Hamilton by railroad route, is advantageously situated on the line of the Welland Canal, here affording a large amount of water-power. This town is a place of great attraction and growing importance, being surrounded by a healthy and rich section of country. Here is a mineral fountain called the "*Artesian Well*," also several large and well-kept hotels, for the accommodation of invalids and seekers of pleasure. The Stevenson House, near the Spring, and the Welland Hotel, are the most frequented by pleasure travelers.

The village contains about 6,000 inhabitants, several fine churches and private edifices, here being exhibited a degree of taste and activity equal to any other town of its size in Canada or the United States If the mineral waters prove as beneficial to invalids as is represented by many who have experienced their beneficial effects, it is no doubt destined to become a popular watering-place during the summer months. The "Well" is situated near the bank of the canal, and is 550 feet in depth; the water being raised by a steam pump to the bath-house, situated on the bank above.

The City of Hamilton, from its geographical position, and its peculiar natural and artificial advantages, lying on Burlington Bay, at the extreme west end of Lake Ontario, has within the last five or six years rapidly increased in wealth and numbers. But a few short years have passed away since the site on which now stands the crowded city, with its stately edifices and its elegant residences, its thronged streets, and its marts and factories teeming with life and business activity, was a dense forest, the residence and hunting-ground of the Indian. It was not many years ago that the waters of its beautiful bay, which now bear upon their bosom magnificent steamers and vessels of every grade, bringing to our port the treasures of other lands, and conveying to Eastern markets the products of the West, were calm and unruffled, save when the red man launched his barque upon the blue expanse, or when lashed into fury by the angry tempest.

Hamilton was first laid out in the year 1813, during the war with the United States, but for many years it progressed but slowly in population and importance. By the census of 1841 it numbered 3,446 inhabitants. During the succeeding four years the population nearly doubled, and by the census of 1861 the numbers had increased to 19,000. From that period to the present the city has progressed with almost unexampled rapidity for Canada.

The city is governed by a mayor and board of aldermen and councilors, together with a police department. The public buildings are a city hall, city hospital, post-office building, custom-house, market building, twenty churches of different denominations, five banks, and a mechanics' institute; many being large edifices, erected in a durable style of architecture. The principal hotels are the Anglo-American, International, and Royal Hotel, situated on James Street.

The *Great Western Railway of Canada*, running from Suspension Bridge to Windsor, has its head offices and machine shops here. A branch of the Great Western Railway extends to Toronto, connecting with the Grand Trunk Railway, running East and West. The *Desjardins Canal*, four miles in length, connects Hamilton with Dundas.

The exports of Hamilton for the year 1861, as shown by the last census, were valued at $1,674,297, and the imports for the same time were $2,656,639. The amount of duties collected was $437,457. Distant from Niagara Falls, 45 miles; Windsor, 183; Toronto 38 miles, and from Montreal, by rail, 372 miles.

Steamers, during the season of navigation, run from Hamilton to Toronto, Kingston, and other ports on Lake Ontario, affording a speedy and delightful mode of conveyance, not only through the lakes, but down the St. Lawrence River to Prescott, Ogdensburgh, and Montreal.

WELLINGTON SQUARE, seven miles below Hamilton, is a place of some importance, it being the outport for Hamilton during the winter months, when the lake is obstructed by ice.

BRONTE, 13 miles below Hamilton, is a small village containing about 400 inhabitants. Here are two public houses, two churches, a grist-mill, a cloth factory, and several lumber yards.

OAKVILLE, 19 miles from Hamilton, and about the same distance from Toronto, is a place of considerable business, having a good harbor. It contains about 1,000 inhabitants; four churches, several public houses and stores; a foundry, and other manufacturing establishments. The country in the rear is healthy and productive, being drained by several fine streams.

PORT CREDIT, 12 miles from Toronto, is a large shipping port for produce of different kinds. It is situated at the mouth of River Credit, here flowing into Lake Ontario. It was once a favorite resort of the Indians, receiving its name, in early times, from the circumstance of the fur traders here meeting the Indians, and delivering to them on *credit* their goods, for which the following year they received their value in furs.

TORONTO.

THE City of TORONTO, and capital of Canada, is favorably situated on Toronto Bay, in 43° 32′ N. lat., and 79° 20′ W. long. from Greenwich. It is 40 miles N.E. Hamilton, 160 W. from Kingston, 333 from Montreal, and 413 from Quebec by railroad route. The bay is a beautiful sheet of water, about 4 miles long and 2 miles wide, separated from the main body of Lake Ontario, except at its entrance, by a long, narrow strip of sandy beach, the southwest termination of which is known as Gibraltar Point, on which is located a light-house.

"*Toronto* signifies, in the Indian language, *a place of n eeting*. In 1793, when surveyed by the elder Bouchette, under the orders of Gov. Simcoe, two Massasauga families were the only inhabitants it contained, and the harbor was a resort for numerous wild fowl, while its waters produced an abundance of fish." It was incorporated as a city in 1834, when it contained 9,254 inhabitants. In 1842 it had increased to 15,436; in 1852, to 30,763; and in 1861, to over 45,000. It is laid out with wide streets, crossing each other at right angles. The esplanade fronting the bay extends for a distance of two miles. The city is lighted with gas, and is well supplied with pure water by companies incorporated for those purposes.

The principal public buildings are the Parliament House, the University of Toronto, Trinity College, Upper Canada College, the Lunatic Asylum, the Custom House, the Post Office, St. James' Church (the English cathedral), and the Roman Catholic Cathedral; besides which there are a great number of churches of different denominations. The Bank of Upper Canada has its head office here, and there are other banks and agencies; also several Fire and Marine Insurance Companies. This is the principal office of the Canada Land Company, which has nearly two millions of acres of land for sale, situated in various parts of the Province. The hotels and public houses are numerous and well kept, making this city a desirable sojourn. The *American Hotel* and the *Queen's Hotel*, both fronting the bay, are the most frequented.

Toronto has become a great thoroughfare by means of steamers and railroads. A constant intercourse is thus kept up with the different ports on Lake Ontario, the Upper Lakes, and the St. Lawrence River. Steamers run from Toronto to Hamilton, St. Catherine's, Niagara, and Lewiston on the west and south; to Rochester and Oswego on the east; and to Cape Vincent, Kingston, Prescott, Montreal, etc., on the northeast.

The *Ontario, Simcoe and Huron Railroad*, 94 miles in length, terminates at Collingwood, on Georgian Bay, connecting with the waters of Lake Huron. The *Grand Trunk Railway* extends northeast to Montreal and Quebec, while its western termination is near Port Sarnia, lying at the foot of Lake Huron. The *Toronto and Hamilton Railroad*, a branch of the *Great Western Railway* of Canada, also terminates here, affording altogether facilities of great benefit to Toronto and the whole of Canada.

The markets of Toronto are abundantly supplied with every description of provisions of the best quality, and at moderate prices. The climate is healthy and delightful during the summer and fall months, being modified by lake breezes.

THE NORTHERN RAILWAY OF CANADA, formerly known as the Ontario, Simcoe and Huron Railroad, extending from Toronto to Collingwood, C. W., does a large local business, in addition to a through traffic with the Upper Lakes, during the season of navigation, which usually lasts from the first of May to the last of November.

The new Steamer ALGOMA, 416 tons burthen, runs from Collingwood to Sault Ste Marie, and thence to Fort William, situated at the head of Lake Superior. This trip, of more than one thousand miles, passing through the Georgian Bay and North Channel, River St. Mary, and Lake Superior, embraces lake and river scenery which for grandeur and beauty is not equaled on this continent. For further particulars, *see Advertisement.*

A Canal has been proposed to connect the Georgian Bay with Lake Ontario, at Toronto. When completed, also a railroad from Lake Superior to the Upper Mississippi, now in progress of construction, there will be an impetus to trade and commerce that will be favorably felt both in Canada and the United States.

PORT WHITBY, 29 miles below Toronto, lies on the line of the Grand Trunk Railway, where is a steamboat landing, at which steamers land on their route from Toronto to Rochester, etc

OSHAWA, 33 miles below Toronto by railroad route, is handsomely situated a short distance from the lake shore and has a good harbor. It contains five churches, two hotels, 15 stores, two woolen factories, two tanneries and a brewery, besides other manufacturing establishments. Population, 2,500.

BOWMANVILLE, 43 miles from Toronto, lying a short distance from the lake, is connected with *Darlington Harbor*, where is a steamboat landing.

PORT HOPE is a port of entry situated on the north shore of Lake Ontario, 62 miles from Toronto and 98 miles from Kingston by railroad route. This is a safe harbor, where steamers land daily from different ports on the lake, which together with sail vessels export large quantities of produce. The village contains a court-house, six churches, four hotels, 40 stores; two flouring-mills, a woolen factory, two iron foundries, a machine-shop, two tanneries, two breweries, and six distilleries. The lumber trade carried on at this port is very extensive and profitable. Population, 3,500. In addition to the *Grand Trunk Railway*, which runs through the town, a railroad runs from Port Hope to Beaverton, situated on Lake Simcoe, a distance of 41 miles, thus opening a fine section of Canada to emigration and trade.

From Port Hope, or Cobourg, going toward Kingston by railroad route, there is to be seen a fine section of Canada, passing through several flourishing towns, and near the Bay of Quinte.

COBOURG, handsomely situated on the north shore of Lake Ontario, nearly opposite the mouth of Genesee River, where the lake attains its greatest width, is 70 miles from Toronto, 90 miles from Kingston, and 263 miles from Montreal by railroad route. It possesses a good harbor and is much frequented by steamers and sailing vessels, it being one of the regular landings for the Royal Mail Steamers, which pass and repass, daily, on their way up and down the lake.

The principal public buildings in Cobourg are the court-house and jail, and the Victoria College, which was established in 1842, by Act of the Provincial Legislature, with power to grant degrees in the arts and sciences; there are also a number of fine church edifices. Here are the most extensive cloth manufactories in the Province; there are also iron, marble, and leather manufactories, with breweries and distilleries, six hotels and taverns, 40 or 50 stores of different kinds, and a number of mechanic shops. Population, 6,000. Few places in Canada present a more beautiful appearance from the water than Cobourg—the landscape being extensive and varied by a most delightful background.

The *Cobourg and Peterboro' Railroad*, 28 miles in length, commences at this place, which, together with the Grand Trunk Railway, tends greatly to benefit Cobourg and the towns lying on the rear, in the vicinity of *Rice Lake*.

COLBORNE, 14 miles below Cobourg, is situated on the line of the Grand Trunk Railway. Here is a good landing for vessels and a flourishing settlement.

On leaving Cobourg for Kingston on the downward trip, the steamer usually runs out into the broad waters of Lake Ontario, soon attaining their greatest width. Often during the prevalence of storms or high winds, the unacclimated voyager experiences sensations any thing but agreeable; sea-sickness often prostrating alike the athletic male and the delicate female. This however, on board the larger class steamers is no serious objection to journeying across Lake Ontario, it being considered the most safe navigation of any of the great lakes.

Nicholas Point and *Island* are passed about 40 miles from Cobourg. Next comes *Wicked Point*, and soon heaves in sight *Point Peter* and *Light*. This light is a conspicuous object for the mariner, who often, when off Prince Edward, the mainland, experiences the full force of easterly and westerly winds.

DUCK ISLAND, attached to Canada is another noted object for the mariner, either descending or ascending Lake Ontario, as this is the first important island to be met on descending from the head of the lake on the Canada side.

Outer Drake and *Inner Drake* are two small islands situated inland toward Prince Edward's Bay.

AMHERST ISLAND, a large and fertile body of land, is next passed on the left, while *Gage Island* and *Grand* or *Wolfe Island* may be seen on the right; these latter islands being situated at the foot of Lake Ontario, or mouth of the St. Lawrence River, where commences the celebrated "*Thousand Islands.*"

The City of KINGSTON, capital of Frontenac Co., Canada, 160 miles from Toronto, and 173 miles from Montreal by railroad route, is very advantageously situated on a beautiful harbor at the northeast extremity of Lake Ontario, and immediately above its outlet, "Cataraqui," or St. Lawrence River, in N. lat. 44° 8', W. long. 76° 40' from Greenwich. "The view of the city and surrounding scenery is not surpassed by the approaches to any other city in America. A few miles above Kingston the waters of Lake Ontario are divided by the first of the long series of islands so well known to Tourists as the "*Thousand Islands*," of which Simcoe and Grand or Wolfe Islands, opposite the city, may be looked upon as strongholds, designed by nature to withstand the encroaches of the waves of Ontario. On approaching from the west, by water, the first object that attracts the traveler's attention is *Fort Henry*, with the naval station of Fort Frederick at its base, and its attendant battlements, fortifications, towers, and redoubts. Fort Henry is a favorite resort for visitors, and its elevated position affords the best view that can be had of the city, lake, and surrounding country "

The principal public buildings are the City Hall, one of the finest and most substantial edifices in Canada, and built of cut limestone at a cost of $92,000. It contains all the public offices of the city, including a spacious hall, capable of seating over 1,000 persons; the court-house is a large stone building, which is about being removed, and another, more in accordance with the wants of the citizens, is to be erected on a ground more central, and its present site occupied by a custom-house and post-office. Here is a Roman Catholic cathedral and several fine church edifices, in all numbering sixteen. Queen's College, under the direction of the Presbyterians, has a president and four professors; the College of Regiopolis (Roman Catholic) has also a president and four professors; the General Hospital, Hotel Dieu, and a nunnery are also in the city, while two miles west is situated the Provincial Penitentiary. It has four banking-houses and several insurance offices; three well-kept hotels, and about 100 stores of different kinds; besides several breweries, distilleries, tanneries, foundries, machine-shops, and a marine railway and ship-yard for the building of lake craft; on *Navy Bay*, which lies between Point Frederick and Point Henry, is the naval dock-yard used for government purposes. Near the Penitentiary is a mineral spring of some celebrity, resembling in its component parts the Cheltenham spring of England; another spring exists which is unusually strong, resembling in some respects the "Artesian Well" of St. Catherine's. It has been analyzed by Prof. Williamson, and found to contain valuable medical properties.—Population, 14,000.

Kingston occupies the site of *Fort Frontenac*, an old French post, this being one of a chain of posts extending from Quebec to Mackinac. Here are owned 20 steamers and about 40 schooners, sailing to and from the port, besides numerous other Canadian and American steamers and sailing vessels. It being the outlet for the productions of the fertile Bay of Quinte, and the *Rideau Canal*, terminating at Kingston, makes it an important and active mart of commerce.

STEAMBOAT ROUTE
FROM KINGSTON TO BELLEVILLE AND PORT TRENTON, PASSING THROUGH THE BAY OF QUINTE.

Landings.	Miles.	Landings.	Miles.
KINGSTON.............	0	PORT TRENTON.......	0
Amherst Island.......	13	BELLEVILLE..........	12
Bath.................	5-18	North Port...........	12-24
Fredericksburg.......	10-28	Indian Woods.........	8-32
Adolphustown.........	4-32	PICTON..............	15-47
Stone Mills..........	3-35	Stone Mills..........	5-52
PICTON..............	5-40	Adolphustown.........	3-55
Indian Woods.........	15-55	Fredericksburg.......	4-59
North Port...........	8-63	Bath.................	10-69
BELLEVILLE...........	12-75	Amherst Island.......	5-74
PORT TRENTON.......	12-87	KINGSTON............	13-87

FARE from Kingston to Picton.............. $1 00
    "   " Belleville............ 1 50

Several steamers leave Kingston daily for Picton, Belleville, Port Trenton, and intermediate ports, during the season of navigation, connecting at Belleville and Port Trenton with the Grand Trunk Railway, and line of stages running to Rice Lake, Peterboro', etc.

On leaving the wharf at Kingston the steamers run in a westerly direction, passing the *Brothers*, to AMHERST ISLAND, 13 miles. This is a large and fertile island, inhabited by an intelligent and prosperous class of citizens. Here commences the BAY OF QUINTE, a long, crooked, and picturesque body of water, into which empties the Napanee, Moira, and Trent rivers.

BATH, 18 miles from Kingston, is situated on the main shore, opposite Amherst Island. It contains about 600 inhabitants, with a fine back country.

FREDERICKSBURG, 28 miles from Kingston, is a settlement on the mainland.

ADOLPHUSTOWN, 32 miles from Kingston, is situated on the mainland, opposite MARYSBURG, located on Prince Edward's Island.

STONE MILLS, 35 miles from Kingston, is situated on Prince Edward's Island, near a most remarkable lake, elevated some 300 feet above the Bay of Quinte. It is called the *Lake of the Mountain*, being half a mile in length, and nearly as wide. It has no perceptible inlet, but discharges a large volume of water, which is used in propelling several mills of different kinds.

PICTON, 40 miles from Kingston, and 35 miles from Belleville by water, is the capital of Prince Edward Co., C. W., being handsomely situated. The Bay of Quinte, which here expands to a considerable width, is called Hallowell Bay. The village contains about 2,000 inhabitants; a court-house and jail, one Episcopal, one Presbyterian, one Methodist, and one Roman Catholic church, two hotels, and several taverns, twelve stores, one steam flouring-mill, one large tannery, and an extensive carriage manufactory.

On leaving Picton, the steamer runs north to the landing called *Indian Woods*, when a westerly course is again pursued to the head of the bay, passing *Morris*, or *Hall's Island*, and several beautiful headlands. Here is another expansion of water called *Hall's Bay*, on Capt. Owen's (R. N.) Chart of Lake Ontario.

BELLEVILLE, Hastings Co., C. W., is advantageously situated at the mouth of the river Moira, 75 miles by steamboat route, and only 47 miles by railroad from Kingston. This is a very thriving town, now containing about 8,000 inhabitants; the county buildings, a town hall and market building; a Methodist seminary, erected in 1855; one Episcopal, two Presbyterian, two Methodist, and one Roman Catholic church; four hotels, and a number of taverns; 50 stores of different kinds, and most kinds of mechanic workshops. The Moira River affords a good water-power, here being situated one woolen factory, three flouring-mills, four saw-mills, one paper-mill, one axe factory, one extensive distillery, three foundries and machine-shops, and a ship-yard. This is a great market for lumber, grain, and other kinds of produce. It is proposed to extend a railroad from Belleville to Lake Simcoe, and thence to the Georgian Bay of Lake Huron.

PORT TRENTON, 87 miles from Kingston by steamboat route, and 59 miles by railroad, is another growing place and port of entry, situated near the head of the Bay of Quinte, at the mouth of Trent River. It contains about 1,200 inhabitants; one Episcopal and one Methodist church; three hotels, ten stores, one grist-mill, one extensive steam saw-mill, one large tannery, two distilleries, a foundry, machine shop, and shipyards. Steamers run from Port Trenton to Kingston. Prescott, Montreal, etc., trans-shipping a large amount of lumber and country produce.

The RIVER TRENT, which is the outlet of Pemedashcontayong, or *Rice Lake*, is a fine stream of water, and is in part navigable for steamers running into the lake. Immense quantities of wild rice are found in the low waters of this lake and its vicinity, which abound in game of different kinds, affording ample sport and profit to the huntsman.

The principal inlet of Rice Lake is called *Otonibee River*, being the outlet of a succession of lakes, the most celebrated of which lies 823 feet above the ocean, and is called *Balsam Lake;* the other bodies of water are called Sturgeon Lake, West Lake, and East Lake. From Balsam Lake to the Bay of Quinte there is a succession of falls of 588 feet descent.

LIST OF STEAMERS.

AMERICAN STEAMERS BUILT ON LAKE ONTARIO AND RIVER ST. LAWRENCE SINCE THEIR INTRODUCTION IN 1816.

Built.	Name.	Tons.	Where built.	Remarks.
1816	Ontario	232	Sacket's Harbor	broken up.
1818	Sophia	75	Sacket's Harbor	broken up.
1823	Martha Ogden	150	Sacket's Harbor	lost in 1832.
1830	Brownville	150	Brownville	broken up.
1831	Charles Carroll	100	Sacket's Harbor	broken up.
"	Paul Pry	50	Ogdensburgh	broken up.
1832	United States	450	Ogdensburgh	broken up.
1833	Black Hawk	200	French Creek	broken up.
1834	Oswego	400	Oswego, N. Y.	broken up.
1836	Oneida	300	Oswego, N. Y.	broken up.
1837	Telegraph	200	Dexter, N. Y.	laid up.
1838	John Marshall	60	Lake Erie	lost in 1844.
1839	St. Lawrence	450	Oswego, N. Y.	broken up.
"	Express	150	Pultneyville	tow boat.
1841	George Clinton	100	Oswego, N. Y.	destroyed.
"	President	60	Oswego, N. Y.	lost in 1844.
1842	Lady of the Lake	425	Oswego, N. Y.	burnt in 1854.
1843	Rochester	350	Oswego, N. Y.	name changed.
1845	Niagara	473	Clayton, N. Y.	—
1847	Cataract	577	Clayton, N. Y.	Lewiston to Ogdensburgh.
1848	Bay State	1,093	Clayton, N. Y.	Lewiston to Ogdensburgh.
"	Ontario	832	Clayton, N. Y.	Lewiston to Ogdensburgh.
1849	Northerner	905	Oswego, N. Y.	—
1853	New York	1,200	Clayton, N. Y.	—

RUNNING ON THE ST. LAWRENCE RIVER.

Name	Tons	Where built	Remarks
Jenny Lind	300	Montreal, C. E.	Ogdensburgh to Montreal.
Montreal	300	Kingston, C. W.	Ogdensburgh to Montreal.
British Queen	300	Grand Island	Ogdensburgh to Montreal.

BRITISH STEAMERS BUILT ON LAKE ONTARIO AND THE RIVER ST. LAWRENCE SINCE 1816.

Built.	Name.	Tons.	Where built.	Remarks.
1816	Frontenac (1st)	500	Kingston, C. W.	broken up.
1817	Charlotte	150	Kingston.	
1819	Dalhousie	350	Prescott.	
1824	Toronto	200	Toronto.	
"	Queenston	350	Queenston.	
1825	Canada (1st)	250	Toronto.	
"	Niagara	400	Brockville.	
1828	Alciope	450	Niagara.	
1829	Sir James Kempt	200	Kingston.	
1830	Great Britain	700	Prescott.	
1831	Iroquois	100	Prescott.	
1832	John By	100	Kingston.	
"	William the Fourth	450	Gananoque	tow boat.
"	Transit	350	Oakville	wrecked.
1833	Britannia	200	Kingston	broken up.
"	Cobourg	500	Cobourg.	
"	Kingston (1st)	200	Kingston.	

Built.	Name.	Tons.	Where built.	Remarks.
1833	Brockville	850	Brockville.	
1834	Com. Barrie	275	Kingston	lost in 1842.
"	Enterprise	200	Kingston	broken up.
"	Union	800	Oakville	changed to barque.
1835	Traveller	850	Niagara	tow boat.
"	St. George	400	Kingston	laid up.
1837	Sir Robert Peel	850	Brockville	burnt in 1838.
"	Gore	200	Niagara	runs on Lake Huron.
"	Queen Victoria	200	Niagara	wrecked.
1838	Experiment	150	Niagara	broken up.
1839	Henry Gildersleeve	250	Kingston	tow boat.
"	Ontario	800	Prescott	name changed.
1840	Highlander (1st)	300	Coteau du Lac	broken up.
"	Albion	200	Brockville.	
"	America (1st)	800	Niagara	tow boat.
"	Sovereign	475	Niagara	broken up.
"	City of Toronto	500	Niagara	tow boat.
"	Prince Edward	200	Kingston	lost in 1848.
1841	Frontenac (2d)	200	Kingston	broken up.
"	Princess Royal	500	Niagara	tow boat.
"	Canada (2d)	450	Prescott	tow boat.
"	Despatch	200		laid up.
1842	Prince of Wales	200	Kingston	name changed.
"	Admiral	400	Niagara	runs on St. Lawrence.
"	Chief Justice Robinson	400	Niagara	
"	Welland (1st)	800		burnt in 1856.
"	Mohawk (iron)	150	Kingston	runs on Lake Erie.
"	Cherokee (gov. steamer)	700	Kingston	sent to Halifax.
1843	Eclipse	400	Niagara	changed to schooner.

TRADE AND NAVIGATION OF THE WELLAND AND ST. LAWRENCE CANALS.

Trade, etc.	Welland Canal. Tons.	Tolls.	St. Lawrence Canal. Tons.	Tolls.
Vessels of all kinds..	1,476.842	$32,823	1,049,230	$13,427
Passengers (No.).......	5,087	401	28,214	1,468
Produce of Forest......	238,213	26,385	381,305	13,172
Farm Stock...........	134	33	1.268	174
Animal Produce.......	9,116	2,367	7,520	1,470
Vegetable Food.......	721,149	163.918	421,265	82,957
Agricultural Products..	6,732	1,662	17,452	2,937
Manufactures.........	171,977	34,746	75.022	12,052
Merchandise..........	96,453	21,501	60,556	10,528
Total am't Tolls....		$283,836		$147,185

STATEMENT showing the total number, national character, and tonnage of vessels which passed on and through the Welland, St. Lawrence, Chambly, Burlington Bay, and Rideau and Ottawa Canals, during the year 1862, and amount of Tolls.

Vessels and Steamers.	Total. No.	Tons.	Am't of Tolls on Vessels.
Canadian.			
Welland Canal	3,355	511,355	$7,363 25
St. Lawrence Canal	10,704	1,028,633	13,271 87
Chambly and St. Ours Lock.....	1,861	115,039	1,277 52
Burlington Bay................	1,835	274.153	1,677 50
St. Ann's Lock................	3,914	236,343	294 30
Rideau and Ottawa............	6,088	371,063	5,781 68
Total Canadian..........	27,757	2,536,586	$32,326 12
American.			
Welland Canal	3,924	965,487	$25,459 78
St. Lawrence Canal	300	29,597	155 96
Chambly and St. Ours Lock.....	657	39,513	486 74
Burlington Bay................	83	12,565	74 00
St. Ann's Lock................	86	5,386	67 33
Rideau and Ottawa............	35	2,262	33 93
Total American..........	5,085	1,045,810	$26,277 74
Gr. Total, American & Canadian..	32,842	3,582,296	$58,603 86

LIST OF STEAMERS, ETC. **161**

LIST OF BRITISH STEAMERS BUILT AND RUNNING ON THE ST. LAWRENCE RIVER, BELOW MONTREAL SINCE 1810.

Built.   Name.   Tons. Where built.   Remarks.
1810 Accommodation.... —.Montreal—broken up.
1812 Swiftsure.......... —.Montreal—broken up.
1814.Malsham........... —.Montreal—broken up.
1816 Car of Com'nerce... —.Montreal—broken up.
1817.Lady Sherbrooke... —.Montreal—broken up.
"   Caledonia .... —.Montreal—broken up.
"   .Telegraph......... —.Montreal—broken up.
1818 New Swiftsure..... —.Montreal broken up.
"   Quebec (1st) ...... —.Quebec—broken up.
1820.Montreal (1st) ..... —.Montreal—broken up.
"   Cham ly .... —.Montreal—broken up.
"   .St. Lawrence (1st).. —.Montreal—broken up.
1822 La Prairie.......... —.Montreal—broken up.
1825.Hercules .... 300.Montreal—broken up.
"   .Edmund Henry..... —.Montreal—broken up.
1826 Waterloo........ ...200 La Prairie, C. E.—lost in the ice.
1829 British America...391.Montreal—broken up.
"   John Molson. ....390.Montreal—broken up.
1832 Voyageur.......... 300 Montreal—broken up.
"   .Canada .... 350.Montreal—broken up.
"   .Canadian Eagle....250 Montreal broken up.
"   .Patriot. ....100 Montreal—broken up.
1833 Britannia......... 135 Montreal—broken up.
1834 John Bull......... 500.Montreal—burnt in 1839.
1836.Princess Victoria.. 171.Montreal—tow boat.
1837.Charlevoix ....200.Montreal—broken up.
1839.Lady Colborne ....250 Montreal—broken up.
"   .Lord Sydenham.... —.Lake Ontario—broken up.
1840.Queen. ....372 Sorel, C. E.—laid up.
1841.Montreal (2d). ....378.Montreal—wrecked 1853.
1842.North America.....181.Montreal - broken up.
1843.Alliance ....192.Montreal—laid up.
"   .St. Louis........ 190 Sorel, C. E.—laid up.
"   .Prince Albert (iron).183 Montreal - Champl in & St. Lawr'nce Ferry
1845.Lord Elgin .... 153.Lake Ontario - Montreal to Kingston.
"   .Quebec (2d) ....400.Quebec—Montreal to Quebec.
"   .Rowland Hill......250.Quebec—tow boat.
1846 John Munn........ 400.Quebec—Montreal to Quebec.
"   .Richelieu ... . 70 Sorel, C. E.—Montreal to Chambly.
1847.Iron Duke (iron)...169.Montreal Champlain & St. Lawr'nce Ferry
"   .Ottawa...........270 Montreal.
1848.Jaques Cartier...... 78 Sorel, C. E.—Montreal to Three Rivers.
1849 Crescent........... 72.Montreal—laid up.
1852.Castor .. .. 75.Montreal—Montreal to Three Rivers.
"   .St. Lawrence (2d)...300..
1854.Montreal (3d).......300.Quebec—Burnt, June 27. 1857.
"   .J. M'Kenzie ....250.Quebec—Montreal to Quebec.
"   .Saguenay ....300.Sorel, C. E.—Quebec to Saguenay.
"   .Princess Royal..... —.Lake Ontario—Quebec to Saguenay.
"   .Huron ....350 Sorel, C. E.
"   .Musk Rat ....150 Montreal—Montreal to Longueil.
1855 Cultivateur........ 60 Montreal—Montreal to Berthier.
'   .Advance.......... —.Quebec—Quebec to River du Loup.
1856.Napoleon ....114.Montreal—Montreal to Quebec.
"   .Victoria...........114.Montreal—Montreal to Quebec.

CANALS OF CANADA, SHOWING THEIR LENGTH, LOCKS, ETC.

Names, etc.	Length in miles.	Locks.	Lockage in feet.	Cost.
WELLAND CANAL.				
Main Trunk, Port Colborne to Pt. Dalhousie	28	27	330	
Dunnville Feeder, junction to Dunnville	21	1	8	£1,061,497
Broad Creek Branch	1½	1	8	
ST. LAWRENCE.				
The Gallops	2	2	8	
Point Iroquois	3	1	6	
Rapid Plat	4	2	11½	£1,052,601
Farren's Point	¾	1	4	
CORNWALL	11½	7	48	
(Long Saut Rapids)				
BEAUHARNOIS	11¼	9	82½	£365,331
(Cascade, Cedars, etc.)				
LA CHINE	8½	5	45	£481,736
Total, from L. Erie to Montreal	69	54	535 feet.	
Add fall not requiring locks			17	
Fall from Montreal to tide-water at Three Riv., C. E.			13	
Grand total			565 feet.	

NOTE.—Lake Huron is elevated nine feet above Lake Erie, and Lake Superior is elevated 26 feet above Lake Huron—making a total elevation above tide-water, or the ocean, of 600 feet, according to recent surveys.

	Length in miles.	Locks.	Lockage in feet.	Cost.
CHAMBLY CANAL	11½	9	74	
(River Richelieu)				
St. Ours Lock, do.		1	5	
ST. ANNE'S LOCK.				
(Ottawa River)		1	3½	
RIDEAU CANAL.				
Kingston to Ottawa City	126	37	457	£965,000
OTTAWA CANAL and LOCKS				£117,647

TRIP FROM KINGSTON TO MONTREAL.

The American steamers on leaving Kingston on their trip to Ogdensburgh run between Grand Island and Howe Island, two large islands belonging to the British, when they enter the American Channel of the St. Lawrence and land at Clayton, situated at the mouth of French Creek, while the Canadian steamers usually run the North or British Channel, passing *Gananoqui*, 20 miles below Kingston. This is usually the first landing made by the British steamers in descending the river, unless they stop to take in wood at some of the numerous islands.

The Thousand Islands.—The remarkable group of islands in the River St. Lawrence called "*The Thousand Islands,*" commences opposite the city of Kingston, and stretches down the river for between 40 and 50 miles, for which distance the St. Lawrence is between six and twelve miles wide. They lie partly in Canada and partly within the bounds of the State of New York, the boundary line between the United States and Canada dividing them into about equal parts.

From an examination of Bayfield's chart of the St. Lawrence River, it appears that Wolfe or Grand Island, belonging to the British, is 18 miles long and from one to six miles wide. This is the largest island of the group, and contains much good land, being inhabited by a number of families. A canal is commenced, extending across this island, to facilitate trade with Cape Vincent.

Gage Island, lying west of Grand Island, is three miles long. On its southwest end may be seen a light-house as you approach Kingston from Toronto or Oswego. The American boats usually run between this island and Wolfe Island, through the *Packet* or *Bateau Channel*.

On Garden Island, opposite Kingston, is situated a large lumber establishment, where may usually be seen vessels taking in lumber, destined for different ports.

Howe Island, also belonging to the British, is eight miles long, and from one to two miles wide, lying near the Canada shore. The usual steamboat route, on ascending and descending the river, is between this island and Wolfe Island, running through the *Kingston* or *British Channel*, a wide expanse of water, extending from near Kingston to French Creek, on the American side.

The *American Channel* runs east of Wolfe or Grand Island, between that and Cape Vincent, where extends the boundary line between the two countries, this being considered the main channel.

Carleton Island, belonging to the United States, is situated nearly opposite Cape Vincent. It contains about 1,200 acres of excellent land, and is an important island, as it commands the American Channel of the St. Lawrence, and has two fine coves or harbors at the upper end, where are extensive lumber stations. Here was erected a fort by the British in 1777, and it became their principal military and naval depôt for Lake Ontario during the Revolutionary War. Some years afterward, the shipping and public stores were removed to Kingston, but the island was retained and occupied by British troops until 1812, when the guard was surprised and taken by a party of New York militia.

The waters of the St. Lawrence among the islands here vary at different seasons from three to four feet in height, exposing some hundreds of islets at its lowest stage.

The fish most abundant are the maskalonge, pickerel, black bass, pike, perch, rock bass, cat-fish, and eels. The maskalonge, pickerel, and black bass are taken by trolling; the pike are taken in nets, and the perch, rock bass, etc , are taken by hook and line.

On the islands are found deer, foxes, raccoons, rabbits, squirrels, muskrats, and minks; also partridges, quail, and wild ducks in abundance.

Grindstone Island, five and a half miles long, belongs to the United States. This is a large island, lying in the middle of the river, a short distance below the mouth of French Creek. Here, it is said, the noted Bill Johnson has his favorite abode, either on the main island, or the small island in its immediate vicinity, called *Johnson's Island.*

WELL'S ISLAND, another large and important island, eight or nine miles in length, is attached to the State of New York; it lies mostly above the village of Alexandria, the boundary line running on its west side, where lies a beautiful body of water, called the "*Lake of the Thousand Islands,*" which is a favorite resort for the angler and sportsman.

THE ADMIRALTY ISLANDS are a group lying below Howe Island, and belong to the British. Here the Canadian Channel becomes a perfect labyrinth for a number of miles, and the navigation would be very dangerous were it not for the great depth of water and bold shores of the islets, and light houses.

The FLEET GROUP, or NAVY ISLANDS, commence opposite Grindstone Island, on the Canadian side of the river, and extends for some distance below to opposite Well's Island. Here the boundary line runs close to the latter island, giving most of the small islands to the British.

The OLD FRIENDS are a small group immediately below Well's Island, belonging to the United States.

The INDIAN GROUP also lie on the American side of the channel, a few miles below the latter islands.

The AMATEUR ISLANDS lie in the middle of the river, opposite Chippewa Creek, and are, in part, attached to the State of New York, and a part belong to Canada, the boundary line running between them.

Immediately below the latter islands the river contracts to one or two miles in width, and the Thousand Islands, of which there are at least fourteen hundred, may be said to terminate, although a large collection of islands called *Brock's Group,* lying mostly on the Canada side, are passed a short distance below the village of Brockville, where the St. Lawrence River is about one mile wide, which width it averages for 30 or 40 miles, until you approach the rapids below Ogdensburgh, when it narrows to about half a mile in width, with banks elevated but a few feet above the water.

"The main stream of the St. Lawrence," says Buckingham, speaking of the Thousand Islands, "is so thickly studded with islands that it is like passing through a vast archipelago, rather than navigating a mighty river. They are for the most part rocky islets, sometimes rising in abrupt cliffs from the water, and so bold and steep that you may run the boat near enough to touch the cliffs from the vessel. A few only are low and flat, but being nearly all wooded, they form a perpetual succession of the most romantically beautiful and picturesque groups that can be conceived."

Among the Thousand Islands are usually found immense quantities of water-fowl and other kinds of wild game, which, during the spring and summer months, afford great pleasure to the sportsman. The fishing is also excellent for the most part of the year. During the months of July and August, pleasure parties from the surrounding country, and strangers from a distance, resort here for their amusement, enjoying themselves to their heart's content by hunting, fishing, and bathing, being surrounded by wild and interesting scenery and invigorating air, not exceeded by any section of the United States or Canada.

The St. Lawrence River, in fact for its entire length of several hundred miles, presents a magnificent appearance, well worthy the attention of the tourist. The *Rapids*, now successfully navigated on their downward trip by steamboats of a large class, returning through the canals, afford a deeply interesting excursion. The cultivated fields and settlements interchanging with bolder features, impart a grandeur as well as variety and beauty to the river and its shores which no other stream on the continent possesses in an equal degree.

BROCKVILLE, 50 miles below Kingston and 125 miles above Montreal by railroad route, is a beautiful and flourishing town of about 5,000 inhabitants; it contains a court-house and jail, a custom-house, several churches, two good hotels, and many fine buildings, besides several extensive manufacturing establishments. Here is a convenient steamboat landing, where the American and British passage-boats usually land on their trips up and down the river, the stream here being about two miles in width.

The *Grand Trunk Railway*, which runs through the town, has added much to the growth and trade of this place. The *Brockville and Ottawa Railroad*, which is in the course of construction, when finished, will further add to its prosperity, the country in the rear being very fertile and heavily timbered, producing large quantities of grain and lumber.

MAITLAND is a small village, five miles below Brockville, on the same side. It contains a church, a public house, and some 300 inhabitants.

The town of PRESCOTT, C. W., is situated on the north bank of the St. Lawrence, directly opposite Ogdensburgh, being 60 miles below Kingston and 113 miles above Montreal by railroad route. This point may be considered as the foot of lake and river navigation for sail vessels, as the Gallop Rapids occur about six miles below, where commences the first of the series of the St. Lawrence canals, terminating with the La Chine Canal, which enters Montreal. Prescott is a port of entry and contains a custom-house, a town-hall, four churches, six public houses, 20 or 30 stores, a foundry and machine-shop, together with several breweries and distilleries, and three extensive laundries. This is also a great depôt for lumber and country produce.

British and American steamers usually land at Prescott several times daily on their route up and down the St. Lawrence. Two steam ferry-boats are also constantly running between this place and Ogdensburgh. The *Grand Trunk Railway* passes through the town, and the *Ottawa and Prescott Railroad*, 53 miles in length, terminates here, affording a speedy and direct route to Ottawa City and the lumber region above.

No section of Canada has fairer prospects of advancement than Brockville and Prescott, if the advantages are embraced of forming lines of railroads to the upper Ottawa country, lying as they do nearer to that heavily timbered region than Montreal.

Fort Wellington, adjoining the lower part of the town, is a strong fortification usually garrisoned by more or less British troops. WINDMILL POINT, one mile and a half below the fort, was the scene of an unfortunate attack by the patriots of 1838, who, after effecting a landing and maintaining their position with great determination for several days, were taken prisoners, many of whom were afterward executed at Kingston, and others transported to Van Dieman's Land.

RAPIDS OF THE ST. LAWRENCE.

On resuming the downward trip, after leaving Prescott or Ogdensburgh, the most interesting objects are presented to view from the deck of the steamer. The depôt buildings of the Northern Railroad of New York, on the one side, and Windmill Point on the Canada side, are quickly passed and the Rapids soon reached.

CHIMNEY ISLAND, four miles below Prescott, is an interesting spot, where may be seen the remains of a fortification, erected by the French during the early settlement of Canada.

The GALLOP RAPIDS, six miles below Prescott or Ogdensburgh, are easily passed by steamboats, although they prevent the navigation of the St. Lawrence by sail vessels. They extend for about two miles, around which is a ship canal on the Canada side of the river, overcoming a descent of seven feet.

MATILDA, eight miles farther, is a convenient steamboat landing on the Canada side of the river, where is a canal one mile and three-quarters in length.

WADDINGTON, on the American shore, 18 miles below Ogdensburgh, lies opposite Ogden's Island, which is passed to the right, descending through the main channel, forming the boundary line. Here commences RAPID PLAT, and extends about two and a half miles. Another canal of the same length is built on the Canada shore, to overcome the descent in the river of eleven and a half feet.

WILLIAMSBURG, seven miles below Matilda, is a regular steamboat landing, where passage-boats usually touch ascending and descending the river. Here is another short canal.

CHRYSLER'S FARM, a few miles below Williamsburg, is the place where was fought a battle in the war of 1812, between the English and Americans, in which the latter were defeated, with considerable loss in killed and wounded.

LOUISVILLE LANDING, 28 miles below Ogdensburgh, is where passengers leave for *Massena Springs*, six miles distant by stage. This is a great resort for invalids during warm weather.

The LONG SAUT RAPIDS, extending from Dickinson's Landing, 40 miles below Prescott, to Cornwall on the Canada side, is one of the longest and most important rapids of the St. Lawrence. They are divided by islands into two channels, the *American Channel* and the *Lost Channel*.* Formerly, the American, or East Channel, was mostly run by steamers in the downward trip, but of late the Lost Channel, on the Canadian side, is mostly used. This channel presents a grand and terrific appearance, the water being lashed into a white foam for several miles, yet still the steamer glides rapidly through them into the quiet and beautiful expanse of water below Cornwall.

The CORNWALL CANAL commences 72 miles above Montreal, on about the 45th degree of north latitude, the dividing line between the United States and Canada. It extends to Dickinson's Landing, 11½ miles, overcoming 48 feet descent in the St. Lawrence. Barnhart Island and Long Saut Island, two large and cultivated bodies of land, belong to the State of New York, while Cornwall Island and Sheek's Island belong to Canada, dividing the waters of the St. Lawrence into two channels, for most of the distance through the rapids.

CORNWALL. 112 miles from Kingston and 70 miles above Montreal, is situated on the northwest side of the river, at the

---

* PASSAGE OF THE LONG SAUT RAPID.—Those who have traveled on the St. Lawrence are aware that between Dickinson's Landing and Cornwall, a distance of from twelve to fourteen miles, there is a long rapid called the *Long Saut*. This rapid is divided into two channels by an island in the center, the channel on the south side being the one which has heretofore been descended by steamers and other large craft passing down the river. Capt. Maxwell, the enterprising commander of the mail steamer "Gildersleeve," having some time ago become impressed with an idea that the channel on the north side of the island was not only practicable for vessels of a large class, but that it was much safer and easier of descent than the channel on the south side, made, with much trouble, soundings and observations, for the purpose of ascertaining whether such was really the case. Having well satisfied himself in the matter, he (with Mr. Hamilton's permission) made a descent down the North Channel, sometimes called *Lost Channel*, in the mail steamer "Gildersleeve." The passage was magnificent, the grandeur and beauty of the Rapid far surpassing even those of the Rapids at the Cedars, the Cascades, or La Chine. Owing to the great rapidity of the current, the water is much rougher than on the south side of the island, but the channel is straighter, and in every respect better than the one heretofore adopted, and there is little doubt that ere long the North Channel will be the one which the main traffic of the river will pass through.—*Montreal Herald.*

lower end of the *Cornwall*, or *St. Lawrence Canal*. The town contains about 2,500 inhabitants, 400 dwelling-houses, a court-house and jail, five churches, twenty stores, and several hotels. This is a regular steamboat landing for American and British steamers. The *Grand Trunk Railway* also passes through the rear part of the town.

St. REGIS, four miles below, on the American side of the river, is situated on the line of the 45th degree of north latitude, the St. Lawrence below this point being entirely in Canada. St. Regis is an Indian village, part of its inhabitants living in the United States and part in Canada. It contains four or five hundred inhabitants, 80 dwelling-houses, one Roman Catholic church, one Protestant church, one tavern, and two stores. Here is a convenient steamboat landing, where during warm weather may sometimes be seen Indian boys, prepared to plunge into the water on having a piece of money thrown overboard: often it is caught by these expert swimmers before reaching the bottom.

LAKE ST. FRANCIS, a most beautiful expanse of water, is an expansion of the St. Lawrence above Coteau du Lac, extending for a number of miles. It is studded with lovely and picturesque islands, giving a variety to the scenery of this river which is almost indescribable. The Indian village of St. Regis, and an island owned by the natives, lie near its upper termination.

LANCASTER, 15 miles below Cornwall, lies on the west side of the lake, or river, here presenting a wide surface, the waters calmly pursuing their course downward before rushing impetuously down the several rapids below *Coteau du Lac*, or the foot of the lake.

At COTEAU DU LAC, 40 miles above Montreal, commences a rapid of the same name, extending about two miles. Seven miles below this commences the *Cedar Rapid*, which extends about three miles. *(See Frontispiece.)* Then comes *Split Rock and Cascade* terminating at the head of Lake St. Louis, where the dark waters of the Ottawa, by one of its mouths, joins the

St. Lawrence. These four rapids, in eleven miles, have a descent of 82½ feet, being overcome by the Beauharnois Canal.

The grandeur of the scenery in the vicinity of these Rapids can not be conceived without being witnessed. The mighty St. Lawrence is here seen in all its magnificence and power, being lashed into a foam for miles by the impetuosity of its current. The *Cedar Rapids** have hitherto been considered the most formidable obstruction to downward-bound craft, but the new South Channel, or McPherson's Channel, as it is now called, affords an additional depth of water. The steamer *Bytown*, Capt. Wm. Sughrue, in 1843, was the first steamboat that descended this channel, which was brought into notice by D. S. McPherson, Esq., one of the late firm of the forwarding-house of McPherson, Crane & Co

BEAUHARNOIS, 24 miles above Montreal, lies at the foot of the Cascade Rapids, where commences the *Beauharnois Canal*, 12 miles in length, overcoming altogether a descent of 82½ feet Between Fond du Lac and Beauharnois. or the foot of the Cascade Rapids, is the most wild and romantic scenery that the St. Lawrence presents.

CAUGHNAWAGA, ten miles above Montreal, is an Indian village, numbering several hundred inhabitants. Here commences the *Montreal and Plattsburgh Railroad*, 52 miles in length. It is proposed to construct a ship canal from this place to the Richelieu River, the outlet of Lake Champlain, thus uniting the waters of the St. Lawrence and Hudson River, *via* Champlain Canal.

LA CHINE, eight miles above Montreal, is situated at the foot of an expansion of the St. Lawrence, called *Lake St. Louis*, where enter the black waters of the Ottawa River, the St. Lawrence presenting a greenish hue, the difference in the color of the waters being plainly visible for many miles below.

The LA CHINE RAPIDS, a few miles above Montreal, are the last rapids of importance that occur on the St. Lawrence. They

---

* It was here that Gen. Amherst's brigade of 800 men, on their way to attack Canada, then in possession of the French, were lost! At Montreal they received the first intelligence of the invasion, by the dead bodies floating down the river past the town.

are now considered the most dangerous and difficult of navigation. These rapids are obviated by the *La Chine Canal*, 8½ miles in length, overcoming a descent of 44½ feet. Canals of a large capacity now run round all the rapids, enabling steamers of a large size to ascend the river, although at a much less speed than the downward trip.

"The St. LAWRENCE is perhaps the only river in the world possessing so great a variety of scenery and character, in the short distance of one hundred and eighty miles—from Kingston to Montreal. The voyage down this portion of the St. Lawrence in a steamer is one of the most exciting and interesting that our country affords to the pleasure-seeking traveler. Starting at daylight from the good old city of Kingston, we are at first enraptured by the lovely and fairy-like scenery of the 'Lake of the Thousand Isles,' and oft we wonder how it is that our helmsman can guide us through the intricate path that lies before him. Surely he will make some mistake, and we shall lose our way, and our steamer wander for ages ere the trackless path be once more discovered. However, we are wrong, and long before the sun has set we have shot the 'Long Saut,' and are passing through the calm and peaceful Lake St. Francis. Gently we glide along, and are lost in pleasing reveries, which grace the scenes of our forenoon's travel. Suddenly we are awakened from our dreams by a pitch, and then a quick jerk of our vessel, and rising to see the cause, we find ourselves receiving warning in the Coteau Rapids, of what we may expect when we reach the CEDARS, a few miles farther on. Now the bell is rung for the engine *to slow* its speed, and glancing toward the beam, we find it merely moving sufficient to keep headway on the vessel; now looking toward the wheelman's house, we see four men standing by the wheel; backward we turn our gaze, and four more stand by the *tiller*, to assist those at the wheel in guiding our craft down the fearful leaps she is about to take. These preparations striking us with dread, we, who are now making our first trip, involuntarily clutch the nearest object for support, and checking our breath, await the first plunge. 'Tis over. We are reeling to and fro, and dancing hither and thither among billows of enormous size, caused solely by the swiftness of the current. With difficulty we keep our feet while rushing down the tortuous channel, through which only we can be preserved from total wreck or certain death. Now turning to the right, to avoid a half-sunken rock, about whose summit the waves are ever dashing, we are apparently running on an island situated immediately before us. On ! on we rush! We must ground! but no; her head is easing off, and as we fly past the island, a daring leap might land us on its shores; and now again we are tossed and whirled about in a sea of foam; we look back to scan the dangers passed, and see a raft far behind, struggling in the waves. While contemplating its dangers, we forget our own, and the lines of Horace appear peculiarly applicable to the Indian who first intrusted his frail canoe to these terrific rapids:

> 'Illi robur et æs triplex
> Circa pectus erat, qui fragilem truci
> Commisit pelago ratem
> Primus ———.'"

RAPIDS OF THE ST. LAWRENCE—EXCITEMENT OF THE TRIP.

Extract from a Correspondent of the Detroit Advertiser—1856.

"LEAVING Hamilton in the evening, on board one of the splendid steamers navigating Lake Ontario, running direct for the St. Lawrence River, a distance of about 180 miles, we had a very pleasant night on the lake, and arrived at Cape Vincent, N. Y., at 7 next morning; discharged some freight, and proceeded to Brockville, Canada, and thence to Ogdensburgh, N. Y., where we arrived about noon; passing from Cape Vincent to Ogdensburgh (*via* the Express Line of steamers), we thread our winding way through among the *Thousand Islands;* here is no monotony, for the scenery is continually changing and ever beautiful.

"I have spoken of the route by which I came to Ogdensburgh; another very pleasant route is by way of the steamer from Detroit to Buffalo, thence to the Niagara Falls, taking the boat at Lewiston. By this route, passengers may see many points of interest, which they do not see in traveling by the direct route.

"On Wednesday, July 17th, we left Ogdensburgh on the steamer MONTREAL, Capt. J. Laflamme, ran across the St. Lawrence to Prescott—then headed down the river to Montreal. At six miles from Ogdensburgh we passed the first rapid (Gallop). This being the first of a series of rapids that we had to pass on our way to Montreal, we had the curiosity to notice the effect the scene had on the passengers. The first with whom we came in contact was a nervous old gentleman, and he was rushing from one side of the boat to the other, with fear and admiration depicted on his countenance, while excitement had taken possession of his whole frame.

"Here is a group of sentimental young ladies; so deeply are they absorbed in drinking in the sickly sentiments of the cheap, yellow-covered literature which they hold in their hands, that they know nothing of the wild and beautiful scene through which we are passing. This is not the case with all, for many are standing or seated near the railing of the deck, looking calmly at the turbulent waters, and discoursing upon the cause of all this commotion; others stand in the background, wishing, but fearing to look at the trembling of the waves. We are now past the first rapid, or the "Gallops," and the water is now in a state of perfect calmness, and so are the passengers.

"The boat stops a few moments at Louisville, 35 miles from Ogdensburgh. At this point the river is divided by an island, and here begins the *Long Saut*, a rapid of nine miles in length; formerly the boats passed down the south side, where the water runs with greater rapidity. The north side is called the 'Lost Channel,' a name given to it by the French boatmen, as they supposed that if a boat drifted into it, it would certainly be lost. A channel has been found on the north side, and now the steamers pass by it in preference to the south channel.

"As we approach the rapid, the grand and lofty tumbling of the waters, as they break upon the projecting rocks, have an angry appearance, and look as if they were preparing to engulph us. We are standing upon the bow of the boat, and are fascinated by the view of the scene, yet we involuntarily turn our eyes to the pilot-house, in front of which, on an elevation, stands the captain, and at the wheel are four strong men. Neither fear nor anxiety is to be perceived in either countenance; but with their eyes fixed upon the landmarks, and their strong hands upon the wheel, they guide the ship through the narrow and crooked channel with unerring precision. The grand and picturesque scene has now brought all to their feet; the novel-readers have dropped their books, and the excitement of reality now surpasses the excitement of their fiction. The nervous man is standing bareheaded against the pilot-house, with both hands elevated, mouth open, and an exclamation upon the end of his tongue, as his tongue refuses to act; but as the boat glides out of the last billow into smooth water, the exclamation drops from his lips, his mouth shuts with a sudden jerk; and as he subsides into a calm he wipes the sweat from his brow, and is glad that he has seen and passed over that rapid. Only a small portion of the Long Saut is very rough, the rest of it has much the appearance of Hell Gate, N. Y.

"After passing the Long Saut, the boat stops a few moments at Cornwall on the Canada side. In a short time after leaving Cornwall, the river widens into a lake, which is called *Lake St. Francis*. This lake is about forty miles in length. Having passed it, the boat stops a few moments at the village of Coteau du Lac.

"Soon after leaving the Coteau, we pass the *Coteau, Cedar,*

Split-Rock, and *Cascade Rapids*. The passage of these rapids is very exciting, particularly the Split-Rock; here, as the boat is by the action of the water lifted above the rocks, and then dropped down among them, the waters covering and then receding and leaving the rocks nearly bare, upon either side, looks fearfully dangerous; the channel is narrow, the current rapid, and the boat is carried along at a 2 40 pace; but the boat is strong, and a skillful pilot is at the helm, and the passage is very quickly and safely made.

"The river again widens, and is called *Lake St. Louis*. At the foot of this lake, on the south side, is the Indian village of Caughnawaga. Here a boat comes off from the village, and brings an Indian named Baptiste. He is a fine-looking man, apparently about sixty years of age; he comes on board to pilot the boat over the *La Chine*, which is the last but most dangerous of the rapids. No man but Baptiste has ever yet piloted a steamer over these rapids. As the boat moves onward to the rapids, all the passengers, even to the novel-readers, are anxious to get a good position in order to have a good view of the heaving, breaking, and laughing waters. As we enter the rapids, we appear to be running upon a small grass-covered rocky island. Indeed, as the bow of the boat is so near that it appears to be impossible to clear it, we look to see if the pilot is at the helm. Yes, there stands the captain at his post in front of the wheel-house, and the Indian pilot, with three other strong men are at the wheel; and as we look at the calm countenance of the Indian, and see that his bright eye does not so much as wink, but is fixed steadily upon his beacon, whatever it may be, and that the wheelsmen are fully under his control we feel that, with his skill, care, and knowledge of the way, w may banish fear from our thoughts.

"Baptiste is a noble Indian; he guides the boats among the islands and the rocks, over the rapids and through the intricate channels, as easily as a skillful horseman reins a high-spirited charger. As quick as thought the boat glides away from those rocks which it appeared impossible to avoid, but the pilot apparently is insensible to fear, though not to the responsibility that rests upon him. He is aware, and all are aware, that one false move and all is lost; for the current is so swift, the seas run so high, and the boat is driven so rapidly, that one touch upon a rock would shiver her to atoms. Although the passage of the rapids appears to be dangerous, a sense of pleasure and excitement takes the place of fear. Just as we left the La Chine Rapids, looking for the nervous man—there he stood, shaking, laughing, and exclaiming, '*that caps the* CLIMAX.' In about half an hour after leaving this last rapid, we enter the harbor of Montreal."

RAILROAD ROUTE FROM MONTREAL TO TORONTO, ETC., VIA GRAND TRUNK RAILWAY.

THE *Grand Trunk Railway of Canada*, extending from Montreal to Toronto, and from the latter place to near Sarnia, situated at the foot of Lake Huron, affords a speedy mode of travel. The following is a description of the route from Montreal westward, ascending the noble St. Lawrence.

The depôt is situated near the termination of the *Victoria Bridge*, about one mile from the center of Montreal. On leaving the depôt the La Chine Canal is soon passed, and then the Montreal and La Chine Railroad, the track of the Grand Trunk Railway extending westerly across the fertile island of Montreal, passing in sight of *Lake St. Louis*, formed by the junction of the Ottawa and St. Lawrence rivers.

ST. ANNE'S, 21 miles from Montreal, is a French-Canadian village, of some four or five hundred inhabitants. Here is a Roman Catholic church, and a number of picturesque edifices situated near the water's edge. The rapids, government lock for steamers, and the railroad bridge, together with the beautiful Ottawa and islands, altogether afford a magnificent view, almost unrivaled for river scenery. A few miles westward may be seen the hills giving the name to the *Lake of the Two Mountains*.

ISLE PEROT, about two miles in width, is next passed over by the upward train, and another branch of the Ottawa crossed, when the cars stop at the

VAUDREUIL STATION, situated about half a mile below the village of the same name. Here a lovely view is obtained of the

Ottawa, its islands, and the hills of the Lake of the Two Mountains in the distance. The railroad track, on leaving the Ottawa, runs through a fertile tract of country for several miles, the village of the CEDARS being passed on the left, some two miles distant.

COTEAU STATION is 37 miles from Montreal and one and a half miles from the landing; here is a scattered settlement of French Canadians, numbering about 500 inhabitants.

LANCASTER, 54 miles from Montreal, is situated on the north shore of Lake St. Francis, an expansion of the St. Lawrence River. Here is a population of about 700 inhabitants, mostly of Scotch descent.

CORNWALL, 68 miles from Montreal, is a thriving town, situated at the foot of the Long Saut Rapids. It contains about 2,500 inhabitants. Here the trains usually meet, and the passengers are furnished refreshments. This is also a convenient steamboat landing, where the Royal Mail Line of steamers stop daily on their trips up and down the St. Lawrence.

Dickinson's Landing, 77 miles; *Aultsburg*, 84 miles; *Williamsburg*, 92 miles; *Matilda*, 99 miles, and *Prescott Junction*, 112 miles, are soon reached and passed by the ascending train.

The line of the Grand Trunk Railway from Vaudreuil to Brockville, a distance of 100 miles, runs through a level section of country, from a half to two miles distant from the St. Lawrence River, which is only seen occasionally from the passing train of cars.

The town of PRESCOTT, 113 miles from Montreal, and 60 miles from Kingston, is advantageously situated on the north bank of the St. Lawrence, opposite the village of Ogdensburgh. It contains a population of about 3,000 inhabitants. (*See page* 259.)

The *Ottawa and Prescott Railroad*, 54 miles in length, extends from Prescott to Ottawa City, intersecting the Grand Trunk Railway one and a half miles from the St. Lawrence River. On leaving Prescott the railroad runs through a level country to *Kemptville*, 23 miles, and thence to Ottawa City, a further distance of 30 miles. This is now the most speedy and favorite route from Montreal to the Upper Ottawa, passengers' baggage being checked through, *via* Prescott.

BROCKVILLE, 125 miles above Montreal, and 208 miles below Toronto, is one of the most important stations on the line of the *Grand Trunk Railway*, it being a flourishing town of about 5,000 inhabitants. The *Brockville and Ottawa Railroad* will extend from this place to Pembroke, situated 100 miles above Ottawa City. The railroad route from Brockville to Kingston, 48 miles, continues along the north shore of Lake Ontario to Cobourg, 90 miles farther, and thence to Toronto, 70 miles; being a total distance of 333 miles

For further information in regard to Kingston, Cobourg, Toronto, etc., see *Trip from Hamilton and Toronto to Kingston, etc.*

MONTREAL.

THE City of MONTREAL, the largest and chief seat of commerce of British America, is favorably situated at the head of ship navigation on the left bank of the St. Lawrence River, here about two miles in width. It lies 170 miles above Quebec and 350 miles below Toronto, by water, in N. lat. 45° 30′, and W. long. 73° 25′ from Greenwich. The site, although not so commanding as Quebec, is in every other respect superior, lying at the foot of a romantic eminence from which it derives its name, called *Mount Royal*, which hill rises in picturesque beauty. about one mile from the city, to the height of 550 feet, forming a prominent object in the picture from every point of view The streets, although somewhat irregular, present a fine and clean appearance. Notre Dame Street, the Broadway of Montreal, is the principal promenade and seat of the fashionable retail trade; it is about one mile in length and has many elegant stores, built of stone in the most durable manner. St. Paul Street, lying nearer the water, is mostly filled with wholesale stores. Great St. James Street is a wide and beautiful avenue, where are located most of the banks and insurance offices; together with hotels and other substantial buildings. McGill Street is filled with stores and offices of different kinds, running across the streets enumerated above. Water Street, Commissioners' Street, and Common Street extend the entire length of the city, facing on the St. Lawrence River and La Chine Canal; at times presenting a pleasing and lively appearance when the harbor and canal are filled with steamers and sail vessels of different kinds. From whatever side the city is approached, either by water or land, the scene is one of much interest; if from the St. Lawrence, Victoria Bridge and islands first attract attention; then the splendid towers of the Cathedral, the tall spires of other churches, the elegant front of Bonsecours

Market, the magnificent stone quay, and the long range of cutstone buildings which front the river, form at once a *tout ensemble* which is unequaled. Pop. in 1861, 90,323.

The public buildings in Montreal are numerous; many of them massive and costly edifices. The most noted is the Roman Catholic or *French Cathedral*, situated on Notre Dame Street, fronting the Place d'Armes; it is built in the Gothic style of architecture, 255 feet in length by 134 in breadth; it has six towers, of which the three belonging to the main front are 220 feet in height. The principal window is 64 feet in height and 32 in breadth. The interior has several desks or altars, and is capable of accommodating from 6 to 7,000 persons, who can disperse by several outlets. "This church boasts the possession of a magnificent set of bells, one of which, weighing thirteen tons, is hung in the western tower, and is the largest bell in America. Under the church, the entire space is occupied by a cemetery—in which the more wealthy of the Roman Catholics are interred." The Seminary of St. Sulpice, adjoining the Cathedral, is a substantial stone building, at present only finished to the extent of half the proposed plan. In this building is transacted all the parochial business, and also the secular affairs connected with the very valuable property belonging to the priests of the seminary. There are several other Roman Catholic churches, mostly belonging to the order of St. Sulpice, to the members of which Montreal chiefly owed its foundation, and who still hold the seigniory of the island on which it stands.

The Protestant churches, consisting of the Church of England or Episcopal, the Church of Scotland (Presbyterian), the Congregational, the Baptist, the Methodist, and other persuasions, are numerous; Montreal being justly celebrated for its church edifices and church-going people. There are also a great number of nunneries and charitable institutions in the city, both under Roman Catholic and Protestant management. The courthouse and prison are new and substantial stone buildings, occupying the site of the former college of the Jesuits. The government house, barracks, ordnance office, six banks, and five market-houses, the principal of which is the Bonsecours Market, are among the remaining public buildings. Nelson's Monument, a colossal statue of the hero of the Nile, is placed on a Doric column, the pedestal of which has bas-reliefs representing naval actions. McGill College is beautifully situated at the base of the mountain, and is richly endowed. Here are also a Baptist college and two Roman Catholic colleges, besides numerous other educational institutions. Montreal has a theater-royal, an exchange building, a penitentiary, a house of industry, a hospital, water works, gas works, a custom-house, a board of trade, scientific institutions, religious and benevolent institutions, and numerous well-kept hotels.

The favorable position of Montreal for trade and commerce, both foreign and domestic, makes it a great thoroughfare for men of business, as well as of the pleasure-seeking community. The facilities afforded by means of the St. Lawrence and Ottawa rivers, in connection with the Grand Trunk Railway and other railroads, open a ready communication, not only with all parts of Canada, but with Portland, Me., Boston, and the city of New York; the latter city being only 400 miles distant, and connected during the season of navigation by two popular lines of travel. The harbor, though not large, is safe and convenient; vessels drawing 15 feet may lie close to the quay, which is a most substantial stone structure of upward one mile in length. The *La Chine Canal*, nine miles long, admits steamers of a large size on their upward trips, they usually running the Rapids on their downward trips from the Lakes above and the Ottawa River. Besides steamers of a large class running to Quebec, steamships run regularly, during the season of navigation, between Montreal and Liverpool, making quick and profitable voyages. The trade through Lake Champlain, mostly by means of the *Champlain and St. Lawrence Railroad*, 44 miles in length, is immense—so much so as to require a ship canal from Caughanawa, or opposite Montreal, to the navigable waters of the Richelieu River, the outlet of Lake Champlain.

The *Montreal and Plattsburgh Railroad*, 52 miles in length uniting with the La Chine Railroad, forms a direct line of travel to Plattsburgh, situated on the west shore of Lake Champlain. The *Montreal and Ottawa Railroad*, under construction, will add greatly to the advantage of Montreal.

The *Victoria Bridge*, now erected across the St. Lawrence River, immediately above the city, is fully completed, and forms one of the wonders of the age ; it crosses the river from Point St. Charles to the south shore, a total length of 10,284 feet, or about 50 yards less than two miles. It is to be built on the tubular principle, and will have a track for railroad cars in the center, while on the outside of the tube there will be a balcony on each side, with a footpath for passengers. The bridge will rest on 24 piers and two abutments of limestone masonry ; the center span being 330 feet long, and 60 feet high from summer water-level, descending at either end at the rate of one in 130. It is in every respect to be built in the most substantial manner, and, when completed, will cost the enormous sum of £1,250,000 sterling, or $6,250,000. The contents of the masonry will be 3,000,000 of cubic feet. The weight of iron in the tubes 8,000 tons. The following are the dimensions of tube through which the trains pass in the middle span, viz. : 22 feet high, 16 feet wide ; at the extreme ends, 19 feet high, 16 feet wide. This gigantic structure is in rapid progress of construction, and, it is understood, will be completed in 1859, or early in 1860.

The drives and inviting excursions about Montreal are numerous, and highly appreciated by visitors from more southern climes. The foremost stands the excursion around the mountain, which stands as a beacon to point out the true position of the city on nearing or departing from this romantic city. Other drives up or down the St. Lawrence, or on almost any part of the fertile island of Montreal, are attended with pleasure and delightful emotions. " Besides these excursions, the tourist will find his time well repaid by a visit to the Saut-au-Recollect, which is a series of Rapids at the northern side of the

island, on a branch of the Ottawa called La Riviere des Prairies
Here, besides the beauty of the scenery, he may see the rafts
from the Ottawa making the descent—an exciting exploit both
to the spectators and hardy crews, though from the rarity of
accidents we must conclude that the skill of the *voyageurs* has
taught them to avoid any real danger."

POPULATION OF MONTREAL—1852.

Males	27,586	Other countries	1,457
Females	30,129		
		Roman Catholics	41,466
Total population	57,715	Protestants	16,196
French Canadians	26,020	Number of houses	7,420
British Canadians	12,494	" families	9,890
English, Irish, & Scotch	17,774		

GRAND TRUNK RAILWAY OF CANADA.

THE GRAND TRUNK RAILWAY, the greatest scheme of its kind in America, embraces in its ramifications the construction of a continuous line of railway from Trois Pistoles, C. E., about 150 miles below Quebec, on the southern side of the river St. Lawrence, the point at which a junction with the proposed *Halifax Railway* is looked forward to—and Port Sarnia, C. W., on Lake Huron, a distance of upward of 800 miles—also a branch line of 50 miles in length, from Belleville to Peterborough, C. W. —and the leasing of the railroad then already built between Montreal and Portland, Me., so that the products of the western points of the Province might be conveyed through Canada to the Atlantic seaboard, without break of guage or bulk. The total length of unbroken railway communication which will thus be obtained, when the St. Lawrence River is spanned by the Victoria Bridge, a structure unequaled in the history of engineering, either in size or in massive proportions—is upward of 1,100 miles. The original capital of the company was £9.500,000, but this being found insufficient, it has been determined to increase this amount to £12,000,000 sterling. or $60,000,000. Of this sum the Province has an interest in the undertaking, in the shape of a guaranty, to an amount of upward of £3,000.000 sterling, or $15,000,000.

GRAND TRUNK RAILWAY AND ITS BRANCHES.

Portland, Me., to Montreal	293 miles.
Quebec and Richmond Division	97 "
Riviere Du Loup Branch	126 "
Montreal to Toronto	333 "
Toronto and Sarnia Division	169 "
Total Distance	1,018 miles.

This important Trunk Railway extends from the shores of the Atlantic Ocean to the foot of Lake Huron, a total distance of 795 miles, connecting with a line of Steamers running from Sarnia to Mackinac, Green Bay, Milwaukee, and Chicago, and other ports on Lakes Huron, Michigan, and Superior, forming altogether the most extensive line of travel on the Continent of America under one direction.

The Division from Montreal to Quebec and the Riviere du Loup extends a distance of 296 miles, connecting with the tide waters of the Gulf of St. Lawrence, opposite the mouth of the Saguenay River.

The *Champlain and St. Lawrence Railroad*, 44 miles in length, running from Montreal to Rouse's Point, N. Y., and the *Lachine and Caughnewago Division* of the railroad running from Caughnewago to the Province Line, 40 miles, and from thence to Plattsburgh, N. Y., are both controlled by the Grand Trunk Railway Company, who have their principal offices in Montreal. For Summer Arrangements, see *Advertisement*.

TRIP FROM MONTREAL TO OTTAWA CITY AND THE UPPER OTTAWA RIVER.

TOURISTS who design to visit the Ottawa River, and view its varied and beautiful scenery, should leave Montreal by steamer, or by the *Grand Trunk Railway*, in the morning for St. Anne's, 21 miles; there taking a steamer for Ottawa City, 90 miles farther; or if desired, continue the railroad route to Prescott, 113 miles from Montreal, and proceed by *Ottawa and Prescott Railroad*. The *La Chine Railroad* also conveys passengers to La Chine, nine miles, from whence steamers depart daily for Ottawa City.

At ST. ANNE'S, 14 miles above La Chine, the steamer passes through a lock 45 feet wide and 180 feet long. Here is a succession of rapids in the river, and several small islands. The village is handsomely situated on the southwest end of the island of Montreal, and is the place where the poet Moore located the scene of his admired *Canadian Boat Song*.*

CANADIAN BOAT SONG.
BY THOMAS MOORE.

Faintly as tolls the evening chime,
Our voices keep tune and our oars keep time;
Soon as the woods on shore look dim,
We'll sing at St. Anne's our parting hymn.
  Row, brothers, row, the stream runs fast,
  The Rapids are near and the daylight's past.

Why should we yet our sail unfurl?
There is not a breath the blue wave to curl;
But when the wind blows off the shore,
Oh! sweetly we'll rest our weary oar.
  Blow, breezes, blow, the stream runs fast,
  The Rapids are near and the daylight's past.

---

* The *voyageurs*, in passing the Rapids of St. Anne, were formerly obliged to take out a part, if not the whole, of their lading, owing to the small depth of water here afforded. It is from this village that the Canadians consider they take their departure on ascending the Ottawa, as it possesses the last church on the island of Montreal, which is dedicated to the tutelar saint of *voyageurs*.

> Ottawa's tide! this trembling moon
> Shall see us float over thy surges soon.
> Saint of this green isle! hear our prayers,
> Oh! grant us cool heavens and favoring airs.
> Blow, breezes, blow, the stream runs fast,
> The Rapids are near and the daylight's past.

Two miles west of St. Anne's commences the *Lake of the Two Mountains*, being an expansion of the Ottawa, about ten miles long and eight miles wide. Here a branch of the river diverges toward the northeast, forming the west boundary of the island of Montreal. Two hills to the north, elevated 400 or 500 feet above the river at the distance of a few miles, give the name to this body of water.

The INDIAN VILLAGE of the Two Mountains is situated on the north side of the Ottawa, about 25 miles west of La Chine. Here reside the remnants of two tribes, the Mohawks and Algonquins. The settlements are divided by a Roman Catholic church, standing near the river side. On the hill toward the north are situated three or four chapels. The highest summit of the hill or mountain, one or two miles distant, is called Calvary, and is visited by the Indians and whites on certain religious festivals of the Roman Catholic Church. Here the river contracts in width to about half a mile, for a distance of one mile, when it again expands, forming the *Upper Lake of the Two Mountains*. About nine miles farther west the river again contracts to half a mile in width.

On the south is passed the settlement of REGAUD, and a mountain of the same name.

CARILLON, eight miles farther, is on the north side of the Ottawa. Here are rapids in the river, and the navigation by steamboat is continued by means of a lock and canal, 12 miles in length.

At POINT FORTUNE, opposite Carillon, passengers going to the Caledonia Springs usually take a stage for L'ORIGINAL, a distance of 18 miles, along the south bank of the Ottawa, which affords some picturesque views.

At GRENVILLE, 12 miles from Carillon, navigation is resumed on the Ottawa River, for a further distance of 58 miles.

The RIDEAU FALLS (the *Curtain*), so called from their resemblance to drapery, is formed by the waters of the Rideau River precipitating itself into the Ottawa, a short distance below the city of Ottawa. This is a beautiful fall of 30 feet, and attracts much notice, being seen to advantage from the steamer ascending the Ottawa.

CHAUDIERE FALLS (the *Boiling Pot*), which are second only to those of Niagara in grandeur and magnificence, are on the Ottawa, immediately above the city. These falls, in connection with the surrounding scenery, render this section of Canada very attractive to tourists seeking health or pleasure.

The City of OTTAWA, C. W., the capital of Canada, occupies a most romantic position on the southwest side of Ottawa River, being 120 miles distant from Montreal, and 54 from Prescott by railway. It is in a naturally strong situation, and could be easily rendered almost impregnable. The city is divided into two parts, like Quebec, known as the Upper and Lower Towns, which are about half a mile apart. The *Rideau Canal* commences here, and is spanned by a handsome stone bridge, forming part of the street which connects the two portions of the town, and it is also connected with HULL, on the Lower Canada side of the river, by a fine suspension bridge

The city is justly celebrated as being a great mart for lumber, in which the Ottawa country abounds. In the neighborhood is found beautiful pale-gray limestone, of which material many of the edifices are constructed, giving a handsome and solid appearance to the place; the streets have been laid out with great regularity, and are very wide. Barrack Hill, a commanding site, is retained by the government, where are situated the new government buildings for the use of the Provincial Parliament of Canada. Here are situated the county buildings, ten churches of different denominations, four or five banking-houses, several well-kept hotels, together with numerous stores and extensive grist-mills, saw-mills, and other manufacturing establishments. Pop. 15,000.

The *Ottawa and Prescott Railway*, 54 miles in length, terminates at Prescott, situated on the St. Lawrence River, directly opposite Ogdensburgh. No other road of its length in America possesses greater advantages than this railway, if right y turned to account, pointing as it does to the State and city of New York.

Stages and *Steamboats* run daily from Ottawa City to different places on the river above the city, affording romantic excursions during the summer and autumn months.

The Union Line of steamers runs from AYLMER, nine miles above Ottawa, to JOACHIN, 150 miles above the city. The proprietors have three iron steamers, with fifty-horse-power engines: one running from Aylmer to Chatts; one from Amprior to Portage Du Fort, and one from Portage Du Fort to Joachin. These boats are not sufficient to do the business that is now offered; and it is a remarkable fact, that while goods are carried in winter on sleighs over this route for 50 cents per 100 pounds, the steamboat charge is $1 25.

VILLAGES ON THE UPPER OTTAWA RIVER.

AYLMER, nine miles above the city on the Lower Canada side, is situated at the outlet of Chaudiere Lake, through which the river flows, has about 1,000 inhabitants, and is the shire town of Ottawa County. Is at the foot of steamboat navigation above the city. There is a good McAdam road from the city to Aylmer.

FITZROY and CHATTS—these villages are connected, and situated 32 miles above the city, with about 500 inhabitants; the river at this place has a fall of 52½ feet.

AMPRIOR, 40 miles above the city. This place has sprung into existence within the last two years: has now 60 dwellings, and 40 more under contract. A railroad is now under contract from Ottawa City to Amprior, to be completed in 1858, and I understand that this is also the point where the Brockville and Pembroke Railroad comes to the river. The river has a fall here of twelve feet To hear the descriptions which are given of this section of the country, one would think that it was the Garden of Eden, and that it was soon to be reclaimed. Those engaged in building up Amprior, predict that it is soon to become the Chicago of Canada.

Portage Du Fort is 60 miles above Ottawa City. The river here has a fall of twelve feet, affording good water-power.

Pembroke, 100 miles above the city, is the next place on the river, and is a point of great importance.

The *Brockville and Ottawa Railroad*, when completed, will terminate at this place, and afford great facilities to the settlements on the Upper Ottawa River and its tributaries

OTTAWA RIVER.

Copied from the CANADIAN TOURIST.

"THIS river, and the vast fertile territory which it drains, has hitherto been, in a great measure, abandoned to the operations of the lumberman, and the comparatively few farmers who have followed his steps ; but, latterly, its capabilities as an agricultural country have gradually attracted a greater degree of attention, which the proposal of connecting its waters with Lake Huron and the Far West will greatly increase. Of the magnitude of the river, the riches of its banks, and the beauty of the scenery, we can not better speak than by making use of the excellent Report lately made by a Committee of the Canadian House of Assembly on Railways :

"'The length of the course of the Ottawa River is about 780 miles. From its source it bends in a southwest course, and after receiving several tributaries from the height of land separating its waters from the Hudson Bay, it enters Lake Temiscaming. From its entrance into this lake downward the course of the Ottawa has been surveyed, and is well known.

"'At the head of the lake the Blanche River falls in, coming about ninety miles from the north. Thirty-four miles farther down the lake it receives the Montreal River, coming one hundred and twenty miles from the northwest. Six miles lower down on the east, or Lower Canada bank, it receives the Keepawa-sippi, a large river which has its origin in a lake of great size, hitherto but partially explored, and known as Lake Keepawa. This lake is connected with another chain of irregularly shaped lakes, from one of which proceeds the River du Moine, which enters the Ottawa about a hundred miles below the mouth of the Keepawa-sippi.

"'From the Long Saut at the foot of Lake Temiscaming, two hundred and thirty-three miles above the city of Ottawa, and three hundred and sixty miles from the mouth of the Ottawa, down to Deux Joachim Rapids, at the head of the Deep River, that is, for eighty-nine miles, the Ottawa, with the exception of seventeen miles below the Long Saut, and some other intervals, is not at present navigable, except for canoes. Besides other tributaries in the interval, at a hundred and ninety-seven miles from Bytown, now called Ottawa, it receives on the west side the Mattawan, which is the highway for canoes going to Lake Huron by Lake Nippissing. From the Mattawan the

Ottawa flows east by south to the head of Deep River Reach, nine miles above which it receives the River du Moine from the north.

"'From the head of Deep River, as this part of the Ottawa is called, to the foot of Upper Allumettes Lake, two miles below the village of Pembroke, is an uninterrupted reach of navigable water, forty-three miles in length. The general direction of the river in this part is southeast. The mountains along the north side of Deep River are upward of a thousand feet in height, and the many wooded islands of Allumettes Lake render the scenery of this part of the Ottawa magnificent and exceedingly picturesque—far surpassing the celebrated Lake of the Thousand Islands on the St. Lawrence.

"'Passing the short rapid of Allumettes, and turning northward round the lower end of Allumettes Island, which is fourteen miles long and eight at its greatest width, and turning down southeast through Coulonge Lake, and passing behind the nearly similar islands of Calumet to the head of Calumet Falls, the Ottawa presents, with the exception of one slight rapid, a reach of fifty miles of navigable water. The mountains on the north side of Coulenge Lake, which rise apparently to the height of fifteen hundred feet, add a degree of grandeur to the scenery, which is in other respects beautiful and varied. In the Upper Allumettes Lake, a hundred and fifteen miles from Ottawa, the river receives from the west the Petawawee, one of its largest tributaries. This river is a hundred and forty miles in length, and drains an area of two thousand two hundred square miles. At Pembroke, nine miles lower down on the same side, an inferior stream, the Indian River, also empties itself into the Ottawa.

"'At the head of Lake Coulonge the Ottawa receives from the north the Black River, a hundred and thirty miles in length, draining an area of eleven hundred and twenty miles, and nine miles lower on the same side the river Coulonge, which is probably a hundred and sixty miles in length, with a valley of eighteen hundred square miles.

"'From the head of the Calumet Falls to Portage du Fort, the head of the steamboat navigation, a distance of eight miles, are impassable rapids. Fifty miles above the city, the Ottawa receives on the west the Bonnechère, a hundred and ten miles in length, draining an area of nine hundred and eighty miles. Eleven miles lower it receives the Madawaska, one of its great feeders, a river two hundred and ten miles in length, and draining four thousand one hundred square miles.

"'Thirty-seven miles above Ottawa there is an interruption in the navigation, caused by three miles of rapids and falls, to pass which a railroad has been made. At the foot of the rap-lds the Ottawa divides among islands into numerous channels, presenting a most imposing array of separate falls.

"'Six miles above Ottawa begin the rapids terminating in the Ottawa *Chaudière Falls*, which, inferior in impressive grandeur to the Falls of Niagara, are, perhaps, more permanently interesting, as presenting greater variety. The greatest height of Chaudière Falls is about forty feet. Arrayed in every imaginable variety of form—in vast, dark masses, in graceful cascades, or in tumbling spray—they have been well described as a hundred rivers struggling for a passage. Not the least interesting feature which they present is the Lost Chaudière, where a body of water, greater in volume than the Thames at London, is quietly sucked down, and disappears under ground.

"'At the city of Ottawa the river receives the Rideau from the west, running a course of a hundred and sixteen miles, and draining an area of thirteen hundred and fifty square miles.'

"The city of OTTAWA is, perhaps, situated more picturesquely than any other in North America, with the exception of Quebec. The view from the Barrack Hill—embracing, as it does, in one *coup d'œil*, the magnificent Falls of the Chaudière, with its clouds of snowy spray, generally spanned by a brilliant rainbow; the Suspension Bridge uniting Upper and Lower Canada; the river above the great Falls, studded with pretty wooded islands, and the distant purple mountains, which divide the waters of the Gatineau from those of the Ottawa—is one of the most beautiful in the world.

"The city, now containing about fourteen thousand inhabitants, sprung up, about thirty years ago, from a collection of shanties inhabited by the laborers and artificers employed by the Royal Engineers to construct the *Rideau Canal*. This canal (terminating at Kingston) was intended by the government of England to be a means of communication between the Lower St. Lawrence and the Lakes, in case the communication on the front should be interrupted. The canal was designed by Colonel By, of the Royal Engineers, and the present city of Ottawa was named Bytown in memory of its founder, until, about two years ago, the inhabitants petitioned the Provincial Parliament to change the name.

"The canal is a splendid specimen of engineering skill, and the masonry of the numerous locks is generally admired for its finish and solidity. Eight of these locks rise one above another directly in the center of the city, the canal being crossed by a handsome stone bridge just above them. The canal, in fact, divides the city into two parts, the Upper and Lower. A large part of the Upper Town is comprised in what is called the Barrack Hill, on which is a small barracks for troops, and some storehouses, the property of the Imperial Government; there is here a parade-ground of several acres, and the summit of the hill, from which is to be seen the beautiful view which we spoke of before, is one of the finest promenades in the world A few very simple fortifications on this hill would make the city of Ottawa almost as impregnable as Quebec.

"Within the last few years a small hamlet has sprung up near the Suspension Bridge, in consequence of the abundant water-power existing there, of which several enterprising persons have availed themselves to erect saw-mills. There is also here a very large iron foundry and machine manufactory.

"Here also are the slides, erected by government, for the passage of timber, in order to avoid the great fall, over which the pieces of timber used to be precipitated singly, to be again collected below at a great trouble and loss. Throughout the whole summer, from morning to night, the 'cribs' of timber, each manned by three or four hardy raftsmen, may be seen darting down these slides; while from the lofty summit of the Barrack Hill the huge rafts, gay with bright streamers floating from their many masts, may be seen on the smooth, dark bosom of the river, the golden-colored timber flashing in the sunbeams.

"In the Lower Town are the principal mercantile establishments, the court-house and jail, the Roman Catholic Cathedral, the Bishop's Palace; a nunnery, to which the General Hospital is attached, and a Roman Catholic college; the Protestant hospital, the Terminus of the Prescott and Ottawa Railway, and the steamboat wharf. Among the objects well worth seeing in this part of the town is a steam saw-mill, of great size, recently erected by an enterprising citizen. In Central Ottawa are the town-hall, the post-office, telegraph office and news-room, to which are attached a library and museum, the latter containing some very interesting geological specimens. In Upper Ottawa are the Episcopal church and the office at which all the business connected with timber cut on the lands of the Crown is transacted. The banks of Upper Canada, British North America, Montreal, and Quebec have agencies in the city.

"During the summer months steamers run daily on the river between Ottawa and Montreal, and between Ottawa and Kingston, by the way of Rideau Canal. A railway train leaves the city every day for Prescott, where those passengers who intend to go to Montreal change into the cars of the Grand Trunk line, and so reach Montreal by railway.

"Travelers who wish to proceed farther up the river can take a carriage or omnibus for Aylmer, a pretty village about nine miles from Ottawa, between which place and Aylmer there is an excellent turnpike road, where they will find a steamer which takes them to the Chatts; from this there is a railway about two miles; they then proceed by another steamer to Portage du Fort; here wagons are used for a short distance, and another steamer takes them to Pembroke, and again another from that point to Deux Joachim, where for the present navigation ceases for any thing larger than a canoe A railroad is under construction, extending from Pembroke to Brockville, situated on the St. Lawrence River.

" Immediately below the city of Ottawa the river Rideau discharges into the Ottawa, falling gently over the edge of a limestone precipice like a beautifully transparent '*curtain*' of water, from which resemblance its name has been derived ; the fall is divided into two portions by a small rocky island, which adds greatly to the picturesqueness of the scene. The Rideau Falls are best seen from a boat.

" A mile lower it receives from the north its greatest tributary, the *Gatineau*, which, with a course probably of four hundred and twenty miles, drains an area of twelve thousand square miles. For about two hundred miles the upper course of this river is in the unknown northern country. At the farthest point surveyed, two hundred and seventeen miles from its mouth, the Gatineau is still a noble stream, a thousand feet wide, diminished in depth, but not in width.

" Eighteen miles lower down the Rivière au Lièvre enters from the north, after running a course of two hundred and sixty miles in length, and draining an area of four thousand one hundred miles. Fifteen miles below it the Ottawa receives the North and South Nation rivers on either side, the former ninety-five and the latter a hundred miles in length. Twenty-two miles farther the river Rouge, ninety miles long, enters from the north. Twenty-one miles lower the Rivière du Nord, a hundred and sixty miles in length, comes in on the same side, and lastly, just above its mouth, it receives the river Assumption, which has a course of a hundred and thirty miles.

" From Ottawa the river is navigable to Grenville, a distance of fifty-eight miles, where the rapids that occur for twelve miles are avoided by a succession of canals. Twenty-three miles lower, at one of the mouths of the Ottawa, a single lock, to avoid a slight rapid (St. Anne's Rapid), gives a passage into Lake St. Louis, an expansion of the St. Lawrence above Montreal.

" The remaining half of the Ottawa's waters find their way to the St. Lawrence, by passing in two channels behind the Island of Montreal and the Isle Jesus, in a course of thirty-one miles. They are interrupted with rapids, still it is by one of them that all the Ottawa lumber passes to market. At Bout de l'Isle, therefore, the Ottawa is finally merged in the St. Lawrence, a hundred and thirty miles below from the city of Ottawa.

"The most prominent characteristic of the Ottawa is its great volume. Even above the town, where it has to receive tributaries equal to the Hudson, the Shannon, the Thames, the Tweed, the Spey, and the Clyde, it displays, when unconfined, a width of half a mile of strong, boiling rapid; and when at the highest, while the north waters are passing, the volume, by calculated approximation, is fully equal to that passing Niagara—that is, double the common volume of the Ganges.

"Taking a bird's-eye view of the valley of the Ottawa, we see spread out before us a country equal to eight times the State of Vermont, or ten times that of Massachusetts, with its great artery, the Ottawa, curving through it, resembling the Rhine in length of course, and the Danube in magnitude.

"This immense region overlies a variety of geological formations, and presents all their characteristic features, from the level uniform surface of the Silurian system, which prevails along a great extent of the Ottawa, to the rugged and romantic ridges in the metamorphic and primitive formations, which stretch far away to the north and the northwest.

"As far as our knowledge of the country extends, we find the greater part of it covered with a luxuriant growth of red and white pine timber, making the most valuable forests in the world, abundantly intersected with large rivers, fitted to convey the timber to market when manufactured.

"The remaining portion of it, if not so valuably wooded, presents a very extensive and advantageous field for settlement. Apart from the numerous townships already surveyed and partly settled, and the large tracts of good land interspersed throughout the timber country, the great region on the upper course of the western tributaries of the Ottawa, behind the red pine country, exceeds the State of New Hampshire in extent, with an equal climate and superior soil. It is generally a beautiful undulating country, wooded with a rich growth of maple, beech, birch, elm, etc., and watered with lakes and streams affording numerous mill-sites and abounding in fish. Flanking on the one side the lumbering country, which presents an excellent market for produce, and adjoining Lake Huron on the other, the situation, though comparatively inland, is highly advantageous. In the diversity of resources, the Ottawa country above described presents unusual attractions alike to agricultural and commercial enterprise."

LAKE GEORGE, OR HORICON.

This romantic sheet of water, whose beauties are almost indescribable, lies mostly in the county of Warren, N. Y., 27 miles north of Saratoga Springs. It is justly celebrated for its varied and beautiful scenery, and for the transparency and purity of its waters. It is 36 miles long, north and south, and from two to three miles wide; and is elevated 243 feet above the tide-water of the Hudson, although its waters flow north into Lake Champlain. It is surrounded by high and picturesque hills, sometimes rising to mountain height, and dotted with numerous islands, said to count as many as there are days in the year; some are of considerable size, and cultivated; while others are only a barren rock, rising majestically out of the surrounding waters. The wild and romantic scenery of this lake is nowhere surpassed. The bed of the lake is a handsome yellowish sand, and the water is so pure and transparent as to render the bottom visible from 30 to 40 feet. Here the delicious salmon-trout, that weigh from five to twenty pounds, are found in great numbers, and of the finest quality. Silver trout, brook trout, pike, pickerel, perch, and several other kinds of fresh water fish, are also abundant. Travelers on the tour from the Springs to Canada should not fail to visit Lake George; by the French called *Lac Sacrament*, on account of the purity of its waters. The steamboat "Minnehaha" runs through the lake, from Caldwell to the landing near the village of Ticonderoga, whence stages run to *Fort Ticonderoga*, at the steamboat landing on Lake Champlain; where steam passage boats, on their route from Whitehall to Burlington and Rouse's Point, touch daily during the season of navigation. This route is varied in scenery, and deeply interesting in historical incidents.

The romantic village of CALDWELL, lying at the south end of the lake, contains a court-house and jail, two churches, and a number of handsome private residences, besides *Fort William Henry Hotel* and the *Lake House*, two popular public houses, which are usually thronged with fashionable visitors during the summer months.

"Lake George abounds with small and beautiful islands, among the most important of which are Diamond Island, Tea Island, and Long Island. Roger's Rock or Slide, and Anthony's Nose, the former on the west and the latter on the east side, are two precipices worthy of note. Howe's Landing, just behind an island at the outlet of the lake, denotes the spot where the unfortunate expedition of Abercrombie landed, and derives its name from Lord Howe, who accompanied and fell in that expedition, in 1758.

"This lake and its vicinity has been the scene of several important battles. One which has been generally known as the *Battle of Lake George*, was fought at the head of the lake in 1755, between the French under the Baron Dieskau, and the English under Sir Wm. Johnson. Dieskau attacked the English in their encampment, but was defeated and slain. The loss of the English was 130 slain, and that of the French about 700. *

"The most shocking transaction in the vicinity of this lake was the *Massacre* at Fort William Henry in 1757. A British and Provincial army having been collected at Fort Edward and Fort William Henry under Gen. Webb, for the reduction of the French works on Lake Champlain, the French sent a large army up the lake under Gen. Montcalm, for their defense. Gen. Webb, then at Fort William Henry, learning from Maj. Putnam that this force had entered Lake George, returned immediately to Fort Edward, and the day following sent Col Monroe, with his regiment, to reinforce the garrison at the lake. The day after Monroe's arrival the French appeared at the fort, laid siege to it, and demanded its surrender. The garrison, consisting of 2,500 men, defended themselves with much bravery for several days, with the expectation of succor from Fort Edward. But as none came, Monroe was obliged on the 9th of August to capitulate. By the articles of capitulation, all the public property was to be delivered to Montcalm, and the garrison were to march out with their arms and baggage, and to be escorted to Fort Edward, on condition of not serving against the French within the period of eighteen months.

"The garrison had no sooner marched out of the fort than a scene of perfidy and barbarity commenced, which it is impossible for language to describe. Regardless of the articles of capitulation, the Indians attached to the French army fell upon

---

* See Thompson's Vermont, Part II., page 8.

LAKE GEORGE, OR HORICON. 199

the defenseless soldiers, plundering and murdering all that fell in their way. The French officers were idle spectators of this bloody scene; nor could all the entreaties of Monroe persuade them to furnish the promised escort. On that fatal day about 1,500 of the English were either murdered by the savages or carried by them into captivity never to return.

"The day following these horrid transactions, Major Putnam was dispatched from Fort Edward with his rangers to watch the motions of the enemy. He reached Lake George just after the rear of the enemy had left the shore, and the scene which was presented he describes as awful indeed. 'The fort was entirely destroyed; the barracks, out-houses, and buildings were a heap of ruins—the cannon, stores, boats, and vessels were all carried away. The fires were still burning—the smoke and stench offensive and suffocating Innumerable fragments of human skulls, and bones and carcasses half consumed, were still frying and broiling in the decaying fires. Dead bodies mangled with scalping-knives and tomahawks, in all the wantonness of Indian barbarity, were everywhere to be seen. More than 100 women, butchered and shockingly mangled, lay upon the ground still weltering in their gore. Devastation, barbarity, and horror everywhere appeared; and the spectacle presented was too diabolical and awful either to be endured or described.'"

STEAMER ON LAKE GEORGE.

A NEW steamboat is being built on Lake George in the place of the JOHN JAY, burned in July last. She is 145 feet long and 26 feet wide. The boiler and furnace are placed in compartments, incased in iron, entirely fire-proof, no expense being spared in order to make her a beautiful and safe passenger boat.

Her name, "MINNE-HA-HA," a romantic one, is selected with great appropriateness from Longfellow's HIAWATHA·

> "With him dwelt his dark-eyed daughter,
> Wayward as the Minnehaha;
> With her moods of shade and sunshine,
> Eyes that frowned and smiled alternate,
> Feet as rapid as the river,
> Tresses flowing like the water,
> And as musical a laughter;
> And he named her from the river,
> From the waterfall he named her
> Minne-ha-ha—*laughing water*."

FALLS OF TICONDEROGA.

The FALLS OF TICONDEROGA, situated on the outlet of Lake George, are well worthy the attention of tourists. Here are two important cascades within the distance of two or three miles, surrounded by mountain scenery of great historic interest. The *Upper Falls*, near the village of Alexandria, are formed by a succession of descents of upward of 200 feet within the distance of a mile, affording water-power unsurpassed by any other locality in the State for safety and a steady flow of water, the stream not being subject to freshets. The *Lower Fall*, in the village of Ticonderoga, has a perpendicular fall of 30 feet, being much used for hydraulic purposes. The ruins of old *Fort Ticonderoga*, two miles below this place, are situated on a point of land at the entrance of the outlet of Lake George into Lake Champlain, standing on an eminence of about 60 feet, overlooking the lake; the ruins are plainly visible from the water, presenting a conspicuous and interesting object. About 1,800 yards southwest stands *Mount Defiance*, rising 750 feet above the lake, overlooking and commanding the site of Fort Ticonderoga. A public house, for the accommodation of visitors, stands near the steamboat landing.

DISTANCES FROM CALDWELL TO ALBANY, *via* SARATOGA SPRINGS.

CALDWELL.........	0	0	ALBANY........... 0	0
Glenn's Falls, *Stage*..	9	9	TROY............. 6	6
Moreau Station " ..	5	14	Cohoes............ 3	9
SARATOGA SPRINGS..	15	29	Waterford.......... 1	10
Ballston Spa........	7	36	Junction Albany R.R 2	12
Mechanicsville.......	13	49	Mechanicsville.. 6	18
Junction Albany R.R.	6	55	Ballston Spa........13	31
Waterford	2	57	SARATOGA SPRINGS.. 7	32
Cohoes............	1	58	Moreau Station......15	53
TROY.............	3	61	Glenn's Falls, *Stage*.. 5	58
ALBANY...........	6	67	CALDWELL " .. 9	67

LAKE CHAMPLAIN.

ONE of the most interesting and lovely bodies of water in North America lies between the States of New York and Vermont, through which runs the boundary line from near Whitehall to lat. 45°, being a distance of 116 miles; it may be said to extend four miles farther, into Canada, making the whole length of the lake 120 miles; varying from half a mile or less to twelve miles in width. Its direction is nearly north and south, and it is a long, narrow, and deep body of water, dotted with a number of islands, the largest of which belong to Vermont. From Whitehall to Crown Point the lake is quite narrow, but here it begins to expand, and soon becomes three miles wide, still increasing northward until near Burlington, where it spreads to its greatest width. *Missisquoi Bay*, an extension of Lake Champlain on the northeast, lies mostly in Canada, above the 45th degree of north latitude. Steamboats of the first class, and sloops of from 50 to 100 tons burden, navigate Lake Champlain its whole length, thence down the Sorelle, or Richelieu River, its outlet, to St. John's, Canada, where steamboat navigation ceases; a total distance of about 140 miles. This lake is also connected with the navigable waters of the Hudson, by means of the Champlain Canal, which extends south, a distance of 63 miles. As you approach near the center of Lake Champlain, a large body of water presents itself to view, bordered by scenery of the most picturesque description; the headlands which are seen to great advantage, and the vast ranges of mountains on either side, are truly grand and romantic. The highest peak of the Green Mountains, called the "*Camel's Hump*," is seen on the east, while the high ranges of the mountains of Essex County are seen on the west. This latter range of mountain peaks, the *Adirondack group*, contains the highest land in the State of New York, rising in some places to the height of 5,000 feet and upward, abounding with iron ore and timber of large growth. In the streams which flow into this lake are frequent waterfalls of great beauty; and the fine headlands, with numerous indentations and bays of singular beauty, only need to be seen to be admired. Its waters are well stored with salmon, salmon trout, sturgeon, pickerel, and other fish.

"Lake Champlain was discovered by Samuel Champlain in July, 1609, having founded the colony of Quebec in 1608; in June, 1809, he, with a number of French and Indians, proceeded in a shallop up the St. Lawrence and river Iroquois, now Richelieu, till stopped by the Chambly Rapids. From this place he determined to proceed in Indian canoes, but the Frenchmen manifested great reluctance, and only two would be persuaded to accompany him. With these and about sixty of the natives, having transported their canoes by the rapids on the 2d of July, and, proceeding southward, on the 4th of July he entered the lake

"CHAMPLAIN and his party proceeded along the west shore, advancing by water during the night and retiring into the forests by day, to avoid being discovered by the Iroquois, between whom and the Canada Indians a war was then carried on. As they drew near the enemy's country they proceeded with great caution, but on the 29th of July, in the evening, they fell in with a large war party of the Iroquois. Both parties drew up to the shore, and the night was spent in preparation for battle, and in singing and taunting each other. In the morning an engagement took place, but the Frenchmen being armed with muskets, it was decided in favor of Champlain and his party, a large number of the Iroquois being slain and several taken prisoners. With these they returned immediately to their shallop. Champlain says that this battle was fought in lat. 43° and some minutes, and the place is supposed to have been on the west shore of Lake George. The present name of Lake Champlain was given by its discoverer during his first visit, as he informs us in his journal. He was not drowned in its waters, as has been sometimes said, but died at Quebec in 1635. One of the Indian names of this lake was *Petawa-Bouque*, signifying alternate land and water, in allusion to the numerous islands and projecting points of land. Another is said to have been *Caniaderi-Guarunte*, signifying the mouth or door of the country. If so, it was very appropriate, as it forms the gate-way between the country on the St. Lawrence and that on the Hudson. In more recent times the Indians called it *Corlear*, in honor of a Dutchman who saved a war party of Canada Indians from being destroyed by the Mohawks in 1665.

"The first steamboat built on this lake commenced running in 1809. The line boats have always been favorably known to travelers either for business or pleasure, for the manner in which they have been managed—their neat and orderly appearance—obliging and attentive officers and efficient crews. At present there are daily lines to and from Whitehall and Rouse's Point, stopping at Ticonderoga, Burlington, Plattsburgh, and intermediate places, connecting with the various railroads —also numerous ferry boats, propellers, and tow boats, besides more than 300 sloops, canal boats, barges, etc."

Champlain Canal connects the waters of the Hudson with Lake Champlain. It is 64 miles long, 40 feet wide at the top and 28 at the bottom, with a navigable *feeder* at Sandy Hill 11 miles long. It has 21 locks, 14 by 90 feet. Rise from the Hudson, 134 feet, fall to the lake, 54; was begun in 1816, finished in 1819, and cost $1,079,872. The route of this canal is interesting on account of its passing through a section of country rendered memorable by important military operations. It passes in part along the line of Burgoyne's advance from Lake Champlain—near the scene of his principal battles—and of his final surrender. It passes near Fort Miller—Fort Edward—the spot where Miss M'Crea was murdered—Fort Anne—the tree to which Gen. Putnam was bound in 1757, etc.

HEIGHT OF THE PRINCIPAL MOUNTAIN PEAKS IN VERMONT—GREEN MOUNTAIN RANGE.

NAME.	Altitude above Sea.
Chin, or North Peak, Mansfield Mountain	4,279 ft.
Camel's Hump, Huntington	4,188 "
Shrewsbury Mountain	4,086 "
Nose, or South Peak, Mansfield Mountain	3,983 "
Killington Peak, Sherburne	3,924 "
Equinox Mountain, Manchester	3,706 "
Ascutney Mt., Windsor	3,320 "

ALTITUDE OF THE PRINCIPAL MOUNTAINS NORTHERN NEW YORK— ADIRONDACK GROUP.

NAME		Altitude above Sea.
Mount Marcy,	Essex County.	5,467 ft.
Mount McIntire		5,183 "
Mount McMartin		5,000 "
Dial Mountain		4,900 "
Whiteface Mt.		4,855 "
Mount Seward, Franklin Co.		4,600 "
Mount Lyon, Clinton Co.		4,000 "

Surface of LAKE CHAMPLAIN, above tide.......... 90 feet.
" LAKE GEORGE " " .... 243 '
" LAKE ONTARIO ' " .... 234 "

LIST OF STEAMERS BUILT AND RUNNING ON LAKE CHAMPLAIN SINCE 1809.

Bui't	Name	Tons.	Where built. Remarks.
1809	Vermont*	167	Burlington, Vt.—sunk Oct., 1815.
1815	Phœnix (1st)	336	Vergennes, Vt.—burnt Sept., 1819.
1817	Champlain	128	Vergennes, Vt.—burnt 1817.
1819	Congress	209	Vergennes, Vt.—broken up.
1820	Phœnix (2d)	346	Vergennes, Vt. broken up.
1825	Gen. Greene	115	Burlington, Vt.—broken up.
1827	Franklin	312	St. Albans, Vt.—broken up.
"	Washington	134	Essex, N. Y.—broken up.
1838	M'Donough	138	St. Albans, Vt.—lost 1841.
1832	Winooski	159	Burlington, Vt.—broken up.
"	Water-Witch	107	Fort Cassin, Vt.—changed to schooner
1837	Burlington	482	Shelburne, Vt.—broken up.
1838	Whitehall	461	Whitehall, N. Y.- broken up.
1843	Saranac	331	Shelburne, Vt.—broken up.
"	Bouquet	81	Essex, N. Y.—broken up.
1845	Francis Saltus	373	Whitehall, N. Y.
1847	United States	566	Shelburne, Vt.
"	Ethan Allen	500	Shelburne, Vt.
1851	Boston	219	Shelburne, Vt.
1852	America	681	Whitehall, N. Y.
1853	Canada	718	Whitehall, N. Y.
1856	Montreal	416	Shelburne, Vt.
"	Oliver Bascom	360	Whitehall, N. Y.

STEAMERS BUILT ON LAKE GEORGE.

Bui't.	Name.	Where built. Remarks.
1817	Caldwell, (1st)	Ticonderoga—burnt 1821.
1824	Mountaineer	Caldwell condemned 1837.
1838	Caldwell, (2d)	Ticonderoga—broken up.
1852	John Jay	burnt, July, 1856
1857	Min-ne-ha-ha	Caldwell.

AMERICAN STEAMERS RUNNING ON LAKE CHAMPLAIN, 1864.

(DAY AND NIGHT LINE.)

Name.	Tons.	From and To.
AMERICA, Capt. H. Mayo	681	Whitehall to Burlington and Rouse's Point.
CANADA, Capt. Wm. Flagg	718	" " "
UNITED STATES, Capt. Wm. Anderson	566	" " "
MONTREAL, —— Mayo	416	Burlington to Plattsburgh.
BOSTON, Capt. Chapin	219	Burlington to Rouse's Point.

---

* Built and run by Capt. John Winants. Fare $7 from Whitehall to St. John's, Can.

FREIGHT BOATS.

Ethan Allen, Capt. Wright. 500   Whitehall to St. John's Can.
Oliver Bascom. " Eldridge, 3.0   "   "
James H Hooker, Propeller   "   "

STEAMBOAT AND RAILROAD ROUTE FROM WHITEHALL TO BURLINGTON, ROUSE'S POINT, AND MONTREAL.

Landings, etc.	Miles.	Stations, etc.	Miles.
WHITEHALL, N. Y. ...	0	MONTREAL, Can.	0
Benson, Vt...........	13	St. John's, "	21
Orwell, "	7–20	Rouse's Point, N. Y...	23–44
Ticonderoga, N. Y....	4–24	Plattsburgh, " ..	25–69
Larabee's Point. Vt...	1–25	Port Kent, " ..	15–84
Crown Point, N. Y....	8–33	BURLINGTON, Vt. ...	10–94
Port Henry, " ...	8–41	Essex, N. Y..........	14–108
Westport, " ...	9–50	Westport, "	12–120
Essex, " ..	12–62	Port Henry, N. Y.....	9–129
BURLINGTON, Vt.....	14–76	Crown Point, "	8–137
Port Kent, N. Y......	10–86	Larabee's Point, Vt...	8–145
Plattsburgh, "	15–101	Ticonderoga, N. Y. ...	1–146
Rouse's Point, N. Y. .	25–126	Orwell,. Vt...........	4–150
St. John's, Can.......	23–149	Benson, "	7–157
MONTREAL, "	21–170	WHITEHALL, N. Y. ...	13–170

USUAL TIME from Whitehall to Rouse's Point, 9 hours.
          Fare...................... . $4 00
"   "   " Rouse's Point to Montreal, 2 hours.
          Fare...................... 2 00

RAILROAD ROUTE FROM WHITEHALL TO ALBANY.

Stations.	Miles.	Total Miles.
WHITEHALL.................	0	0
Fort Anne.................	11	11
Fort Edward...............	12	23
Moreau Station............	1	24
SARATOGA SPRINGS..........	15	39
Ballston Spa	7	46
Mechanicsville.............	13	59
Waterford	8	67
TROY	4	71
ALBANY...................	6	77

Usual Time, 3½ hours. Fare, $2 38.

The village of WHITEHALL, 77 miles north of Albany by railroad route, is situated in a narrow valley at the head of Lake Champlain, and at the junction of the Champlain Canal with the lake, being a secure and important naval station in time of war. The village was incorporated in 1820, and now contains four churches, three hotels, a bank, 30 stores of different kinds, several storehouses, and extensive forwarding houses; two ship-yards and two dry docks, where are built and repaired steamboats, lake craft, and canal boats; machine-shops, brick-yards, tanneries, and other manufacturing establishments Population about 4,000.

Besides the daily line of steamers running from Whitehall to Burlington, Plattsburgh, and Rouse's Point on the north, the *Saratoga and Whitehall Railroad* extends 40 miles south, to Saratoga Springs, and a branch railroad extends east to Rutland, Vt., connecting with the Rutland and Burlington Railroad, thus forming speedy facilities for reaching New York and Boston by railroad routes.

In the immediate vicinity of Whitehall are high and rugged hills, while to the south lies the valley formed by *Wood Creek*, heading near the banks of the Hudson. Through this valley, during the old French War of 1759, and the Revolutionary War of 1776, the French, the British, and the American armies each marshaled their forces preparatory to attack, or on their retreat. This place was formerly called *Skeenesborough.* The Indian name was said to be *Kah-sha-quah-na*, or *place where dip fish.* Here, during the Revolutionary War, for a time, was the rendezvous of the American forces; this point and Lake George being the only two accessible approaches from Canada, by the invading foe, under Gen. Burgoyne. Here. too, during the old French War, Gen. Putnam distinguished him self, both in battle and in an adroit escape from Indian foes, having, it is said, plunged into the lake about one mile north of Skeenesborough, and swam his horse to the opposite shore, thus eluding their pursuit. Peaceful pursuits and pleasure now render this place a great thoroughfare

TRIP FROM WHITEHALL TO BURLINGTON AND ROUSE'S POINT.

This excursion, during the summer months, is the most grand and interesting of any of similar extent in North America—passing through a romantic lake, with high mountains in the distance, and past scenes rendered classic by their associations with events that occurred during the old French and Revolutionary wars.

On leaving the new steamboat wharf, about one mile north of Whitehall, an interest is at once excited in the breast of all intelligent travelers. The hills rise abruptly to the height of several hundred feet, while the lake or outlet of Wood Creek is hemmed in for several miles by rocky cliffs. The *Elbow*, the *Narrows*, the *Pulpit*, and other names, are given to the most interesting points.

Benson, 13 miles below Whitehall, is the first steamboat landing. Here the waters begin to widen to about half a mile in width.

Orwell, seven miles farther, is another steamboat landing. Here the lake widens from one to two miles.

Ticonderoga, 24 miles north of Whitehall, and four miles east of the foot of Lake George, is a sacred and romantic spot, where is a convenient steamboat landing and a good hotel, besides the celebrated ruins of the old Fort.

Fort Ticonderoga.—The ruins of this old fortification are situated in the town of Ticonderoga, Essex Co., on the west side of Lake Champlain, at the entrance of the outlet of Lake George, 24 miles north of Whitehall. This place was originally called *Che-on-der-o-ga* by the Indians, signifying, in their language, *noise*, and applied to the falls in the outlet of Lake George; its name was afterward slightly changed by the French into its present appellation, which it has borne ever since it was first occupied and fortified by them in 1756. The fort was at first named *Fort Carillon*, but afterward called Fort Ticonderoga by the English and Americans This fortification cost the French government a large sum of money, and was considered very strong, both by nature and art. It stands on a point of land elevated 70 feet above Lake Champlain, being surrounded on three sides by water, and on the northwest it was defended by strong breastworks. *Mount Independence*, on the opposite or east side of the lake, was also fortified, and some of the intrenchments are still visible, elevated 110 feet above the lake, and overlooking the peninsula of Ticonderoga. After several sanguinary conflicts in this vicinity, and under the very walls of the fort, in which several thousand lives were sacrificed, this important military position was tamely evacuated by the French in 1759, and given up to the British army under Lord Amherst; who retained possession until it was taken by surprise by Col. Ethan Allen, of the American army, in 1775. He is said to have entered the fort through a subterraneous passage from the south, extending to the lake; surprising the commandant in his bed before he was aware of his danger, and in his characteristic way required the officer to surrender. He asked to whom? "*Why, to Jehovah and the Continental Congress, to be sure,*" was his laconic reply. In 1777, the British army, under Gen. Burgoyne, on their route to Saratoga, appeared in array before Ticonderoga, when Gen. St. Clair, the American commander, was forced to evacuate; the enemy having erected a battery on *Mount Defiance*, in the rear, elevated 720 feet above the lake, which overlooked and completely commanded this fortification, which was before considered almost impregnable; it then remained in the hands of the British until the close of the war Since that time it has been suffered to go to decay, and now presents one of the most interesting ruins of the kind in this country, and is annually visited by a great number of travelers Near by, delightfully situated on the lake shore, is a well-kept hotel for the accommodation of visitors. Here steamboats, during the season of navigation, daily land and receive passengers on their route from Whitehall to Rouse's Point.

The following account of the DEFEAT OF THE BRITISH AT TICONDEROGA, IN 1759, is taken from the "*Memoirs of an American Lady*," written by Mrs. Grant:

" The army, under the command of Gen. Abercrombie, crossed Lake George on the 5th of July, and landed without opposition. They proceeded in four columns to Ticonderoga, and displayed a spectacle unprecedented in the New World. An army of sixteen thousand men, regulars and provincials, with a train of artillery, and all the necessary provisions for an active campaign or regular siege, followed by a fleet of batteaux, pontons, etc. They set out wrong, however, by not having Indian guides, who are alone to be depended on in such a place. In a short time the columns fell in upon each other, and occasioned much confusion. The advance guard of the French, which had retired before them, were equally bewildered, and falling in with each other in this confusion, a skirmish ensued, in which the French lost above three hundred men, and the English, though successful in this first rencontre, lost as much as it was possible to lose, in one man—for here it was that the valiant Lord Howe, the second in command, fell mortally wounded. He was shot from behind a tree, probably by some Indian; and the whole army were inconsolable for a loss they too well knew to be irreparable.

" The fort is in a situation of peculiar natural strength; it lies on a little peninsula, with Lake Champlain on one side, and a narrow opening communicating with Lake George on the other. This garrison, which was well prepared for attack, and almost impregnable from situation, was defended by between four and five thousand men. An engineer sent to reconnoiter was of opinion that it might be attacked without waiting for the artillery. The fatal resolution was taken without consulting those who were best qualified to judge.

" I can not enter into the dreadful detail of what followed. Certainly never was infatuation equal to this. The forty-second regiment was then in the height of deserved reputation, and commanded by a veteran of great experience and military skill, Col. Gordon Graham, who had the first point of attack assigned to him. He was wounded at the first onset, and of the survivors, every officer retired wounded off the field. Of the fifty-fifth regiment, ten officers were killed, including all the field officers. No human beings could show more determined courage than this brave army did—standing four hours under a constant discharge of cannon and musketry from barricades, on which it was impossible for them to make the least impression. Gen. Abercrombie saw the fruitless waste of blood that was every hour increasing, and ordered a retreat, which was very precipitate; so much so, that they crossed the lake, and regained their camp on the other side, the same night. Two thousand men were killed, wounded, or taken in this disastrous engagement; which was, however, quickly succeeded by the dear-bought conquest of Quebec, where fell both the rival commanders, WOLFE and MONTCALM."

Mount Defiance, about one mile southwest of Fort Ticonderoga, on the south side of the outlet to Lake George, is a bold promontory, elevated about 800 feet above the level of the lake While the ascent from the water or eastern face is quite steep and difficult, the approach from the west is easy. It was from this quarter that Gen. Burgoyne, in 1777, ascended this mountain and planted several pieces of artillery—obliging the Americans to evacuate the fort, which was before considered almost impregnable. The top of this eminence gives a grand view of Lake Champlain and the surrounding country, and is well worthy of a visit, which can easily be accomplished on foot.

The village of TICONDEROGA, two miles west of Lake Champlain, is situated on the outlet of Lake George, where is a thriving settlement, surrounded by picturesque mountain scenery. One or two miles farther west, on the road to Lake George, is situated another village, called *Upper Ticonderoga*, or *Alexandria*. Here is a most beautiful fall of water, affording immense hydraulic power, a small part of which is only used for propelling machinery. The steamboat landing, at the foot of Lake George, is about one mile west of the latter place, the whole distance to Lake Champlain being four miles. The distance to Caldwell, at the head of Lake George, is 36 miles.

LARABEE'S POINT, Vt., two mile from the landing at Fort Ticonderoga, on the opposite side of the lake, is a regular steamboat landing. Here the lake expands from one to two miles in width.

CHIMNEY POINT, nine miles north of Ticonderoga, is also another landing on the east side of the lake, although not now frequented by the steamers.

"Here the French commenced their first settlement upon the lake in 1731. When Crown Point fell into the hands of the English, in 1759, this settlement was abandoned, and the remains of the chimneys, which they had erected in their huts, probably suggested to the first English settlers the name of *Chimney Point.* The *stone windmill,* mentioned by Kalm as being one or two musket-shots to the east of Fort Frederick, and as having five or six small cannon mounted in it in 1749, and which has been supposed to have given name to this point, was most probably at the place opposite, marked by the ruins of what is called *Grenadier's Battery.*"

CROWN POINT, 16 miles north of Ticonderoga, on the west side of Lake Champlain, presents an interesting appearance from the water. The ruins of the old fortifications are situated on a neck of land running into the lake; the embankments are visible, and indicate an immense amount of labor expended to render this point invulnerable to an approaching foe, whether by land or water; yet it was taken by surprise at the commencement of the Revolutionary struggle.

"The French first established themselves here in 1731, and erected a fort which they called *Fort St. Frederick,* from Frederick Maurepas, the French Secretary of State. At this place the French kept a garrison, and from it, during the colonial wars, sent out their parties of French and Indians to destroy the frontier English settlements and massacre the inhabitants. When Kalm visited this place in 1749, there was considerable settlement around the fort, with well-cultivated gardens. Within the fort was a neat little church. The fort was built upon the brow of a steep bank of the lake, but a short distance from the water, and the remains of its bomb-proof covered way, ovens, etc., are still to be seen, though in a very dilapidated state. The small circle to the southeast of this denotes the site of Grenadier's Battery, and the two small parallelograms to the southwest of the latter place, the situation of two strong redoubts.

"On the approach of the British army under Gen. Amherst, in 1759, the French abandoned this fort and retired to the north end of the lake. Amherst took immediate possession, but instead of repairing the old works, began a new fort, which was called *Crown Point,* about 200 yards to the southwest, on higher and more commanding ground. This fort was never completed, as is evident from an examination of the ditch, glacis, etc., at the present day, although it has been said that the British government expended here no less than £2,000,000 sterling

"This fort was taken by surprise by a party of Green Mountain Boys, under Seth Warner, on the same day that Ticonderoga surrendered to Ethan Allen.

"The width of the peninsula upon which these works stood is one mile, and is in no part much elevated above the site of the principal fort, but there is a considerable mountain on the west side of Bulwagga Bay, the nearest summit of which is only 1¾ miles from the fort, and elevated 400 feet above it. The highest is distant 2¼ miles, and elevated 900 feet. The whole peninsula is made up of dark limestone, covered in most parts with only a slight depth of earth, so that works upon it can not be assailed by regular advances. The width between Crown Point and Chimney Point is only about half a mile. From Crown Point to Split Rock the average width of the lake is about three and a half miles."

PORT HENRY, on the west side of the lake, is situated on *Cedar Point*, at the mouth of *Bulwagga Bay*, which separates Crown Point from the mainland. Here are the works of the *Port Henry Iron Company*, with iron ore of good quality in the vicinity.

WESTPORT, 50 miles north of Whitehall, is situated on Northwest Bay, on the west side of Lake Champlain. It contains 700 or 800 inhabitants, and is a thriving place. A horse ferry-boat here plies across the lake, running to Basin Harbor, Vermont.

BASIN HARBOR, one of the best on the lake, is in the town of Ferrisburgh, Vt., and is five miles west from the city of *Vergennes*, and is the landing for it.

FORT CASSIN, three miles north of Basin Harbor, and on the north side of the mouth of Otter Creek, was formerly a landing place of passengers for Vergennes. It is eight miles from the city of Vergennes, where Macdonough's fleet was fitted out, with which he gained his victory. Fort Cassin takes its name from Lieut. Cassin, of the navy, who, with a small breastwork at this place, and less than 200 men, commanded by himself and Capt. Thornton, of the artillery, on the 14th of May, 1814, repulsed a large British force in an attempt to enter the creek for the purpose of destroying the American flotilla before it should be ready for service.

SPLIT ROCK has been regarded as one of the greatest natural curiosities on the lake, and is one which did not escape the notice of the earliest French explorers. *Rocher Fendu* occupies a conspicuous place on Charlevoix's map of 1744. The part detached contains about half an acre, rises about 30 feet above the water, is covered with bushes, and is separated about twelve feet from the main rock. Some have supposed the chasm to have been produced by the breaking off of the promontory in consequence of being undermined by the lake, or by some great convulsion of nature. But the slightest examination shows that the rocky point was here originally crossed by what geologists call a dike, the materials of which have been washed out, forming a chasm in the more solid rock, through which the lake flows when high The chasm, instead of being unfathomable, as some have represented, is so shallow that no water flows through when the lake is low. A few rods south of Split Rock stands a light-house. The width of the lake between Split Rock and Thompson's Point is only about a mile. From this place the width of the lake increases toward the north, and at *McNeil's Ferry*, between Charlotte landing and the village of Essex, it wants 20 rods of three miles.

The village of ESSEX, 61 miles from Whitehall, is handsomely situated on the west side of Lake Champlain, opposite *Charlotte Landing*, with which it is connected by a horse ferry-boat. Population about 700. The lake here expands to three or four miles in width, and presents a large expanse of water toward the north. The *Green Mountains* of Vermont, and the *Adirondack Group* of Essex County, are here seen stretching north and south in vast mountain peaks and ridges. The *Camel's Hump*, being one of the highest peaks of the former, is overlooked by Mount Marcy, on the New York side of the lake, the latter being elevated 5,467 feet, or upward of one mile above the tide waters of the Hudson; and near it this noble river has its most northern source.

FOUR BROTHERS are four small islands lying about seven miles southwest from Burlington, and being out of the usual line of navigation, they are resorted to by gulls and other water-fowl for the purpose of raising their young. On Charlevoix's map of 1744 they are called *Isle de Quatre Vents.*

JUNIPER ISLAND lies about three miles southwest from Burlington—is composed of slate rock, with precipitous banks about thirty feet high, and covered with about a dozen acres of good soil. A light-house was erected here in 1826.

ROCK DUNDER is a solitary rock rising out of the water, between Juniper Island and Pottier's Point, to the height of about thirty feet.

BURLINGTON, Vt., 80 miles from Whitehall, 25 miles from Plattsburgh, and 50 miles from Rouse's Point by steamboat route, is delightfully situated on Burlington Bay, on the east shore of Lake Champlain, and is the most important place in the State. It possesses a convenient and safe harbor for steamboats and lake craft. The United States government have here erected a breakwater, which protects the shipping from westerly winds, and is a great addition to the security of the harbor. In 1860 it contained a population of 7,713 inhabitants; the University of Vermont, founded in 1791, occupying four spacious edifices, and having a medical school attached to it; the Episcopal institute, a court-house and jail, eight churches of different denominations, an academy, and two female seminaries; three banking-houses, several well-kept hotels, and a number of stores of different kinds, besides several factories and mills, and almost every kind of mechanic establishments. About 1½ miles distant, on the falls of the Onion River, is a thriving manufacturing place called *Winooski*, where are located several large factories and mills.

Burlington is, no doubt, destined rapidly to increase in wealth and population, from the fact of here centering several important lines of railroad travel, extending from Boston by two routes, through Montpelier and through Rutland. This railroad and steamboat communication extends across Lake Champlain to Plattsburgh and Rouse's Point, running north to Montreal, Canada, and west to Ogdensburgh, N. Y.

Its advantages are now great, and its situation most beautiful, overlooking the lake, with its bays, islands, and adjacent scenery—the passing steamboats and other vessels—and possesses a beauty of location probably unsurpassed by any other place in the Union. In trade and commerce it is closely allied with the interests of the State of New York. Steamboats stop here daily on their route from Whitehall to Rouse's Point; a steamboat also plies from this place to Port Kent, on the opposite side of the lake, a distance of ten miles, and thence to Plattsburgh, 25 miles.

The principal hotels in Burlington are the American Hotel the Lake House, and the Howard House.

Travelers wishing to visit *Mansfield Mountain*, 20 miles northeast of Burlington, or the *Camel's Hump*, in the town of Huntington, about the same distance in a southeast direction, can easily obtain conveyances to either of the above romantic resorts. From the summit of both are obtained beautiful and sublime views of the surrounding country and Lake Champlain, said to fully equal the prospect from the White Mountains of New Hampshire. The Vermont Central Railroad route, between Burlington, Montpelier, and Windsor, runs near the base of the latter mountain.

The *White Mountains* of New Hampshire, about 120 miles east of Burlington, are reached from this place by railroad and stage, passing over the *Vermont Central Railroad* to White River Junction, and from thence up the valley of the Connecticut River to Wells' River, where commences the *White Mountain Railroad*, extending to Littleton, N. H. From Littleton stages run to the Notch of the White Mountains, a farther distance of 20 miles. This line of travel can be extended through to Portland, Me., passing over a romantic section of country.

Mount Mansfield is known as the first in dignity, beauty, and grandeur of all the Green Hills of Vermont. It consists of three prominent peaks lying in a line nearly north and south, which, viewed from the valley near Stowe, has a resemblance to the profile of the human face turned upward. From this fact the three summits have received the names of "Chin," "Nose," and "Forehead." The Chin is about 4.500 feet high; the Nose or middle summit about 4,260 feet, and the Forehead or south peak about 160 feet lower than the Nose. No written description can adequately describe the extent, variety, and beauty of scenery visible from the Chin; but it is sufficient to say that a more extensive, delightful, and charming view is not to be found on the Continent. Standing on the summit in a clear day, and looking westward, the most prominent of all the objects that fill the eye of the beholder, is Lake Champlain. It seems but a short way off, but in reality is eighteen or twenty miles to the nearest point; while far to the north and south, 40 or 50 miles distant, its smooth surface, like high polished masses of silver, reflect the rays of the evening sun, and give light and beauty to the scene. Occupying the intervening space between the Lake and the base of the mountain, spread out like a map under the feet of the observer, are forests, cultivated fields, villages, and streams of water, comprising the richest agricultural region of Vermont. Beyond Lake Champlain, stretching to the north and south as far as the eye can see, rise the majestic and picturesque Adirondack Mountains, which furnish an appropriate background to the picture and terminate the view in that direction.

Turning to the east, a vast extent of country stretches away to the Connecticut River, mapped out with bright fields of grain, pleasant openings, dark forests, streams, roads, houses and church spires, with hills and valleys interspersed; and far beyond, 60 or 70 miles distant, the eye rests upon Mount Washington, which lifts its blue peak on the extreme verge of the horizon, and forms a marked feature of the eastern landscape.

THE GREEN MOUNTAINS.

"Hail, land of Green Mountains! whose valleys and streams
Are as fair as the muse ever pictured in dreams;
Where the stranger oft sighs with emotion sincere—
Ah, would that my own native home had been here!

Hail, land of the lovely, the equal, the brave,
Never trod by the foe, never tilled by the s'ave;
Where the lore of the world to the hamlet is brought,
And speech is as free as the pinions of thought."

* * * * * * * * *

PORT KENT is advantageously situated on the west side of Lake Champlain, 12 miles south of the village of Plattsburgh. It contains about 400 inhabitants and 50 dwelling-houses. The site of this place is beautiful, commanding one of the finest views on Champlain, extending to the opposite shore of Vermont.

Immediately south of the landing at Port Kent lies *Trembleu Point*, the commencement of the Clinton range of mountains.

KEESEVILLE, situated on both sides of the Au Sable River, is four miles west of Port Kent. It contains about 3,000 inhabitants, 400 dwelling-houses, one Congregational, one Baptist, one Methodist, and one Roman Catholic church; an incorporated academy, one banking-house, two taverns, and 20 stores and groceries. The water-power at this place is very great, and advantageously used by several extensive manufacturing establishments. There are two flouring-mills, four extensive saw-mills, which make annually about half a million of market boards, an iron foundry, one furnace, and a machine-shop, together with most other kinds of mechanic workshops.

At BIRMINGHAM, two miles below Keeseville, is a succession of picturesque falls, in all about 150 feet descent. Immediately below the lower falls the river enters a deep ravine of singular and romantic beauty Through the chasm thus formed by the wearing of the waters, or some convulsion of nature, the rocks rise from 75 to 150 feet, almost perpendicular, for a distance of about two miles, averaging about 50 feet in width, altogether forming a great natural curiosity. In addition to the above, there are other ravines in this vicinity of singular formation.

From Port Kent to Plattsburgh the course is along the western shore of the lake, passing several islands.

PORT JACKSON, the only intermediate landing place, is nearly west of the south end of *Valcour Island*, noted for a severe naval conflict, on the 11th of October, 1776, between the American flotilla under General Arnold, and the British under Capt. Prindle. The battle was fought a little north of Port Jackson.

" Five or six miles nearly east from Port Jackson was the scene of the conflagration of the steamer Phœnix on the 5th of

September, 1819. On the morning of the accident, the Phœnix left Burlington about one o'clock, against a strong north wind. About 3 o'clock, while off nearly west of the south end of Grand Isle, the boat was discovered to be on fire, and all efforts to extinguish it were unavailing. There were at this time 44 persons on board, 31 of whom entered the small boats, and succeeded, with considerable difficulty, in reaching a small island about a mile to the windward, called Providence Island. The remaining 13 were soon obliged to commit themselves to the water upon bits of plank and such other things as were within their reach. The small boats returned just after daylight, and succeeded in saving six of those who had managed to keep themselves afloat. The remaining seven were drowned. The wreck drifted southward and lodged on a reef extending from Colchester Point. This is the only accident worthy of notice which has occurred during 46 years of steam navigation on this lake."

PLATTSBURGH, Clinton Co., N. Y., is situated on both sides of the Saranac River, 100 miles north of Whitehall and 25 miles south of Rouse's Point by steamboat route It was incorporated as a village in 1815, and now contains about 4,000 inhabitants. 500 dwelling-houses, a court-house, jail, and county clerk's office; a town-hall, one Presbyterian, one Episcopal, one Methodist, and two Roman Catholic churches; an incorporated academy, 50 stores of different kinds, and six public houses, the principal of which are the Cumberland House and Fouquet's Hotel; two banks and one insurance office. Here are situated, on the Saranac, using water-power, two flouring-mills, one woolen factory. one fulling-mill, two saw-mills, two machine-shops, and one foundry; there are also two tanneries, one soap manufactory, three printing-offices, together with almost every other kind of mechanic workshops. The water-power at this place is very great, the Saranac River here having a succession of falls, making a total descent of about 40 feet. The surrounding country is rich in agricultural and mineral productions; iron ore of fine quality is procured in different parts of the county. This is also a United States military post, where the government has erected extensive stone barracks, near the lake shore, and a permanent breakwater for the protection of the harbor in Cumberland Bay.

WHITEHALL TO ROUSE'S POINT. 219

Steamers run daily, during the season of navigation, from Plattsburgh to Burlington and Whitehall on the south, and to St. Albans and Rouse's Point on the north, connecting with different railroads. The *Plattsburgh and Montreal Railroad* extends in a northerly direction to Mooer's Junction, and thence across the Canada line to Caughnawaga and Montreal, a total distance of 62 miles.

RAILROAD ROUTE FROM PLATTSBURGH TO MONTREAL.

Stations.	Miles.	Total Miles.
PLATTSBURGH	0	0
West Chazy	10	10
Mooer's Junction	10	20
Hemingford, Canada	6	26
St. Remi	15	41
Caughnawaga	11	52
La Chine	2	54
MONTREAL	8	62

Usual Time, three hours. Fare, $2 10.

Plattsburgh was the scene of an important engagement between the British and American armies, in September, 1814, which resulted in the defeat of the British, under the command of Sir George Prevost, and the capture of the British fleet under Com. Downie, who was killed in the action. The American army was commanded by Maj. Gen. Macomb, and the fleet by Com. McDonough.

NAVAL ENGAGEMENT AND BATTLE OF PLATTSBURGH,
SEPT. 11, 1814.

Copied from Palmer's "HISTORY OF LAKE CHAMPLAIN."

"WHEN the British army reached Plattsburgh, their gunboats had advanced as far as the Isle La Motte, where they remained, under command of Capt. Pring. On the 8th Sept., Captain Downie reached that place with the rest of the fleet, and on the morning of the 11th the whole weighed anchor and stood south to attack the Americans, who lay in Cumberland Bay, off Plattsburgh.

"As the British vessels rounded Cumberland Head, about

eight o'clock in the morning, they found McDonough at anchor a little south of the mouth of the Saranac River, and abreast, but out of gun-shot, of the forts. His vessels lay in a line running north from Crab Island, and nearly parallel with the west shore. The brig *Eagle*, Captain Henley, lay at the head of the line, inside the point of the Head. This vessel mounted twenty guns and had on board one hundred and fifty men. Next to her, and on the south, lay McDonough's flag-ship, the *Saratoga*, mounting twenty-six guns, with two hundred and twelve men. Next south was the schooner *Ticonderoga*, of seventeen guns, Lieutenant Cassin, with one hundred and ten men, and next to her, and at the southern extremity of the line, lay the sloop *Preble*, Lieutenant Charles Budd. This vessel carried seven guns, and was manned by thirty men. She lay so near the shoal extending northeast from Crab Island, as to prevent the enemy from turning that end of the line. To the rear of the line were ten gun-boats, six of which mounted one long twenty-four pounder, and one eighteen pound Columbiad each; the other four carried one twelve pounder. The gun-boats had, on an average, thirty-five men each. Two of the gun-boats lay a little north and in rear of the Eagle, to sustain the head of the line; the others were placed opposite the intervals between the different vessels, and about forty rods to their rear. The larger vessels were at anchor, while the gun-boats were kept in position by their sweeps.

"The British fleet was composed of the frigate *Confiance*, carrying thirty-seven guns,* with over three hundred men, commanded by Captain Downie; the brig *Linnet*, Captain Pring, of sixteen guns and 120 men; the sloop *Chub*, Lieutenant McGhee, and the sloop *Finch*, Lieutenant Hicks, carrying eleven guns and about forty-five men each. To these vessels were added twelve gun-boats of about forty-five men each. Eight of them carried two guns, and four one gun each. Thus the force of the Americans consisted of one ship, one brig, one schooner, one sloop, and ten gun-boats, manned by eight hundred and eighty-two men, and carrying in all eighty-six guns. The British had one frigate, one brig, two sloops, and twelve gun-boats, manned by over one thousand men, and carrying in all ninety-five guns. The metal of the vessels on both sides was unusually heavy. The Saratoga mounted eight long twenty-fours, six forty-twos, and twelve thirty-twos, while the Confiance had the gun-deck of a heavy frigate, with thirty long twenty-fours upon it. She also had a spacious topgallant forecastle, and a poop that came no farther forward than the mizen

---

* There were thirty-nine guns on board the Confiance, but two of them were not mounted.—*Cooper*.

mast. On the first were a long twenty-four on a circle, and four heavy carronades; two heavy carronades were mounted on the poop.

"When the British fleet appeared in sight, the Finch led and kept in a course toward Crab Island, while the other vessels hove to opposite the point of Cumberland Head, to allow the gun-boats to come up, and to receive final instructions as to the plan of attack. The vessels then filled and headed in toward the American fleet, passing inside of the point of Cumberland Head; the Chub laying her course a little to windward of the Eagle, in order to support the Linnet, which stood directly toward that vessel. Captain Downie had determined to lay the Confiance athwart the Saratoga, but the wind baffling, he was obliged to anchor at about two cables' length from that ship. The Finch, which had run about half way to Crab Island, tacked and took her station, with the gun-boats, opposite the Ticonderoga and Preble.

"As the British vessels approached they received the fire of the American fleet; the brig Eagle firing first, and being soon followed by the Saratoga, and the sloop and schooner.* The Linnet poured her broadside into the Saratoga as she passed that ship to take her position opposite the Eagle. Captain Downie brought his vessel into action in the most gallant manner, and did not fire a gun until he was perfectly secured, although his vessel suffered severely from the fire of the Americans As soon, however, as the Confiance had been brought into position, she discharged all her larboard guns, at nearly the same instant. The effect of this broadside, thrown from long twenty-four pounders, double shotted, in smooth water, was terrible. The Saratoga trembled to her very keel; about forty of her crew were disabled, including her first Lieutenant, Mr. Gamble, who was killed while sighting the bow-gun.

"Soon after the commencement of the engagement, the Chub, while maneuvering near the head of the American line, received a broadside from the Eagle, which so crippled her that she drifted down between the opposing vessels and struck. She was taken possession of by Mr. Charles Platt, one of the Saratoga's midshipmen, and was towed in shore and anchored. The Chub

---

* The first gun fired on board the Saratoga was a long twenty-four, which McDonough himself sighted. The shot is said to have struck the Confiance near the outer hawse-hole, and to have passed the length of her deck, killing and wounding several men, and carrying away the wheel. In clearing the decks of the Saratoga, some hen coops were thrown overboard, and the poultry permitted to run at large. Star led by the report of the opening gun of the Eagle, a young cock flew upon a gun slide, clapped his wings and crowed. The men gave three cheers, and considered the little incidence as a happy omen.—*Cooper's Naval History and Niles' Register.*

had suffered severely; nearly half of her men having been killed or wounded. About an hour later the Finch was driven from her position by the Ticonderoga, and, being badly injured, drifted upon the shoal near Crab Island, where she grounded. After being fired into from the small battery on the island, she struck, and was taken possession of by the invalids who manned the battery.*

" After the loss of the Finch, the British gun-boats made several efforts to close, and succeeded in compelling the sloop Preble to cut her cables and to anchor in shore of the line, where she was of no more service during the engagement. The gun boats, emboldened by this success, now directed their efforts toward the Ticonderoga, against which they made several very gallant assaults, bringing the boats, upon two or three occasions, within a few feet of the schooner's side. They were, however, as often beaten back, and the schooner, during the remainder of the day, completely covered that extremity of the line.

" While these changes were taking place at the lower end of the line, a change was also made at the other extremity. The Eagle, having lost her springs, and finding herself exposed to the fire of both the Linnet and Confiance, dropped down and anchored between the Saratoga and Ticonderoga, and a little in shore of both. From this position she opened afresh on the Confiance and the British gun-boats, with her larboard guns. This change relieved the brig, but left the Saratoga exposed to the whole fire of the Linnet, which sprung her broadsides in such a manner as to rake the ship on her bows.

" The fire from the Saratoga and Confiance now began materially to lessen, as gun after gun on both vessels became disabled, until at last the Saratoga had not a single available gun, and the Confiance was but little better off. It therefore became necessary that both vessels should wind, to continue the action with any success. This the Saratoga did after considerable delay, but the Confiance was less fortunate, as the only effect of her efforts was to force the vessel ahead. As soon as the Sara-

---

* Mr. Alison (History of England, vol. 4), referring to this event, says: " The Finch, a British *brig*, grounded out of shot and *did not engage;*" and again, " The Finch struck on a reef of rocks and could not get into action." Had Mr. Alison taken the trouble to read Capt. Pring's official account of the engagement, he would have found in it the following statement: " Lieutenant Hicks, of the Finch, had the mortification to strike on a reef of rocks, to the eastward of Crab Island, about the middle of the engagement, which prevented his rendering that assistance to the squadron that might, from an officer of such ability, have been expected." It is very convenient for the English historian to convert a small sloop of eleven guns and forty men into a *brig*, and to keep that large vessel out of the action altogether, but, as I have before said, such statements are unnecessary to preserve the well-earned reputation of the British navy for bravery or gallantry in action.

toga came around she poured a fresh broadside from her larboard guns into the Confiance, which stood the fire for a few minutes and then struck. The ship then brought her guns to bear on the Linnet, which surrendered in about fifteen minutes afterward. At this time the British gun-boats lay half a mile in the rear, where they had been driven by the sharp fire of the Ticonderoga and Eagle. These boats lowered their colors as soon as they found the larger vessels had submitted; but not being pursued, for the American gun-boats were sent to aid the Confiance and Linnet, which were reported to be in a sinking condition, they escaped, together with a store sloop, which lay near the point of Cumberland Head during the battle.

" The engagement continued for two hours and a half, and was the most severely fought naval battle of the war. The Saratoga had twenty-eight men killed and twenty-nine wounded; the Eagle thirteen killed and twenty wounded; the Ticonderoga six killed and six wounded, and the Preble two killed. The loss on the gun-boats was three killed and three wounded. Total killed and wounded, one hundred and ten, being equal to every eighth man in the fleet. Besides, the Saratoga had been hulled fifty-five times, and was twice on fire; the Eagle was hulled thirty-nine times. The carnage and destruction had been as great on the other side. The Confiance had forty-one men killed and eighty-three wounded; the Linnet reported her casualties at ten killed and fourteen wounded, but the killed and wounded probably exceeded fifty; the Chub was reported at six killed and ten wounded, and the Finch at two wounded. No account is given of the loss on the gun-boats, but from their close and severe contest with the Ticonderoga, it must have been large. The total of killed and wounded on the British side was equal to at least one fifth of the whole number of men in their fleet. The Confiance had been hulled one hundred and five times. So severe had been the contest, that at the close of the action there was not a mast in either fleet fit for use.*

" Among those killed on the side of the British were Captain Downie. who fell soon after the action commenced, Captain Alexander Anderson of the Marines, Midshipman William Gunn of the Confiance, and Lieutenant William Paul and Boatswain Charles Jackson of the Linnet. Among the wounded were Midshipman Lee of the Confiance, Midshipman John Sinclair of the

---

* I could only look at the enemy's galleys going off, in a shattered condition; for there was not a mast in either squadron that could stand to make sail on; the lower rigging being nearly all shot away, hung down as though it had been just placed over the mast head.—*McDonough's Report of the Battle.* Our masts, yards, and sails were so shattered, that one looked like so many bunches of matches, and the other like a bundle of rags.—*Letter of Midshipman Lee of the Confiance.*

Linnet, and Lieutenant James McGhee of the Chub. The American officers killed were Peter Gamble, 1st Lieutenant of the Saratoga, John Stansbury, 1st Lieutenant of the Ticonderoga, Midshipman James M. Baldwin, and Sailing Master Rogers Carter. Referring to the death of three of these officers, Mr. Cooper, in his History of the Navy, says : ' Lieutenant Gamble was on his knees, sighting the bow-gun, when a shot entered the port, split the quoin, drove a portion of it against his breast, and laid him dead on the quarter-deck without breaking his skin. Fifteen minutes later one of the American shot struck the muzzle of a twenty-four on the Confiance, dismounted it, sending it bodily inboard against the groin of Captain Downie, killing him also without breaking the skin. Lieutenant Stansbury suddenly disappeared from the bulwarks forward, while superintending some duty with the springs of the Ticonderoga. Two days after the action, his body rose to the surface of the water, and it was found that it had been cut in two by a round shot.'

"It is said that scarcely an individual escaped on board of either the Confiance or Saratoga without some injury. Macdonough was twice knocked down; once by the spanker-boom, which was cut in two by a shot, and fell upon his back as he was bending his body to sight a gun; and again by the head of a gunner, which was driven against him, and knocked him into the scuppers. Mr. Brum, the sailing-master of the Saratoga, had his clothes torn off by a splinter while winding the ship. Mr. Vallette, acting Lieutenant, had a shot-box, on which he was standing, knocked from under his feet, and he too was once knocked down by the head of a seaman. Very few escaped without some accident, and it appears to have been agreed on both sides, to call no man wounded who could keep out of the hospital.* Midshipman Lee of the Confiance, who was wounded in the action, thus describes the condition of that vessel : 'The havoc on both sides is dreadful. I don't think there are more than five of our men, out of three hundred, but what are killed or wounded. Never was a shower of hail so thick as the shot whistling about our ears. Were you to see my jacket, waistcoat, and trowsers, you would be astonished how I escaped as I did, for they are literally torn all to rags with shot and splinters; the upper part of my hat was also shot away. There is one of our marines who was in the Trafalgar action with Lord Nelson, who says it was a mere *fleabite* in comparison with this."†

---

* Cooper's Naval History.
† Letter to his brother, published in *Niles' Register*, vol. 8. The result of the engagement depended, from the first, upon the Saratoga and Con-

The officers, on both sides, who fell in the several encounters by land and water, on the memorable occasion above mentioned, were buried in the public cemetery adjacent to the village of Plattsburgh; but their graves were left, under the pressing exigencies of that time, without any permanent monument, or stone of memorial. That community, long discontented with an omission which seemed to betoken an apathy not at all in unison with real feelings, at last determined to make amends for their neglect, and fulfill all the rites of sepulture. Accordingly, a little previous to the return of the anniversary of the battle, in 1843, meetings were held at which it was resolved to celebrate the day, by placing marble monuments, with appropriate inscriptions, at the several graves, and thus render to the brave and devoted dead the remaining public honors so eminently their due, and so long left unpaid. This design was carried into effect under the superintendence of the Clinton County Military Association, and the anniversary rendered deeply interesting by the placing of these monuments, with appropriate ceremonies and religious services, accompanied by commemoration addresses.

The graves are arranged in the form of a parallelogram, with that of Capt Downie, the commander of the British flotilla, in the center, as the officer of highest rank. The names of the others, so far as known, are as follow: Of our own countrymen, Lt. George W. Runk, of the U. S. A.; Lt. Peter Gamble, U. S. N.; Lt John Stansbury, U. S. N.; Sailing Master Rogers Carter, U. S. N.; Midshipman James M. Baldwin, U. S. N.; Pilot Joseph Barron, U. S. N., and another pilot, name not known. Of the British army, Col. Wellington, 3d Regt Buffs, Capt. Purchess, 76th Regt., Lieutenant R. Kingsbury, 3d Regt. Buffs; and of the British navy, Capt. Alex. Anderson and three Lieutenants, names not known.

---

flance. When McDonough anchored his vessel, he not only attached springs to the cables, but also laid a kedge broad off on each bow of the Saratoga, and brought the hawsers in upon the two quarters To this timely precaution e was indebted for the victory, for without the larboard hawser he could not have brought his fresh broadside into action.

The beautiful lines of an Irish poet of the last century (Collins), can never be more appropriate than to this occasion:

> "How sleep the brave who sink to rest,
> By all their country's wishes blest!
> When spring with dewy fingers cold,
> Returns to deck their hallowed mold.
> She there shall dress a sweeter sod
> Than fancy's feet have ever trod.
> There honor comes, a pilgrim gray,
> To bless the turf that wraps their clay,
> And memory shall awhile repair
> To dwell a weeping hermit there.

CUMBERLAND HEAD is a peninsula extending two or three miles into the lake, opposite the village of Plattsburgh, forming *Cumberland Bay*, into which empties the Saranac River.

CRAB, or HOSPITAL ISLAND lies two miles south, and near the track of the steamers on their way to and from the landing at Plattsburgh. It was on a line nearly north and south between Cumberland Head and Crab Island that the British and American fleets encountered each other, on the 11th of September, 1814, a day which brought so much honor to the American flag.

SOUTH HERO and NORTH HERO are the names of two Islands belonging to the jurisdiction of Vermont. The former is connected by a ferry, and on the east side with the main shore of Vermont by a bridge.

CHAZY LANDING, 16 miles north of Plattsburgh, is a convenient steamboat landing, on the west side of Lake Champlain.

ISLE AU MOTTE, opposite the above landing, is a fine island, also attached to Vermont. It is 6 miles long and 2 miles wide, containing much good land, and a valuable quarry of marble.

The village of ROUSE'S POINT, in the town of Champlain, 25 miles north of Plattsburgh, and 125 miles from Whitehall, is situated on the west side of Lake Champlain, about one mile south of the Canada line, and has a convenient steamboat landing, a very large depôt building, and a well kept hotel. It is surrounded in part by a level and fertile region, which extends west to the St. Lawrence River. One mile north of the village is a fort and military position commanding the navigable channel of the lake. In 1815 the government of the United States commenced the construction of a strong fortress at Rouse's Point; but on running out the boundary line between the United States and Canada, under the treaty of Ghent, this point was found to be north of the 45th degree of north latitude, and the works were suspended.

United States Boundary Line.—"This line was fixed in 1842, by treaty negotiated by Lord Ashburton and Mr. Webster, on the old line formerly supposed to be the 45th parallel of latitude. Immediately after the close of the last war the United States government commenced building a fort on a low point to the northward of Rouse's Point landing, which should completely command the passage up the lake. By the survey of this line in 1818, it was found that this point was north of the 45th parallel, and the work was consequently abandoned; but by the late treaty the fort was secured to the United States, and the work has recently been resumed. An opening through the woods like a road, on the east side of the lake, and about 200 rods north of the fort, marks the place of the *Line* as now established."

At Rouse's Point is erected a long and substantial drawbridge, crossing the foot of Lake Champlain, for the accommodation of the railroad traffic passing from Montreal and Ogdensburgh to New York and Boston. During the winter months this bridge affords the exclusive thoroughfare at this point between Canada and the Eastern States.

The railroads which here terminate are the *Vermont and Canada Railroad*, connecting with the Vermont Central Railroad; the *Northern Railroad* of New York, 118 miles in length, terminating at Ogdensburgh; and the *Champlain and St. Lawrence Railroad*, 44 miles in length, terminating opposite Montreal.

On arriving and departing from Rouse's Point, travelers are subjected to the inconvenience of having their baggage examined by custom-house officers; this is a great port of entry as well as thoroughfare.

The town of ALBURGH, Vt., is a triangular body of land projecting from Canada into Lake Champlain, by which it is surrounded, excepting on the Canada side. On the eastern shore lies the village of *Alburgh*, a port of entry, and a few miles north is *Alburgh Springs*, where is a small settlement and several hotels. This justly celebrated watering-place lies near the Missisquoi Bay, and is easily reached by railroad, being situated seven miles east of Rouse's Point and 16 miles west of St. Albans, Vt.

HIGHGATE SPRINGS, three miles from Swanton Station and 17 miles from Rouse's Point, near the village of Highgate, Vt., is another and favorite watering-place, attracting much attention. It is situated near Missisquoi Bay, affording fine fishing-grounds, and an opportunity to enjoy aquatic sports and hunting.

MISSISQUOI BAY, connecting with Lake Champlain on the north, is a large and romantic sheet of water lying mostly in Canada, or north of the 45th degree of north latitude. This bay and its surrounding shores afford most romantic and delightful scenery, varied by high land and picturesque points. Hunting, fishing, or pleasure sailing can here be enjoyed by those fond of such sports, while the invigorating climate gives strength and elasticity to the weak and debilitated. During the summer and autumn months a steamer runs around the bay, landing at *Phillipsburgh*, Can., *Highgate*, Vt., and other landings.

ASH ISLAND, four miles north of Rouse's Point, is considered the foot of Lake Champlain. Here the Richelieu, or St. John's River, as the outlet of Lake Champlain is called, is about half a mile wide. The land on both sides of the stream seems almost level with the water, and presents this low and flat surface for many miles.

ISLE AUX NOIX, situated in the Richelieu River, 12 miles north of Rouse's Point, is the first steamboat landing after entering Canada. Here is a strong fortification commanding the channel of the river, and occupied by British troops.

RAILROAD ROUTE FROM ROUSE'S POINT TO OGDENSBURGH, via NORTHERN RAILROAD.

Stations.	Miles.	Total Miles.
ROUSE'S POINT	0	0
Mooer's Junction	12	12
Chazy	11	23
Summit	14	37
Chateaugay	9	46
MALONE	11	57
Brush's Mills	11	68
Stockholm	14	82
Potsdam Junction	11	93
Lisbon	16	109
OGDENSBURGH	9	118

USUAL TIME, 5 hours. FARE, $3 50.

On leaving Rouse's Point for St. John's and Montreal, the line of the *Champlain and St. Lawrence Railroad* extends along the west side of the Sorel or Richelieu River, over a level and productive section of country, passing La Colle, six miles from Rouse's Point.

ST. JOHN'S or DORCHESTER, 150 miles from Whitehall. is advantageously situated on the west side of the Richelieu River, at the foot of navigation; a bridge connecting it with the village of *St. Anthanase*, on the opposite shore. It is 23 miles north of the American line, 22 miles southeast of Montreal, and contains about 2,200 inhabitants, 275 dwelling-houses, a custom-house, and extensive barracks for soldiers, one Episcopal, one Roman Catholic, and one Methodist church; ten hotels and taverns, ten stores, and two forwarding houses, one extensive glass factory, one stone factory, two tanneries, and mechanics shops of different kinds.

The *Chambly Canal* extends from St. John's to Chambly, on the northwest side of the Richelieu River, a distance of 12 miles. It was completed in 1843, at a cost of about $400,000. There are nine locks on this canal 120 feet long, 24 feet wide, and six feet deep; lift ten feet each, making a total descent of 90 feet in 12 miles. This canal was constructed by the Provincial government. It affords navigation for vessels of 100 tons burden between Lake Champlain and the St. Lawrence River, thus furnishing an uninterrupted water communication from New York to Quebec.

The railroad from St John's to Montreal, 21 miles in length, extends over a level section of country, the St. Lawrence River soon coming in sight.

The aspect of the St. Lawrence is truly grand and interesting, as you approach it on the south from Rouse's Point. Toward the west is seen the La Chine Rapid, one of the most dangerous on the river. Opposite Montreal it is two miles wide, embosoming the beautiful island of St. Helen, which is fortified and garrisoned by British troops.

As you approach Montreal by water, the new Victoria Bridge, the city, shipping, and wharves are seen to great advantage. The latter—the wharves—probably exceed any thing of the kind in America, consisting of a range of massive and solid masonry extending along the river for upward of a mile.

THE following beautiful lines, descriptive of one of the sources of *human happiness*, is from the gifted pen of N. P. WILLIS, and may be appropriately inserted at this place:

> " 'Tis to have
> Attentive and believing faculties;
> To go abroad rejoicing in the joy
> Of beautiful and well-created things;
> To love the voice of waters, and the sheen
> Of silver fountains leaping to the sea;
> To thrill with the rich melody of birds,
> Living their life of music;/to be glad
> In the gay sunshine, reverent in the storm;
> To see a beauty in the stirring leaf,
> And find calm thoughts beneath the whispering tree;
> To see, and hear, and breathe the evidence
> Of God's deep wisdom in the natural world."

TABLE OF DISTANCES BETWEEN ALBANY AND MONTREAL.

Places.	Miles.	From Albany.	From Montreal.
ALBANY	0	0	248
Troy	6	6	242
Saratoga Springs	32	38	210
Whitehall	40	78	170
Ticonderoga	24	102	146
BURLINGTON, Vt	51	153	95
Plattsburgh, N. Y.	25	178	70
Rouse's Point, "	25	203	45
St. John's, Canada	23	226	22
MONTREAL	22	248	0

TABLE OF DISTANCES FROM MONTREAL TO QUEBEC, BY WATER.

	Miles.	Total
MONTREAL	0	0
To Varennes	0	15 Miles.
WILLIAM HENRY	30	45 "
Lake St. Peter	8	53 "
St. Francis	30	83 "
THREE RIVERS	7	90 "
St. Anne	20	110 "
Richelieu Rapids	15	125 "
Cape Sante	15	140 "
Cape Rouge	22	162 "
QUEBEC	8	170 "

RAILROAD ROUTE FROM MONTREAL TO QUEBEC, WHITE MOUNTAINS, AND PORTLAND, MAINE, *via* GRAND TRUNK RAILWAY.

Stations.	Miles.	Total Miles.
MONTREAL	0	0
Longueuil	2	2
St. Hyacinthe	30	32
Richmond	42	74
QUEBEC	97	171
Sherbrooke	24	98
Boundary Line	30	128
ISLAND POND, Vt.	17	145
Northumberland	27	172
GORHAM (White Mt. Station)	31	203
South Paris	43	246
Danville Junction	20	266
PORTLAND	28	294

RAILROAD ROUTE FROM MONTREAL TO TORONTO, via GRAND TRUNK RAILWAY.

Stations.	Miles.	Stations.	Miles.
MONTREAL	0	TORONTO	0
Blue Bonnets	5	York	6
Pointe Claire	15	Scarboro'	13
St. Anne's (*Ottawa River*)	21	Port Union	17
Vaudreuil	24	Port Whitby	29
Cedars (road to)	29	OSHAWA	33
Coteau Landing	37	Bowmanville	43
River Beaudette	44	Newcastle	47
Lancaster	54	Port Britain	59
CORNWALL	68	PORT HOPE	62
Dickinson's Landing	77	COBOURG	70
Aultsville	84	Grafton	77
Williamsburg	92	Colborne	84
Matilda	99	Trenton	101
Edwardsburg	104	BELLEVILLE	113
Prescott Junction	112	Shannonville	120
PRESCOTT	113	Napanee	134
Maitland	120	Ernestown	145
BROCKVILLE	125	Collins Bay	153
Mallorytown	137	KINGSTON	160
Lansdowne	146	Kingston Mills	164
Gananoque	155	Gananoque	178
Kingston Mills	169	Lansdowne	187
KINGSTON	173	Mallorytown	196
Collins Bay	180	BROCKVILLE	208
Ernestown	188	Maitland	213
Napanee	199	PRESCOTT	220
Shannonville	213	Prescott Junction	221
BELLEVILLE	220	Edwardsburg	229
Trenton	232	Matilda	234
Colborne	249	Williamsburg	241
Grafton	256	Aultsville	249
COBOURG	263	Dickinson's Landing	256
PORT HOPE	271	CORNWALL	265
Port Britain	274	Lancaster	279
Newcastle	286	River Beaudette	289
Bowmanville	290	Coteau Landing	296
OSHAWA	300	Cedars (road to)	304
Port Whitby	304	Vaudreuil (*Ottawa Riv'r*)	309
Port Union	316	St. Anne's	312
Scarboro'	320	Pointe Claire	318
York	327	Blue Bonnets	328
TORONTO	333	MONTREAL	333

USUAL TIME, 15 hours. FARE, $10

TRIP FROM MONTREAL TO QUEBEC.

THIS interesting trip is, during the warm season, one of a most delightful character. To be fully enjoyed, however, it should be performed during daylight; but, unfortunately, the evening line of steamers usually alone performs the trips, leaving Montreal at seven o'clock P. M., and Quebec two hours earlier. "Both banks are low and uninteresting in a scenic point of view, but lined with the neat, whitewashed cottages of the French-Canadian peasantry, built so closely to each other as to suggest the idea of a continuous village on either bank; with here and there a thicker grouping of houses round the parish church. Darkness, however, soon closes the view, and the traveler only knows that he is rapidly borne along on the now united and smooth waters of two mighty rivers, better known by the inhabitants on its banks as the *La Grande Rivière.*"

On leaving Montreal for Quebec and the intermediate landings, in one of the many splendid steamers which navigate the St. Lawrence, you have a fine view of the beautiful fortified island of ST. HELEN, situated mid-stream opposite the city; and as you are borne along on the majestic current of the mighty river, its thickly settled and cultivated shores compel the admiring attention of the traveler, by the aspect presented by their lines of settlements on each side, for the whole distance of 170 miles from city to city.

LONGUEUIL, on the opposite side of the river from Montreal, is connected with the city by a commodious ferry—this being the present terminus of the *Grand Trunk Railway,* leading to Quebec and Portland, Me., the two routes diverging at Richmond, C. E.—thus forming a speedy line of travel both to *Quebec* on the northeast, and the *White Mountains* of New Hampshire on the southeast.

The RAPIDS OF ST. MARY are entered immediately below St Helen's Island; and. although not formidable to steam vessels, they often retard the ordinary river craft for many days in ascending.

LONGUE POINT and POINT AUX TREMBLES, on the island of Montreal, are successively passed on the left, and BOUCHERVILLE on the opposite shore.

The ISLAND OF ST. THERESA lies in the St. Lawrence, a short distance from the northern termination of the *island* of Montreal, and 15 miles below the *city*, near the lower mouth of the Ottawa River.

VARENNES, on the southeast side of the river, 15 miles from Montreal, is a beautiful place, and was formerly much resorted to for the mineral springs in its vicinity. The massive church, with its two spires, surrounded by a cluster of neat dwellings presents a fine appearance from the river. Other objects of interest are seen in the distance; the hills back of Montreal are still visible; and the *Mountain of Rouville*, rising grandly in the southeast, its summit crowned with an immense cross, seen for many miles, greatly exalts the character and expression of the whole prospect.

WILLIAM HENRY, or SOREL, 45 miles below Montreal, stands on the site of an old fort, built in 1665, at the mouth of the Richelieu River. It is regularly laid out with streets crossing each other at right angles. This town was first settled in 1685, and now contains about 3,000 inhabitants. It is no doubt destined to increase, as a canal, with locks, is now constructed from Chambly to St. John's, affording an uninterrupted water communication with Lake Champlain. The fort at this place was taken and occupied in May, 1776, by a party of the American army, in their retreat from Quebec on the death of Gen. Montgomery.

Leaving the mouth of the Richelieu and proceeding down the St. Lawrence, several islands are passed in succession, and then you enter

LAKE ST. PETER, 50 miles below Montreal. This sheet of

water, which is but an expansion of the river, is about 25 miles long and 12 to 15 miles wide, while the average breadth of the river proper, from Montreal to Quebec, is about two miles, and the scene which its waters present has some features peculiar enough to be noticed. In addition to the more customary forms of steamboats, of ships, and other sea-going vessels, and of the craft usually employed in the navigation of large rivers, the waters of the St. Lawrence, more than any other even on this forest-covered continent, are frequented by enormous timber-rafts, commonly borne along on their way to market by the force of the current alone, though occasionally aided by spreading a sail, or by huge oars called sweeps. These floating islands of timber, with huts here and there rising from their low surface, for the accommodation of the raft-men, and another singular sort of craft with long, low hulls, nowhere else known, and designed chiefly for the transport of timber of great length, contribute the more remarkable and picturesque features to the animating spectacle presented by the navigation of this noble river; while, from its high latitude, and from the characteristic phenomena of northern skies, the ordinary, as well as the more grotesque, features referred to are accompanied by contrasts in the golden grandeur of the sunsets, and in the varied splendor of the northern lights, both of which are so frequent and so remarkable, that they may be very fairly regarded as habitual, and from which the scenery of the St. Lawrence derives a magnificence and beauty probably unequaled.

PORT ST. FRANCIS, 83 miles below Montreal, is the next steamboat landing. Here the river again contracts to its usual width.

THREE RIVERS, about half way between Montreal and Quebec, is situated on the north side of the St. Lawrence, at the mouth of the river St. Maurice; nearly opposite to which, and of smaller volume, enters the river Becancour. Three Rivers is an old town, having been settled by the French in 1618. Here is a court-house and jail, a convent, a Roman Catholic church, and three Protestant churches; a mechanics' institute, an academy, several public houses, 40 stores, lumber-yards, a ship-yard and foundry; also, other manufacturing establishments. The town contains about 6,000 inhabitants, and is a place of considerable trade and importance.

This place has become a great lumber mart, caused by the opening up of the great timber country in its rear, on the banks of the St. Maurice. A visit to the wild and romantic *Falls of Shawanagenne*, about 25 miles up this river, will be found interesting; it may be easily accomplished in one day, the road leading through a forest for most of the way, with here and there a hamlet to vary the scene. A part of the journey is usually performed in a bark canoe propelled by Indians. On arriving at the falls, nothing but grandeur and solitude strikes the imagination.

St. Anne, 25 miles below Three Rivers, stands on the north bank of the St. Lawrence, at the mouth of a river of the same name.

The Richelieu Rapids, 45 miles above Quebec, extend some eight or ten miles. The channel of the river is here very narrow and intricate, huge rocks being visible in many places during low water. In order to guide the mariner safely through these rapids, beacon lights are stationed at the more critical points of the passage.

Cape Sante, 30 miles from Quebec, is on the north side of the St. Lawrence, and on the opposite side is a settlement called St. Trois. The banks of the river are here elevated some 60 or 80 feet above the water, and are almost perpendicular, from which the land extends away for many miles, with an almost level surface.

Cape Rouge, eight miles above Quebec, is next passed on the left, when the citadel of Quebec comes into view, presenting a sight at once grand and deeply interesting, from the historical events with which it is associated.

The Chaudiere River, on the right, is much visited for the sake of its beautiful falls, situated a short distance from its entrance into the St. Lawrence.

WOLFE'S COVE, two miles above Quebec, on the same side, is an interesting spot to strangers, for here the lamented *Wolfe* landed with his gallant army, in 1759, and ascended to the Plains of Abraham, where he fell a victim to his heroic enterprise. But he fell not alone. France mourned an equal loss in the fall of the brave and generous *Montcalm*.

As the steamer approaches the wharf, the line of shipping, extending usually for two or three miles, gives life and interest to the scene below—while the towering citadel above produces emotions of wonder and delight. The city, or Lower Town, only as yet partly seen, soon opens to view, hugging the base of the rocky promontory.

QUEBEC.

THE City of QUEBEC, a seaport, and most important naval and military depôt, is situated on the left bank of the river St. Lawrence, at the point where it is joined by the St. Charles, 170 miles below Montreal, and about 400 miles from the Gulf, in N. lat. 46° 49′ 12″, W. long. 71° 15′ 45″. Population in 1831, 25,916; in 1844, 32,876; in 1852, 42,000, and in 1861, contained 51,109, of which about 2,000 are soldiers.

As a fortress, Quebec may be justly ranked in the first class. Words can hardly express the strength of its position without the aid of technical terms. The citadel, the Gibraltar of America, is approached by a zigzag pathway, with thirty-two pounders staring you in the face at every turn. When inside the fortress, it looks like a world of itself. The officers' barrack is a fine building, overlooking the St. Lawrence. The soldiers quarters are under the ramparts. The armories, magazines, and warlike implements are immense. The military authorities are energetically at work putting the fortifications of Quebec into repair. The Quebec *Mercury*, of a late date, says: "There is hardly a point at which the fortifications are not being repaired or improved. A new and very strong blockhouse is making below the flag-staff, and very extensive works, of by no means ancient construction, above that point, have been condemned, and are now rebuilding in a more formidable manner, near where a new battery and draw-bridge outlet from the citadel have lately been constructed, communicating with the city over the northeastern glacis."

"The city is built on the extremity of a ridge terminating in the angle formed by the junction of the two rivers on the point called Cape Diamond, which here rises to the height of about 340 feet above the St. Lawrence. The cape is surmounted by the citadel, and the city extends from it principally in a N.E. direction, down to the water's edge. The old town, which lies wholly without the walls, partly at the foot of Cape Diamond, and around to the St. Charles, has narrow and, in parts, steep streets. The ascent from the upper to the lower portion of the city which crosses the line of the fortifications is by a winding street and by a flight of steps; the streets in this section, though narrow, are generally clean, and well paved or macadamized. The public buildings and most of the houses are built of stone. The line of the fortifications stretches nearly across the peninsula in the west, and runs along a ridge between the upper and lower parts of the city. It is intersected by five gates, and has an inner circuit of about 2½ miles. Beyond the ramparts on the west are the extensive suburbs of St. Roch, St. John, and St. Louis. Durham Terrace commands a picturesque view, having the lower part of the city in the foreground; and the shores and waters of the St. Lawrence extending far in the distance. The Public Garden, on Des Carrieres Street, contains an elegant monument erected to the memory of Wolfe and Montcalm. It is 65 feet high, and its design is very chaste and beautiful. This spot attracts great attention, and should be visited by every stranger. The Esplanade, railed off from, and situated between D'Auteuil Street and the ramparts, affords delightful views of the surrounding country and river scenery.

"There are 174 streets in the city and suburbs, the principal of which are the following: St. John Street, the principal seat of the retail trade; St. Louis Street, occupied by lawyers' offices and private dwellings, is handsome and well-built; D'Auteuil Street, facing the Esplanade in the upper town, and in the lower town, St. Peter Street, in which most of the banks, insurance companies, and merchants' offices are situated. There are also many other fine streets, and the appearance of the city has been much improved since the great fire of 1845 when nearly 2,000 buildings were destroyed, which have been replaced by others of a superior description. The streets are lighted with gas, and the city is well supplied with water from the St. Charles River. The Parliament House (destroyed by fire 1853) was an elegant pile of buildings, forming three sides of a square, now about being rebuilt in a much improved style. The Court House and City Hall are substantial stone edifices, St. Louis Street, upper town. The Marine Hospital, a fine stone building, will accommodate 400 patients. The Lunatic Asylum at Beauport, 2½ miles from the city, is an extensive building, inclosed in a park of 200 acres. The Quebec Musical Hall, recently erected, is a substantial and well-built edifice, fitted for musical entertainments, etc. The Quebec Exchange, the Canadian Institute, the Literary and Historical Society, the Quebec Library Association, the Advocates' Library, etc., are among the most noted and interesting institutions of Quebec.

"The Roman Catholic Cathedral is a large and commodious building, but with no great pretensions to beauty of architecture; the interior is handsomely fitted up, and has several fine paintings; the church will seat 4,000 persons. It has a fine choir and a good organ. The Episcopal Cathedral is a handsome edifice, 135 feet by 75 feet. It was erected in 1804, and will seat between 3,000 and 4,000 persons. Trinity Church is a neat stone building, erected in 1824; it is handsomely fitted up. St. Andrew, Presbyterian Church, is 95 by 48 feet, and will accommodate about 1,200 persons. There were, in 1852, one Baptist, one Congregational, four Episcopal, one Free Presbyterian, two Methodist, one Presbyterian, and five Roman Catholic churches. Quebec has three banks, and several bank agencies, two savings' banks, and a number of insurance agencies. The hotels are numerous, and several of them well-kept, being usually thronged with visitors from the United States and foreign parts during warm weather.

"There are three nunneries, one of which, the Hotel Dieu, is a very valuable hospital; the nuns acting as nurses to the sick in these establishments, and as instructresses of young females. There are numerous religious and benevolent institutions, an exchange, a board of trade, a mechanics' institute, etc. Among the establishments for educational purposes, the first place is due to the University of Quebec; it has a principal, and professors of theology, rhetoric, and mathematics, with five regents for the Latin and Greek classes.

"Though not a manufacturing town, Quebec has various distilleries, breweries, with tobacco, soap and candle works, and numbers of fine vessels have been launched from its ship-yards. The climate, though on the whole good and healthy, is extremely hot in summer and cold in winter. The majority of the population is of French extraction, and the French language is mostly spoken in the best circles, and the Roman Catholic religion predominates."

Steamships and other sea-going vessels of the largest burden come up to the wharves of Quebec. Its harbor or basin between the city and the island of Orleans is of great extent, having in general about 28 fathoms water, the tide rising from 16 to 18 feet at neaps, and from 24 to 30 feet at spring tides. The commerce of the city is very extensive, the lumber trade alone giving employment to a great number of ships during the season of navigation, from May to November. Quebec has a regular intercourse, by means of steamers, with Montreal and ports higher up the St. Lawrence and the Ottawa River; also with Halifax, Liverpool, and other ports on both sides the Atlantic.

The *Grand Trunk Railway* is now so far finished as to afford speedy communication with the Riviere du Loup, below Quebec, with Portland Me., Montreal, Kingston, Toronto, etc., Its passenger and freight depôts are situated at Point Levi, opposite Quebec, the two places being connected by steam ferries. Steamers also run to different ports below Quebec, and during warm weather make trips to the lower St. Lawrence and Saguenay rivers.

The following description of the city of Quebec is taken from Mr. Buckingham's late interesting work on CANADA, etc.:

"The situation of Quebec is highly advantageous, in a commercial as well as a military point of view, and its appearance is very imposing, from whatever quarter it is first approached. Though at a distance of four hundred miles up from the sea, the magnificent river on which it is seated is three miles in breadth a little below the town, and narrows in to about a mile in breadth immediately abreast of the citadel; having, in both these parts, sufficient depth of water for the largest ships in the world—a rise and fall of twenty feet in its tides—and space enough in its capacious basin, between Cape Diamond on the one hand, and the Isle of Orleans on the other, to afford room and anchorage for a thousand sail of vessels at a time, sheltered from all winds, and perfectly secure! A small river, the St. Charles, has its junction with the St Lawrence a little to the north of the promontory of Cape Diamond, and affords a favorable spot for ship-building and repairs, as well as an excellent winter-harbor for ships lying up dismantled.

"The citadel of Quebec occupies the highest point of Cape Diamond, being elevated 350 feet above the river, and presenting almost perpendicular cliffs toward the water. The city is but It from the water's edge along the foot of these cliffs, round the point of the promontory, and ascending upward from thence to the very borders of the citadel itself. It is divided into the Lower and Upper Town, the former including all that is below the ramparts or fortified lines, the latter comprehending all that is above and within that barrier. Besides these, there is a large suburb, separated from Quebec proper by the ramparts, and some open lawn beyond these on the west, called the suburb of St. Roch, on the right bank of the river St. Charles, the only portion of the whole that is built on level ground.

"On landing at Quebec, therefore, the traveler has to wind his way up through steep, narrow, and tortuous streets, with still narrower alleys on his right and left, till he reaches the fortified line or barrier. Here he enters by Prescott Gate, on the right of which, after passing through it, he sees the imposing structure of the New Parliament House (since destroyed by fire), with its lofty cupola and fine architectural front; and on the left, a double flight of mean and straggling wooden steps, leading to one of the oldest streets, as an avenue to the Place d'Armes. Going across this last, he passes the English and French cathedrals, the government offices, and palace of justice on his right; and has the site of the old castle of St. Lewis, and the platform overlooking the harbor, on his left Passing by these, and continually ascending for about half a mile beyond, he reaches the ramparts and gates on the upper side of the city; and going through these, he comes to the open lawn in front of the glacis, beyond which is the suburb of St. Roch, on the level ground along the southern bank of the St. Charles River.

"The plan of the city is as irregular as the greatest enemy of symmetry could desire. The steepness of the ascent from the river to the plain above is no doubt one cause of this, because it was only by making the ascending streets winding and tortuous that they could be got over at all; but besides this, the inequalities in the surface even of the Upper Town led to other irregularities in the form and direction of the streets; while the large space occupied by the old religious establishments, still further curtailing the lines in different directions, so cut up the area, that there is not a single street in all Quebec which can compare in length, breadth, or general good appearance to the King Street of Toronto or the Notre Dame of Montreal. The streets of Quebec are, therefore, in general short, narrow, crooked, steep, wretchedly paved in the center, still worse provided with sidewalks, and not lighted with lamps at night The private dwellings are in general destitute of architectural beauty, and small and incommodious; some few are of wood, none of brick, but the greatest number are of rough-hewn stone, with high, steep roofs, containing a double row of projecting garret windows, very lofty chimneys, and the roofs principally covered with sheets of tin. The shops are also small and mean, and greatly inferior in the extent and variety of their contents to those of Montreal and Toronto; though the prices charged are, as we thought, higher here than in either of these.

"The public buildings are scattered over the city with so much irregularity, that their position seems to be as much the effect of accident as design. Several of them, however, are so prominently placed and advantageously seen, that they relieve, in some degree, the general monotony of the mass of ordinary houses, and are thus far ornamental to the town; while the spires of the churches, the dome of the Parliament House, and other elevated points rising from the general surface, with their tinned roofs glittering in the sun, give a liveliness and variety to the picture presented by the city, from every point of view, which no other place in Canada, and indeed few places on the globe, present.

"The earliest of the public buildings erected in Quebec was undoubtedly the castle of St. Lewis, of which Champlain laid the foundation on the 6th of May, 1624. The position chosen for it was a most commanding one, on the very edge of an almost perpendicular precipice of rock 200 feet above the river, yet close to its edge; as, between the cliff and the stream, there is only just room enough for one narrow avenue, called Champlain Street. The castle erected here was regarded as the palace of the French governors, who received in it the fealty and homage of the several seigneurs holding their lands according to the feudal tenure of the times. Nor is this practice discontinued; for, according to Mr. Hawkins, in his *Picture of Quebec*, the sovereignty of England having succeeded to that of France, with all its ancient rights and privileges, the king's representative, in the person of the English governor, receives the same homage at the present day as was paid by the seigneurs of former times; this being one of the conditions on which the feudal tenure is sustained. His words are these:

"'Fealty and homage are rendered at this day (1834) by the seigneurs to the governor, as the representative of the sovereign, in the following form: His Excellency being in full dress, and seated in a state-chair, surrounded by his staff, and attended by the Attorney-General, the Seigneur in an evening dress, and wearing a sword, is introduced into his presence by the Inspector-General of the Royal Domain and Clerk of the Land Roll. Having delivered up his sword, he kneels on one knee before the Governor, and placing his right hand between those of the Governor, he repeats aloud the ancient oath of fidelity; after which a solemn act is drawn up in a register kept for that purpose, which is signed by the Governor and Seigneur, and countersigned by the proper officers.'

" In this castle the French and English governors resided till 1809, when it was found necessary to erect a temporary new building for their use while the old one underwent repair; and £10,000 were expended for this purpose under the administration of Sir James Craig. After this it continued to be the seat of government as before; and all the proclamations and ordinances issued, and all the messages sent to the legislative assemblies by the governor in the king's name, were dated from the castle of Quebec. It was also the scene of all the public levees and private entertainments of the governors and their families; and was therefore the constant resort of all the gay and fashionable society of the province. In 1834, however, this ancient edifice was entirely destroyed by a fire, which broke out on the 23d of January, in the depth of winter, when Lord Aylmer occupied it as his official residence; and notwithstanding every exertion made to save it, the thermometer being at 22° below zero, and the fire-engines only capable of being worked by a constant supply of warm water, the castle was soon reduced to ashes. It has never since been rebuilt; but Lord Durham, during his short stay here, had the site cleared of the ruined heaps that still covered it, and the whole area of the former edifice leveled, floored with wood, and converted into a beautiful platform, with a fine iron railing at the edge of the precipice, making it one of the most beautiful promenades imaginable—commanding an extensive view of the St. Lawrence down as far as the island of Orleans—the harbor filled with ships immediately before it, and the opposite bank of the river, with Point Levi, the village of D'Aubigny, and the road leading up through one continuous line of cottages to the Falls of Chaudière.

" The site on which the Parliament House stood is of even earlier date than that of the castle of St. Lewis; there being good reason to believe that it occupied the first spot of ground which was cleared by Champlain for his fort, on founding the city in 1608. Here, too, as at the castle, the site stands on a mass of rock made level by art, and extending to the brink of a perpendicular precipice, of about 100 feet above the river, the narrowest part of which is commanded by its guns. Along the edge of this precipice, beyond the area occupied by the late Parliament House, still runs the Grand Battery of Quebec, the promenade on which, and the view from its platform, is scarcely inferior to that already described on the site of the old castle of St. Lewis."

PLAINS OF ABRAHAM.—This celebrated battle-field lies a short distance southwest of the citadel. A monument is here erected on the spot where Gen. Wolfe is said to have died, with this simple inscription: "*Here fell Wolfe victorious.*" A beautiful monument is also erected, of recent date, to the memories of both Wolfe and Montcalm, within the city walls, with this inscription: "*Immortal memory of Wolfe and Montcalm.*"

WOLFE'S MONUMENT—QUEBEC.

"HERE FELL WOLFE VICTORIOUS."

A broken column! few and brief
  The words inscribed upon its stone
Yet speaks it of the dying chief.
  Triumphant tales alone!

It tells unfading glory shed
  Upon the hero's parting hour;
Dying beside the host he led,
  To victory and to power!

The trumpet's tone, the battle shout,
  All sounds of triumph come again,
As shines the brief inscription out,
  Upon the storied plain.

The clashing sword, the cannon's roar,
  The beating of the wild war drum;
And the last shout, "They fly!" once more
  On fancy's vision come.

And marching round the hero's bed,
  With banners floating free and fair
Are seen the host he nobly led
  For England's glory there.

But years have passed, and silence reigns
  Where once was heard the battle cheer;
Of all the trophies naught remains—
  This, only this, is here.

A broken column! brief, yet high
  The eulogy its words convey;
Thus in the triumph hour to die,
  Breathes not of earth's decay.

Wolfe fell in the moment of victory, and Montcalm, who was mortally wounded in the action, expired soon after. The French, panic-struck by the loss of the battle and the death of their commander-in-chief, surrendered the city before even a single battery had been opened against it. This important event, which transferred the possession of Canada from the French to the English nation, occurred on the 13th Sept., 1759

The following is an English account of the attack on Quebec by Montgomery and Arnold, in 1775 and 1776:

"At the period of the American Revolution, it is well known that Canada did not join the revolted colonies, but continued firm in her allegiance to the Crown; and hence it became the land of refuge to the many loyalists who were driven from the United States by the success of their war of Independence. As it was believed, however, by the Americans of that day, that an attack on Quebec would be successful, and if so, would induce all Canada to join their cause, such an attack was planned, and its execution committed to two American generals, Montgomery and Arnold. The British troops usually retained in Canada for its defense had been sent on to Boston, so that the province was almost destitute of military force, there being scattered throughout all Canada only about 800 men. In this state of things Gen. Montgomery advanced from Lake Champlain on St. John's, and after a short resistance took it; he then marched on against Montreal, which being perfectly defenseless, surrendered to the American arms on the 12th of November, 1775. At the same time Gen. Arnold was known to Montgomery to be advancing toward Quebec, from the New England States, by way of the Kennebec River through Maine, which at this late period of the year was a most daring undertaking. After passing thirty-two days in the wild forests and swamps, and suffering almost incredible hardships and privations in this hitherto untrodden wilderness, Arnold and his followers reached the banks of the St. Lawrence, by the Chaudière River, on the 4th of November, in the same year. From thence they descended to Point Levi, opposite to Quebec, where they arrived on the 9th, crossed over on the night of the 13th, and landed 500 men at Wolfe's Cove without being perceived either by the sentries or from the ships of war.

"On the 1st of December this force was joined by a much larger one under General Montgomery, from Montreal. By these two the city was invested, and several bombardments of it made with shot and shells. but without producing much effect. A night attack was at length determined on by Montgomery on the southern, and Arnold on the northern, side of the Lower Town. Both attacks were made with great courage and impetuosity, but both failed. In the former, Gen. Montgomery and nearly all his personal staff were killed; in the latter. Gen. Arnold was wounded, and with most of his followers taken prisoners. The loss of the Americans in these attacks was upward of 100 killed and wounded, and of the British, only one naval officer killed, and seventeen men killed and wounded. The Americans did not, however, give up the attempt to reduce Quebec; as, during all the winter following they continued to receive reinforcements, and to invest the town; and in the spring of the year ensuing, May, 1776. they renewed their attack on the citadel. Gen. Carleton, the English commander of the garrison, having received an important accession to his force by the arrival of a small squadron under the command of Sir Charles Douglas, bringing to his aid provisions, ammunition, and men, was enabled to baffle every attempt made on the city, and ultimately to make a sally on the enemy, when they retreated, and abandoned their post.

"This was the last attack made on Quebec by any foreign foe, and as since that period the citadel has been gradually strengthened and improved, under every successive governor of the province, it is now in a condition to resist ten times the force ever yet brought against it, and could not, so long as it contained supplies of provisions, and an adequate number of brave and faithful men, be conquered by any force likely to be brought against it from this continent."

GENERAL MONTGOMERY.—A tablet has been placed on the rock of Cape Diamond, near the spot where General Montgomery fell, with his two aids-de-camp, Majors McPherson and Cheeseman, at Pres-de-ville, in the attack upon Quebec by the American forces, in the winter of 1775-6.

The tablet is raised about fifty feet from the road, and bears the following inscription:

HERE

MAJOR-GENERAL MONTGOMERY FELL,

DECEMBER 31ST, 1775.

"It has long been a matter of surprise to our neighbors of the United States, who, during the summer months, pour in a continual stream of visitors to our celebrated city, that no clue could be found by them to indicate the spot where Montgomery fell. The event must ever remain memorable in our colonial history as terminating the last hostile struggle before the city of Quebec.

"Quebec is much indebted to the late Mr. Hawkins for the labor he has bestowed in bringing before the public the various historical reminiscences connected with the city, and this tablet, erected by him, is a fresh proof of the interest he takes in perpetuating the recollection of every incident connected with the many warlike and memorable events illuming the annals of our American Gibraltar." *See* HAWKINS' QUEBEC.

VICINITY OF QUEBEC.

QUEBEC, the *Ultima Thule* of most travelers, stands not alone in regard to attractions of interest. In the Vicinity, within a few hours' ride, are located waterfalls and varied scenery of the most romantic character, while the banks of the Lower St. Lawrence and Saguenay rivers stand unrivaled in scenic grandeur

EXCURSION TO CAPE ROUGE.

On this excursion you leave the city by the St. Lewis Gate, and cross the Plains of Abraham to the right of the spot where Wolfe fell. A mile from the gate is the *Race Course*, which is thronged during the spring and fall races; and a mile farther, a road branching to the left leads to *Wolfe's Cove*, celebrated as the place where he landed with his army previous to the capture of Quebec, but now occupied by an extensive ship-yard and lumber-yard. The road beyond runs for some distance through a fine grove, with avenues leading to various pleasant country residences overlooking the river, of which you catch as you pass along occasional glimpses, together with the opposite shore in the neighborhood of the Chaudière Falls.

Returning by the St. Foi road, and facing toward the city, the prospect is far wider and more magnificent. Below and to the left stretches the fine cultivated valley of the St. Charles, bounded on the northwest by a picturesque range of mountains, the settlements reaching to their very base, with villages and church spires scattered over the intervening region; in another direction appear the Falls of the Montmorenci and the Isle of Orleans, and in front spreads the harbor of Quebec, with the bold cliffs of Cape Diamond and Point Levi rising perpendicularly on each side, the former crowned with impregnable bulwarks.

The FALLS OF LORETTE, situated eight miles northwest of Quebec, are visited by many strangers with delight, though but a small volume of water. They have a descent of about 50 feet, and are surrounded by very fine scenery, peculiar to this section of Canada.

The *Indian Village*, at the falls, is inhabited by the remains of the once powerful tribe of the Hurons.

The hills or mountains on the northwest of Lorette may be said to be the bounds of white settlements in North America, although, at no distant period, the upper Saguenay River and Lake St. John will, no doubt, be reached in this direction by railroad.

FALLS OF MONTMORENCI.

In going to the Falls of Montmorenci, which should be visited by every lover of picturesque natural scenery, you pass through the suburbs of Quebec, mostly inhabited by French Canadians, and cross the river St. Charles, near its mouth, by a wooden toll bridge. Here are situated on the roadside several pretty country residences, on the route to *Beauport*, which is a long scattered village about half way between Quebec and Montmorenci, although for most of the distance there are dwellings so contiguous as to appear like one continued settlement. At Beauport there is a Roman Catholic church with three spires; and a little farther north may be seen a neat monument and cross near the road, where are frequently found persons kneeling at their devotions.

The celebrated MONTMORENCI FALLS, situated eight miles below Quebec, is a grand cataract. The river is but 60 feet wide, but the height of the falls is 240 feet. The effect on the beholder, says Professor Silliman, is delightful. All strangers at Quebec proceed to visit Montmorenci.

"The effect of the view of these falls on the beholder is most delightful. The river, at some distance, seems suspended in the air, in a sheet of billowy foam, and, contrasted as it is, with the black frowning abyss into which it falls, it is an object of the highest interest. The sheet of foam, which first breaks over the ridge, is more and more divided as it plunges and is dashed against the successive layers of rock, which it almost completely vails from view; the spray becomes very delicate and abundant from top to bottom, hanging over and revolving around the torrent till it becomes lighter and more evanescent than the whitest fleecy clouds of summer, than the finest attenuated web, than the lightest gossamer, constituting the most airy and sumptuous drapery that can be imagined. Yet, like the drapery of some of the Grecian statues, which, while it vails, exhibits more forcibly the form beneath, this does not hide, but exalts. the effects produced by this noble cataract

"Those who visit the falls in the winter, see one fine feature added to the scene, although they may lose some others. The spray freezes, and forms a regular cone of one hundred feet or upward in height, standing immediately at the bottom of the cataract, like some huge giant of fabulous notoriety."

The *Natural Steps*, in the vicinity of the falls above, are an object of much interest, and there are many excellent fishing places on the river, rendering it a favorite resort of the lovers of angling and romantic scenery. There are also historical incidents connected with this neighborhood, which render it almost classic ground.

There are extensive saw-mills on the south bank of the river below the falls, which are propelled by water-power taken from the stream above, and conveyed for about half a mile in a raceway. These mills have upward of a hundred saws in motion at a time, and are said to be capable of completing an entire cargo of planks in a single day! In winter, the spray rising from the falls is congealed, and often presents a conical mass of ice 100 feet and upward in height. It was on the high grounds north of the falls that Gen. Wolfe met his first repulse, when he attacked the French, a short time before his triumph on the Plains of Abraham. He was here driven back, and compelled to re-embark, with the loss of 700 engaged in the assault.

On returning to Quebec there is afforded a splendid view of the city and citadel; the St. Lawrence, and the opposite shore above and below Point Levi; the beautiful island of Orleans, opposite the falls, and the rich valley of the St. Charles.

The FALLS OF ST. ANNE are situated on the river of the same name, on the north side of the St. Lawrence, 24 miles below Quebec, and presents a singular variety of wild and beautiful scenery, both in themselves and their immediate neighborhood. By leaving Quebec early in the day, the tourist can visit the Falls of Montmorenci, and the objects contiguous, and reach St. Anne the same evening, leaving the next morning to visit the falls, and the remainder of the day to return to Quebec

LAKE ST. CHARLES, 13 miles north of Quebec, is a favorite resort of tourists, particularly of those who are fond of angling, as the lake abounds with fine trout. Parties intending to remain any length of time would do well to bring some of the good things to be found in the larders of Quebec with them, as it is not at all times that the supplies in the vicinity are all that can be desired.

The CHAUDIERE FALLS, on the river Chaudière, nine miles above Quebec, situated on the opposite side of the St. Lawrence, are very beautiful, and much visited. They are 130 feet high The cataract is a fierce and noisy one. The following is Col. Bouchette's description:

"The continued action of the water has worn the rock into deep excavations, that give a globular figure to the revolving bodies of white foam as they descend, and greatly increase the beautiful effect of the fall; the spray thrown up being quickly spread by the wind, produces in the sunshine a most splendid variety of prismatic colors. The dark-hued foliage of the woods, that on each side press close upon the margin of the river, forms a striking contrast with the snow-like effulgence of the falling torrent; the hurried motion of the flood, agitated among the rocks and hollows, as it forces its way toward the St. Lawrence, and the incessant sound occasioned by the cataract itself, form a combination that strikes forcibly upon the senses, and amply gratifies the curiosity of the admiring spectator."

On visiting the above falls, the tourist crosses the river to *Point Levi*, and then obtains a conveyance for the excursion, passing up the St. Lawrence for a few miles.

DISTANCES FROM QUEBEC TO KAKOUNA, CHICOUTIMI, ETC.

		Miles.
QUEBEC to	GROSSE-ISLE	30
"	ST. THOMAS	10-40
"	River Ouelle	32-72
"	MURRAY BAY	12-84
"	KAMOURASKA	6-90
"	RIVIERE DU LOUP	20-110
"	KAKOUNA	10-120
"	TADOUSAC	130
"	HA-HA BAY	54-184
"	CHICOUTIMI	16-200

TABLE OF DISTANCES. 251

TABLE OF DISTANCES BETWEEN QUEBEC AND KINGSTON via ST. LAWRENCE RIVER.

Places.	Miles.	From Quebec.	Places.	Miles.	From Kingston.
QUEBEC	0	0	KINGSTON	0	0
Richelieu Rapids	45	45	Gananoque	22	22
THREE RIVERS	35	80	(Thousand Islands.)		
Lake St. Peter	30	110	BROCKVILLE	30	52
WILLIAM HENRY	15	125	Maitland	5	57
MONTREAL	45	170	PRESCOTT, or		
LA CHINE, via Canal.	9	179	OGDENSBURGH	7	64
Beauharnois	18	197	Gallop Rapids	6	70
Cascade Rapids	1	198	Point Iroquois	6	76
Split Rock "	3	201	MATILDA	2	78
Cedar "	2	203	Rapid Plat	5	83
COTEAU DU LAC	5	208	WILLIAMSBURG	2	85
Lancaster	16	224	Farren's Point	11	96
St. Regis	13	237	Dickinson's Landing.	4	100
(N. Y. State Line.)			(Long Saut Rapid.)		
CORNWALL	3	240	CORNWALL	10	110
(Long Saut Rapid.)			St. Regis	3	113
Dickinson's Landing.	10	250	(N. Y. State Line.)		
Farren's Point	4	254	Lancaster	13	126
WILLIAMSBURG	11	265	COTEAU DU LAC	16	142
Rapid Plat	2	267	Cedar Rapids	5	147
MATILDA	5	272	Split Rock "	2	149
Point Iroquois	2	274	Cascade "	3	152
Gallop Rapids	6	280	Beauharnois	1	153
PRESCOTT or			LA CHINE	18	171
OGDENSBURGH	6	286	MONTREAL	9	180
Maitland	7	293	WILLIAM HENRY	45	225
BROCKVILLE	5	298	Lake St. Peter	10	235
(Thousand Islands.)			THREE RIVERS	35	270
Gananoque	30	328	Richelieu Rapids	35	305
KINGSTON	22	350	QUEBEC	45	350

DISTANCE from QUEBEC to NIAGARA FALLS, 570 miles. Descent in the St. Lawrence River, from Kingston to Quebec, 234 feet.

Cape Trinity and Point Eternity, Saguenay River.—Canada.

TRIP FROM QUEBEC TO THE SAGUENAY RIVER.

As a trip down the St. Lawrence to Riviere du Loup, Kakouna, and the far-famed river Saguenay has, within the last few years, become a fashionable and exceedingly interesting steamboat excursion, we subjoin an account of such trip made by the author some few years since.

As the steamboat left the wharf, she took a graceful turn up stream, passing a 74 gun-ship of the Royal Navy, and then descended, running close under Point Levi, affording a fine view of the city and citadel of Quebec.

The beautiful line of settlements below the city, on the same side of the river, next attracts attention ; the view in the distance being bounded by hills, apparently elevated 1,500 to 2,000 feet above the waters of the St. Lawrence.

The romantic *Falls of Montmorenci*, seven miles below Quebec, are seen to great advantage from the deck of the steamer, plunging over an almost perpendicular precipice of 240 feet directly into this great river. Immediately below, on the bank of the St. Lawrence, was fought a severe battle between the English and French armies, a short time previous to the capture of Quebec by Gen. Wolfe, in 1759, in which the British were repulsed with considerable loss.

The ISLAND OF ORLEANS is next passed on the left, descending the river through the principal ship channel. This is a fertile tract, 20 miles long by five or six wide, and in part covered with a beautiful growth of forest. It rises from 50 to 100 feet above the water, and the stream of the St. Lawrence being here divided, the aspect of the shores at once reminds you of the scenery of the Hudson River above the Highlands. It has a population of about 7,000 souls, and produces the finest fruit in Lower Canada, excepting that raised in the vicinity of Montreal.

St. Patrick's Hole, eleven miles below Quebec, on the Orleans shore, affords a fine anchorage for vessels of the largest size. It was here, some 30 years ago, that the immense timber ship was built, supposed to be the largest vessel, by far, that ever crossed the Atlantic.

The Parish of St. Laurent, 14 miles below Quebec, is handsomely situated on the southeast side of the island, which is settled exclusively by French Canadians, mostly engaged in cultivating the soil. The dwellings have a remarkably neat look, being one story high, with both roof and sides painted white.

The southeast shore of the St. Lawrence, for many miles below Point Levi, presents a succession of villages and hamlets, consisting each of a cluster of houses with a church standing in the midst, and with its aspect of guardianship and guidance to the families dwelling around, imparting to the landscape a moral expression, which greatly enhances its picturesque beauty.

The vessels usually seen on this part of the St. Lawrence are of the larger class of merchant ships. The arrivals at the port of Quebec average some 1,400 to 1,500 annually, mostly from Great Britain, and besides other colonial produce, they carry back immense quantities of timber and lumber.

Madam Island, 26 miles from Quebec, is one of several small islands lying below Orleans. The river here widens to ten miles, which gradually increases all the way to its mouth; and for most of the distance there are two ship channels, called the *north* and *south channels*, the latter being the best and most navigated.

Cape Tourment, 30 miles below Quebec, is a bold promontory on the northwest side of the river rising to the height of about 2,000 feet, and seen at a great distance. Here the scenery is truly grand.

Grosse Island, opposite Cape Tourment, is the *Quarantine station* for vessels ascending the river, and it has a hospital, a Roman Catholic chapel, and other buildings usually connected with such an establishment.

St Thomas, 40 miles from Quebec, on the southeast shore, is situated at the mouth of a stream called *South River*. The shore of the St. Lawrence is lined with a succession of dwellings for many miles below, with high grounds rising in the distance, beyond which may occasionally be seen the hills formerly claimed by the Americans, as the boundary between the State of Maine and Canada. Here terminates the *Grand Trunk Railway* for the present, but will be extended soon some 100 miles farther, to Trois Pistoles.

Crane Island, 45 miles below Quebec, is fertile and settled. Its north end is adorned with the delightful residence of the *Seigneur*.

Goose Island, 50 miles from Quebec, is owned by the Nuns, and is cultivated as a farm, by tenants.

The Pillars, 60 miles below Quebec, is the name given to several small rocky islets, on one of which stands a light-house. Here the scenery is peculiarly grand and interesting. The vast estuary of the river below looks indeed like an opening to the ocean The shores for some ten miles onward are studded with shining residences, while the hills in the distance, on both sides, resemble very much the scenery bordering the widest part of Lake Champlain.

Sixty-five miles below Quebec is the remarkable channel called the *Traverse*. A floating light guides the mariner by night through this narrow and dangerous passage.

Isle aux Coudres (Isle of Filberts) is a large body of land lying toward the north shore, opposite the Bay of St. Paul's, and about 65 miles from Quebec. It is said that when Jacques Cartier anchored here, on his first voyage of discovery up the St. Lawrence, he gave this island the name it yet bears, from the quantity of filberts, or hazel nuts, which he found there.

St. Anne stands on the southeast shore, on a bay of the same name. Here is a Catholic college and a settlement of considerable size, about 70 miles from Quebec.

As you approach Goose Cape, 75 miles below Quebec, the banks of the river seem to decline in the distance; the river now being free of islands, presents a large expanse of water, here being about 18 miles wide.

MURRAY BAY, 80 miles below Quebec, lies on the northwest side of the St. Lawrence, at the mouth of a river of the same name. This is a fine section of country, producing wheat and other kinds of grain in abundance. Beyond this place is seen a beautiful range of hills, terminating at Cape Eagle and Cape Salmon on the east. This delightful place has become, within a few years, a fashionable summer resort for the Canadians.

KAMOURASKA, situated 90 miles below Quebec, on the southeast side of the river, contains about 1,500 inhabitants, and is surrounded by a fruitful district. Vessels can land here only at high water; at low water, passengers are taken ashore in small boats. In the rear of this village are seen abrupt and sterile hills with little or no verdure. In front are two or three small islands, chiefly resorted to for fishing and bathing, this being a favorite resort, during the summer months, for the citizens of Montreal and Quebec, and is no doubt destined to become a fashionable watering-place, where sea-bathing can be enjoyed by invalids and seekers of pleasure.

About 105 miles below Quebec are the *Pilgrim Islands*, a group of rocky islets which are passed to the right. On the left, a few miles below, is *Hare Island*, near the middle of the river.

The settlement at the RIVIERE DU LOUP, 110 miles below Quebec, on the southeast side of the St. Lawrence, contains about 1,500 inhabitants. Here commences the great road from the St. Lawrence River to the St. John's, by the way of the Madawaska River and settlement.

CACONA or KAKOUNA, 120 miles below Quebec is a fashionable sea-bathing resort.

RED ISLAND lies off the mouth of the Saguenay, this being the first island of the small group met on ascending the St. Lawrence. It is destitute of a light, and has caused many shipwrecks during the prevalence of fogs and storms, so frequent on the lower part of the river and Gulf of St. Lawrence. GREEN ISLAND lies nearly opposite Red Island, on the southeast.

RIVER DU LOUP AND KAKOUNA.

From the pen of a talented Correspondent of the Montreal Gazette.

"RIVIERE DU LOUP is a prettily situated village, taking its name from its river, which river has been made available for the purposes of an extensive saw-mill, a water-power being created by its precipitation over a ridge of rocks, which form the very beautiful Riviere du Loup Falls. There are a few " English" settlers (the word being used in its general sense as distinguishing from " French"), and a clergyman of the Church of England is stationed here. Six miles from Riviere du Loup is the village of " KAKOUNA," to adopt the Indian and more euphonious name, which is effectually supplanting the corruptions of " Cacona" and " Cocona" now in vogue. Kakouna is formed into a village, from the invariable custom of placing the houses on the front of the farms. It is prettily situated on a high ridge, along which passes the highway. Behind the ridge on which the village stands, gently slopes a valley, which is well cultivated, ascending gradually till it attains a considerable elevation at the rear concession, where another village and church are placed. In front of the Kakouna ridge a curtain of trees intervenes between the village and the beach. The view from Kakouna is very pleasing. The river stretches out before it in a noble width of twenty-five miles. The farther shore is a continuous succession of mountains. Amid them opens up the scarcely visible embouchure of the Saguenay. Up the river the pilgrim rocks look grim and solitary. Midway, *Hare Island* rises from the surrounding waters. Below, Kakouna Island projects into the river, forming a bay. Sunset at Kakouna sometimes presents an enchanting spectacle. The gently rippling waters gleam and shine with the sparkling luster derived from the rays of the declining sun. The brilliant coloring and changeful hues of the evening sky appear to rest upon the somber mountains, which, begirt midway with a zone of gray mist, contrast strangely with the gleaming dark blue river which laves their base. Far as the eye can reach, the wide expanse glitters, as if set with gems of every hue—its calm repose unbroken, save by the numerous vessels which, with their white sails floating on the breeze, proclaim the industry of man and his power over the elements, or by the shores of the islets which, bathed in light, rise from its surface. When a storm, too, rises, the river wears a peculiar grandeur, and the mind is irresistibly impressed with a sense of its majesty, and led to a contemplation from nature up to nature's God.

" But, to pass on from this digression, a word or two as to the advantages of Riviere du Loup and Kakouna as watering-places. Now easy of access, with a telegraph at Riviere du Loup and a daily mail, these places are every year becoming more resorted to. There is now much increased accommodation at Kakouna, where are two large and commodious hotels, and a good boarding-house. These contain many visitors, but many families are accommodated in the farm-houses—renting these and providing for themselves. This is a comfortable and independent plan. The houses are improving in accommodation; the practice is beginning to be established of the Canadian families having a smaller house, to which they betake themselves so as to give to the visitors control of the whole of the farm-house. A few home comforts will naturally be wanting, but life in Kakouna is not without its attractions, and the deprivation of a few comforts makes one appreciate them more keenly when regained. A baker leaves regularly at the houses good bread. Beef, poultry, mutton, salmon, herrings, pigeon, sardines, eggs, milk, and butter present a bill of fare that shows there is no danger of starving, while strawberries, raspberries, and blueberries are besides to be had in the greatest abundance. The strawberry grows in peculiar profusion, and of a singularly excellent quality, attaining often a large size. The children of the village reap a harvest while they continue. The sportsman will not find much game, through trout are abundant in the streams and lakes. There are, it may be remarked, attractive places for walks and drives, however. But the main recommendation of the two places in question, is the comparative moderation of the temperature, and the fact that open air exercise can, at all periods of the day, be enjoyed. The heat is never excessive, but the air of the evening is often decidedly cool. On the whole, these watering-places of the St. Lawrence will no doubt continue to attract a steady annual stream of visitors, desirous of luxuriating in a cool atmosphere and enjoying sea-bathing, while other places on the Lower St. Lawrence, presenting equal or greater advantages, will no doubt in due course come into notice, and prove desirable places of resort so soon as the necessary facilities for reaching them shall have been supplied."

As you approach the mouth of the SAGUENAY RIVER, the waters take a very black hue, perceivable for many miles below, and extending far into the St. Lawrence. Just within the mouth of the river, near Tadousac, there is a round mountain peak, called *Tête du Boule*, about 800 feet high, while on the opposite bank there is another bold eminence.

TADOUSAC, 140 miles below Quebec, is situated on the northwest shore of the St. Lawrence, at the mouth of the Saguenay River. This is a post belonging to the Hudson Bay Company.

and is the residence of one of its partners and an agent. They alone are allowed to trade with the Indians in the interior, who occasionally visit this place, but more frequently Chicoutimi, at the head of navigation on the Saguenay, and the post at the Lake of St. John, where some of the company's agents also reside. At Tadousac is a Roman Catholic chapel, a store, and warehouse, and some eight or ten dwellings. Here is erected a flag-staff, surrounded by several pieces of cannon, on an eminence elevated about 50 feet and overlooking the inner harbor, where is a sufficient depth of water to float the largest vessels. This place was early settled by the French, who are said to have here erected the first dwelling built of stone and mortar in Canada, and the remains of it are still to be seen. The view is exceedingly picturesque from this point. The southern shore of the St. Lawrence, may be traced even with the naked eye for many a league—the undulating lines of snow-white cottages stretching far away, both east and west—while the scene is rendered gay and animated by the frequent passage of the merchant vessel plowing its way toward the port of Quebec, or hurrying upon the descending tide to the Gulf—while from the summit of the hill upon which Tadousac stands, the sublime and impressive scenery of the Saguenay rises into view.

We extract from the Report of the Commissioners for exploring the Saguenay, published in 1829, the following :

"Upon landing at Tadousac, we proceeded immediately to examine a few of the geognostical characters of the country. The only place of residence here is erected on a bank of sandy alluvium, elevated about fifty feet above the river, and forming a flat terrace at the base of the mountain, which suddenly emerges at a short distance behind. The rocks of which these mountains are composed is granite, either of a red or gray color, depending upon that of the feldspar. On the shore were seen small deposits of magnetic iron. Here bases were measured, and the requisite angle taken, for determining the height of the most elevated point, on either side of the Saguenay, at its mouth, and this was found to be 912 feet on the westerly side, and 588 on the opposite."

L'ANCE A L'EAU, or WATER HARBOR, situated on the Saguenay, about a half a mile above Tadousac, is the name of a settlement where is an extensive lumber establishment.

The ST. LAWRENCE RIVER, below the mouth of the Saguenay, assumes an imposing appearance, gradually widening until its breadth exceeds one hundred miles.

THE SAGUENAY.

" THIS river has its mouth, according to common computation, 120 miles below Quebec, on the north shore of the St. Lawrence, in latitude 48 deg. 6 min. 38 sec. long., 70 deg. 40 min. west from Greenwich. It discharges a much greater body of water than any other river that falls into the St. Lawrence. Indeed, it is the largest river in North America, the St. Lawrence excepted, east of the Alleghanies.

" It takes the name of Saguenay only below *Lake St. John*, which lies about 120 miles N. by W. of Quebec. From Tadousac, a distance of about 140 miles to the lake, the course of the river is nearly east and west, Tadousac being, as before stated, in lat. 48 deg. 6 min. 38 sec., and the south side of Lake St. John in 48 deg. 23 min. 12 sec., giving only 16 miles to the north of Tadousac."

This lake, which is nearly circular, is about 40 miles across, and it is the center of an extensive region, the waters of which flow into it from the north, the west, and the south, in twelve principal rivers, being discharged to the east by the Saguenay.

The streams which flow into this lake from the south, the west, and the northwest have their sources in a mountainous tract which ranges nearly east and west for a long distance, and then, far in the west, bends northwardly, separating these waters from those which seek the St. Lawrence above Quebec and the Ottawa; and regarding them in their still wider relations, they are part of the extensive range of highlands which divide the basin of the St. Lawrence from that of Hudson Bay and its tributaries.

" The country, the waters of which are discharged into the St. Lawrence by the Saguenay, is more extensive than all the rest of Lower Canada ; but it has till lately contained, probably, not more than a few hundred Indian families, who live by hunting and fishing, and exchange their surplus with lessees of the King's Post, for a few articles of imported produce.

"The passage of the waters of the Saguenay from below the Ha-Ha Bay to the St. Lawrence, a distance of fifty miles, is one of the wonders of nature. They penetrate through a mountainous tract, composed of sienite granite, forming an immense canal in many places, with banks of perpendicular rocks rising from a thousand to fifteen hundred feet above the surface of the river, which is from a hundred to a hundred and fifty fathoms deep nearly the whole way, and from a mile to three miles broad. The power and pride of man is as much humbled in some parts of this tremendous chasm, as in the immediate presence of Niagara Falls. In many places the largest vessel may run close to the perpendicular rocks, with 100 fathoms water. There are, however, several coves with good anchorage. In Ha-Ha Bay the navy of England might ride, in from five to eighty fathoms. At twelve miles below Chicoutimi, which is distant 68 miles from Tadousac, the spring tide rises 18 feet, and there is from 10 to 50 fathoms at low water. The tide rises and the river is navigable seven miles above Chicoutimi, where the rapids of the outlet of Lake St. John commence. At this point a range of highlands crosses the Saguenay, extending along the head waters of the Malbay, the Gouffre, the Jacques Cartier, St. Anne, Batiscan, and St. Maurice, and forming the south and western side of the basin of Lake St. John, with the Hudson Bay highlands on the north and east.

"It is only within a few years that there have been any agricultural settlers in the Saguenay country. At present there are a few hundred families of *squatters* from the north shore below Quebec, chiefly induced to go in by employment in lumbering, etc., for Mr. Price's numerous saw-mills. At Ha-Ha Bay there is a church, and about 150 families, and openings are made at various places on the river. The soil is of disintegrated clay and granite, with limestone in some places. The general level of the land above Ha-Ha Bay, as far as the eye can reach from the river, is not higher than the island of Orleans, although more broken. The timber mixed, hard and soft, and of a middling growth. The climate is milder, if anything, than at Quebec. With the exception of the ridge crossing below Lake St. John, already mentioned, the country to a great extent round the lake, but particularly on the southwest side, is of the same character.

"On entering the Saguenay from Tadousac, which is about one mile wide at its mouth, the hills soon rise abruptly from the water's edge, from 500 to 1,000 feet above the tide-way, presenting an appearance somewhat similar to the entrance from the north into the ' Highlands' of the Hudson River, with which most travelers are familiar, divested, however, of all appearance of habitation for many miles, and the Saguenay averaging twice the width of the Hudson."

TETE DU BOULE, a round mountain peak, rises on the north side of the river, about one mile from its mouth. Here the rocks and hills are mostly bare, but the verdure increases as you ascend.

About three miles from Tadousac, the river inclines to the north for a few miles, then resumes its western course to Chicoutimi, a distance of sixty-eight miles from the St. Lawrence, and being in many places three miles in width, with a great depth of water, until you arrive at the bar, about sixty miles from its mouth.

The TWO PROFILES, seen on the north shore, a few miles up, and elevated several hundred feet above the water, bear a striking resemblance to the human face.

ST. LOUIS ISLAND presents a rocky and rugged appearance. It lies eighteen miles above Tadousac, and may be passed by large vessels on either side. Here, it is said, fine trout may be taken in large quantities.

At the mouth of the river Marguerite, on the north shore, and at St. John's Bay, on the south, are lumber establishments —the latter 28 miles above the mouth of the Saguenay.

At the distance of 34 miles from Tadousac, on the south shore of the river, are two enormous masses of rock called ETERNITY POINT and CAPE TRINITY. They rise from the water's edge to the height of some 1,500 feet, and so abruptly that they can almost be touched with the hand from the deck of the passing steamer. The aspect of these mountain cliffs is beyond expression grand. No man can pass along their base, and lift his eyes up their vast height, without awe--without experiencing the most intense emotions of sublimity. Sheltered between them is a lovely recess of the shore called Trinity Cove, its sequestered and lonely beauty enhanced by its strong contrast with the wild grandeur of the rest of the scene. (*See Engraving.*)

TRINITY CAPE takes its name from the three peaks of its summit, bearing some resemblance to three human heads ; and the name of ETERNITY POINT is abundantly indicated by the huge pile of ever-during rock of which it is composed. The whole scene—the majestic river, a hundred fathoms deep, rolling along the base and in the shadows of the vast and beetling cliffs, bearing on their rocky fronts the impress of Almighty power and everlasting duration—the whole scene at this place is unsurpassed for its magnificence and solemn beauty.

Continuing up the Saguenay, STATUE POINT is next passed, where formerly was to be seen a rock in a niche, high above the water, which resembled a huge human figure. The niche is still visible, but the figure has fallen into the deep water.

The TABLEAU is an upright rock, rising almost perpendicularly from the water, to the height of several hundred feet, situated on the south shore.

The scenery in this vicinity, and for several miles below, is exceedingly grand and picturesque—high and precipitous hills, clothed with a stunted growth of forest trees, and all around a wild solitude, unbroken by a sign of habitation or life, except occasionally a huge porpoise showing his back above the wave, and the water-fowl peculiar to these northern latitudes.

Fifty-eight miles from Tadousac opens the HA-HA, or GREAT BAY, as it is sometimes called. It is entered on the left, while the Saguenay proper comes down on the right. At the head of the bay there is a large settlement, with several extensive saw-mills.

The Bay of Ha-Ha—a name by no means euphonious or worthy of the locality—contains a numerous population for so new a country. Two villages appear at the farther extremity, the population whereof must number at least five hundred souls; it is situated about sixty miles above the entrance, and so closely does it resemble the Saguenay, that it is only when the traveler has arrived at its extremity that the mistake is perceived. The streams which flow into this bay furnish the various saw-mills with the power of preparing deals for the

English market—and it is not an uncommon occurrence to behold three or four square-rigged vessels busily engaged loading on English account. All the lumber establishments throughout the country are owned by the firm of Messrs. Price & Co., of Quebec, and although they entered the trade in the first instance with the intent of furthering their own interests, the result has been that the men they employed have become settlers, and brought into cultivation a large tract of arable land.

From the entrance to Ha-Ha Bay to Chicoutimi, a distance of about twelve miles, the banks of the river are less rugged and are clothed with more verdure, and openings may now be seen on both shores, with occasionally a habitation. About eight miles below Chicoutimi there is a bar, which can be passed by vessels of a large size only when the tide is up, this being the first impediment to navigation in ascending this noble river, which for grandeur of scenery and depth of water may vie with any other stream on the American continent.

CHICOUTIMI, 68 miles from Tadousac, situated at the junction of the Chicoutimi River with the Saguenay, where is a picturesque water-fall, is another post occupied by the Hudson Bay Company, which has a resident agent stationed here. The settlement now contains an extensive saw-mill, a few dwellings, and a venerable-looking Roman Catholic chapel, of small dimensions, erected in 1727. It is one of those stations where, in former days, the indefatigable Jesuits established a home for themselves; a church yet remains to attest their religious zeal. This edifice is believed to have been one of the first erected in Canada. The locality selected is singularly picturesque and romantic. On one side the Saguenay pours down its mighty flood, the shores on either side covered to the water's edge with the most luxuriant foliage, while, on the other side, a safe and commodious bay receives the mountain torrent of the Chicoutimi River.

The church, a peculiarly agreeable object in so remote a spot, stands about 100 yards from the margin of the stream, in the center of a plat of green-sward set out with shrubbery, and forest trees crown the rising ground in the rear. Here assemble at stated periods the children of the soil; some from the region of the far north—the faith which their fathers were taught in earlier ages leading them to reverence a spot hallowed by traditional associations.

The steamboat navigation of the Saguenay ends here, as the river above this is obstructed by rapids and falls. Fifty miles above Chicoutimi, the river issues from LAKE ST. JOHN, which is a fine expanse of water of about 30 miles in length, and, in the widest part, the same in breadth, its superficial area being over 500 square miles. The rivers *Mistasine*, *Assuapmoussoin*, *Peribonea*, and *Ouatchoanish*, all of which are large streams, and many smaller ones, empty into Lake St. John, and as its only outlet is the Saguenay, which also receives many considerable streams in its course, the great depth and volume of water in that river may be thus accounted for. A *portage road*, or foot-path, runs from Chicoutimi to the Hudson Bay Company's station on Lake St. John.

Lake St. John, the *Saguenay*, and the rivers which they receive, abound in excellent fish, consisting of white fish, bass, trout, doré, carp, pike, eels, and others; the favorite salmon, during the spring and summer months, ascends the Saguenay for a considerable distance, and are taken in large quantities and shipped to Quebec; also cured and sent to European markets.

"The region of the Saguenay can not long remain silent and unoccupied. It is destined to become the home of an active and enterprising race. The climate is well adapted to the purposes of agriculture, and the virgin soil can not fail to repay the labors of the farmer. The aspect of the country around Chicoutimi is divested of the rugged and rocky character which distinguishes the banks of the Saguenay for the first 50 miles, and as the traveler advances inland, the appearance of the country indicates a superior soil—while the climate in the vicinity of Lake St. John approaches very closely to that of the Montreal district."

Taken altogether, few excursions can afford more interest to the tourist and seeker of pleasure, than a visit to Chicoutimi and its vicinity. Besides having a view of the magnificent scenery of the St. Lawrence, here may be seen a picturesque water-fall, and if fond of angling or hunting, the visitor may enjoy himself to his heart's content—surrounded by a vast wilderness, as yet almost unbroken by the haunts of man.

MURRAY BAY—TADOUSAC—HA-HA BAY, ETC.

The following letter was written by a gentleman of Philadelphia :

"On Wednesday morning, 25th July, 1855, we left Quebec for the lower St. Lawrence and Saguenay rivers. At eight o'clock, precisely, the steamer Saguenay shot out from the landing, and rounding under the stern of the French frigate *La Capricieuse* made her way down the St. Lawrence. The tin roofs and spires of Quebec gradually grew smaller in the distance, and the blue tops of the Green Mountains, miles away in Vermont, broke on the sight. As we steamed down the river, we had a fine view of Quebec with its precipitous hill, crowned with battlements, whose immense guns were leveled at us in the harbor. The magnificent basin before the city was dotted with craft laden with other tributaries of the St. Lawrence. A few miles below Quebec the river is divided by the island of Orleans, which is at first hilly and covered with trees, but as we pass along, its shores becomes flat and under cultivation. Its lands are held under the old French tenure, and its inhabitants are Canadian French. A singularity of division in lands which the tourist will observe through Eastern Canada, presents itself very prominently in this island. The lands of the French population, at the owner's death, are divided equally among the children; and in order that each child may have a portion of the river front, a farm is cut up into narrow strips running sometimes a mile in length by twenty yards in breadth. Upon the front the house is built, and the island shore is therefore a continuous line of little wooden houses, backed by cultivated fields

"In about an hour after passing the island of Orleans, we came to Grosse Isle, upon which is located the Quarantine Station of Canada. Several large vessels were anchored in the stream, undergoing the precautionary measures against infectious or contagious diseases. Ample accommodations are erected upon the shore for emigrants suffering from ship-fever or similar disorders, and the Lazaretto arrangements of Quebec seem to be of the most perfect kind. On the mainland, behind Grosse Isle, Cape Tourment lifts its cloud-capped summit 1,800 feet into the air. The boat stopped at *Murray Bay* to land passengers and freight. This place seems to be the Cape May of Canada, where the citizens of Quebec and Montreal resort in great numbers, for salt-water bathing. The long pier that stretches into the river was crowded with ladies expecting friends and relatives by the boat. During the summer, the ladies of Canada, of every class, when at watering-places, wear straw hats, with rims of enormous breadth, which afford a marked contrast to the minute fixtures which American ladies affect. The scene was highly picturesque, and called forth much complimentary notice from traveling Americans who were aboard. We arrived at *Riviere du Loup*, another watering-place, about dusk, and anchored in the stream to await daylight. At three o'clock we again started for the mouth of the Saguenay, which is directly across the St. Lawrence from Riviere du Loup. The St. Lawrence is twenty-one miles wide at this point. About five o'clock we reached *Tadousac*, which is situated on the point of land formed by the confluence of the Saguenay and St. Lawrence At this place the French first settled in Canada, and a little red-spired church was pointed out to us as being the first church erected north of the St. Lawrence, and the oldest ecclesiastical edifice in America.

"Leaving the St. Lawrence at this point, we plunged between high ridges into the Saguenay, and continued for five hours to float over its mirror-like expanse. It is a singular fact that the depth of the Saguenay is about seven hundred feet greater than that of the St. Lawrence, into which it empties, and in certain parts a fathom line of one thousand feet fails to touch bottom. The perpendicular mountains that hem it in, rise directly out of the water, without an intervening shore, and the steamboat can glide rapidly along within a yard of the solid land. *Cape Eternity*, about thirty-five miles above Tadousac, is one of the most striking objects upon the route. It is a huge mass of granite, without flaw or fissure, rising eighteen hundred feet in the air. Hardy birches and pines cling tenaciously to its barren sides, giving the only indication of life in the vicinity. The boat arrived at this point while we were at breakfast, and the pilot ran into a little cove beside it, so as to give the passengers a view of it from every side, then rounding directly beneath the overhanging mass, we shot out into the stream to gaze at its heavy summit from the distance. There was a feeling of indescribable awe in watching the receding boulder, as we sped up the stream, and many an admiring gaze was flung backward, even after a sudden bend in the river had hid it from our view. Tête du Boule, the Two Profiles, the Tableau,

Cape Trinity, and Statue Point, are each attractive objects that excite the admiration of the tourist.

"Near eleven o'clock in the forenoon we arrived before the little town which lies at the head of *Ha-Ha Bay*, about 60 miles from the St. Lawrence, and having dropped our anchor, the passengers were sent ashore by the ship's boats. The town is merely an establishment for lumbering purposes, and is owned by William Price, Esq., of Quebec, who is the most extensive lumber merchant in Canada. All the saw-mills upon the Saguenay belong to this gentleman. He keeps constantly employed at his various mills about 3,000 persons, and freights over 100 vessels annually with lumber. As only a few minutes were allowed us, before starting on our return to the St. Lawrence, we preferred remaining upon the steamer's deck and inspecting the town and adjacent country with the aid of a lorgnette. About Ha-Ha Bay the cliffs almost disappear and some indications of agricultural attempts are manifest, but a sterile soil and a bleak atmosphere always militate with tillage and farming in this region The Governor-General of Canada, Sir Edmund Head, was expected to visit the Saguenay on this trip, and as we ran up before the town a salute of guns was fired, and the English colors run up the flagstaff on shore In return for the compliment, Capt. Simard decorated his steamer with flags of almost every nation, and we left Ha-Ha Bay about noon, in a gala attire of floating bunting. At five o'clock in the afternoon we touched at Tadousac, and in two hours after anchored at the pier of Riviere du Loup, to wait for the morning. Early on Friday, July 27, we started for Quebec, and made the 114 miles before four o'clock in the afternoon.

"The greater part of American tourists make a great mistake in omitting the Saguenay River. They miss the finest scenery on this continent, which they can view by an additional expense of $12 only. The fare on board the boat is of excellent quality, and the berths large and comfortable. It is worth a visit to the Saguenay to taste the salmon, that but an hour before was gliding in its native element. As a matter of information to those wishing to make the trip in future seasons, we may say that a thick over-coat is an absolute necessity From eleven o'clock in the morning until four in the afternoon the temperature is agreeable, but not too warm; during the other hours of the day and night it will compare exactly with our November. Coming from warmer climates, the tourist can not be too careful to prepare for sudden changes of temperature. We can not close our imperfect sketch of the Saguenay without a word of thanks to Capt. Simard, who commands the steamer Saguenay. To our numerous questions he politely returned us full and satisfactory answers, and we are greatly indebted to him for much valuable information We cordially commend him and his boat to the attentions of all American travelers who may hereafter visit Quebec. From all classes of Canadians, both French and English, we met with the politest treatment, and can vouch for their hospitality and good-will. In conversation with numerous intelligent persons from Quebec and Montreal, we discover that the American character is greatly admired in Canada, and an earnest hope is indulged that the amicable commercial relations now in process of formation between the two countries will tend to introduce some of our finer national characteristics into Canadian affairs. While they are eminently loyal to their sovereign, they yet rejoice in the active energy of the Yankee race, and esteem it a privilege to live in such close juxtaposition to a nationality whose rapid rise and hardy vigor reflect honor on the Anglo-Saxon blood. The kindly feeling beyond doubt is reciprocated in the United States, and that, too, from a nobler motive than commercial and mercantile gain—from the fraternal feeling inseparable from nations descended from a common stock. Whether or not the time will ever come when Colonial Canada will be a sovereign State, and part of our rapidly expanding confederacy, remains to be seen. If the course of events should take such a turn, we will acquire a territory rich in mineral and agricultural resources, and one geographically adapted for unexampled greatness; if not, we are sure of a faithful ally and a firm unwavering friend." J. M. G.

ANTICOSTI.

ANTICOSTI, about 400 miles below Quebec, is a large and important island in the Gulf of St. Lawrence, lying W.S.W. and E.S.E., in the widest part of its estuary, between the meridians of 61° 45′ and 64° 15′ W., and dividing the entrance of the river into two channels, from twenty to forty miles in width. It is about 125 miles in length; its extreme breadth is 30 miles; its superficial area 1,530.000 acres. Its surface is in general low, and covered with forests of stunted fir, white cedar, and poplar, or alluvial flats clothed with cranberry and blueberry bushes; but the timber is of inferior quality, and the soil is mostly poor. Bears, foxes, hares, martins, sea-otters, partridges, curlews, plover, and snipe are numerous. The geological formation is a shell limestone mixed with clay, and in some places wholly composed of encrinites. The northern coast is bold and high, presenting magnificent limestone cliffs, which sometimes rise to the height of 500 feet. The severity of the climate is so great that any grain is usually nipped in the bud. In the month of June, ice of considerable thickness is frequently formed during the night; and summer is always far advanced before the snow disappears. Winter commences in the early part of November, and continues till the middle of March; the thermometer ranging during this season from 20° above to 20° below zero. The shores are then surrounded with ice, and all communication with them is cut off. Its shores present a few small creeks, but throughout an extent of 300 miles there is neither bay nor harbor sufficient to protect ships; while the powerful stream setting constantly from the St. Lawrence, the shoals which surround this island, and the heavy snow-storms which here occur in the fall of the year, with its position across the mouth of the river, render it the frequent scene of shipwrecks, and the sailing past it " the worst part of the voyage to or from Canada." (Bonnycastle.) "The bearings of its extreme points are as follows: west point, N. lat. 49° 52' 29", W. long. 64° 36' 54"; variation 22° 55' W. East point, N. lat. 49° 8' 30", W. long. 61° 44' 56"; variation 24° 38' W. North point, N. lat. 49° 57' 38", W. long. 65° 14' 1". Southwest point, N. lat. 49° 23', W. long. 63° 43' An elevated and magnificent light-house, with a revolving light, now occupies this point of the island; and another has been erected on the E. coast. Spring tides rise ten feet; neaps, seven feet. This island formerly belonged to Labrador, but was annexed to Lower Canada in 1825, and now forms part of the county of Saguenay. Its name is probably a corruption of the Indian name *Naticostee*. It is first noticed in 1535, by Cartier, who gave it the name of Assumption." (Bouchette.)

GULF OF ST. LAWRENCE.—On passing along the south side of the island of Anticosti, entering the Gulf of St. Lawrence, the shores of GASPE are seen in the distance. This is an important district and headland, jutting out into the Gulf, and running round into the *Bay of Chaleurs*, comprehending 350 miles of coast; the whole extent is said to abound with fish of different kinds, and during the fishing season a large number of vessels and men are engaged in taking and curing fish for exportation.

Below where the Saguenay joins the St. Lawrence, the distance from shore to shore across the latter stream exceeds twenty miles, and the width goes on increasing till it expands to forty miles, from Cape Chatte to Cape des Monts Pelles, some three hundred miles below Quebec. From thence it goes on still further expanding, till it reaches the breadth of about 120 miles from shore to shore, in a line drawn from the extreme point of Gaspe due north across the western edge of the island of Anticosti, and so on to the coast of Labrador.

The grand trip from the Upper Lakes to the Gulf of St. Lawrence is thus spoken of by a late writer, on terminating the voyage: "Through this magnificent mouth of the river we passed into the *Gulf of St. Lawrence*, having thus traced the noble stream, from the island of Mackinac, in the strait of Michilimackinac, at the head of Lake Huron, down to the island of Anticosti, a distance of at least 2,000 miles, through a chain of the most splendid lakes in the world, and with almost every variety of scenery along its majestic course."

PROPOSED CANAL FROM THE HEAD OF NAVIGATION ON THE SAGUENAY RIVER TO LAKE ST. JOHN.

A MEETING was recently held at Ha-Ha Bay, on the Saguenay, for the purpose of agitating for the construction of a ship canal between that interesting village and the Lake St. John. The country in the vicinity of the lake is covered with valuable timber, and is eminently adapted for settlement, while the streams abound in salmon, trout, and other kinds of fish of a delicious flavor.

RAILROAD AND STEAMBOAT ROUTES,

From NEW YORK to Niagara Falls, Toronto, Montreal, Quebec, and the White Mountains of New Hampshire, forming a round trip by returning *via* Portland and Boston to New York; or *via* Lake Champlain.

ROUTES AND DISTANCES.

New York to Albany, *steamboat route*	150 miles.
Albany to Niagara Falls, *railroad route*	306 "
Niagara Falls to Toronto, Canada, *steamboat route*	50 "
Toronto to Montreal, *railroad or steamer*	333 "
Montreal to Quebec, " "	170 "
Quebec or Montreal to White M'ts, *railroad route*	202 "
White Mountains to Portland, Me., " "	91 "
Portland to Boston, " "	108 "
Boston to New York, *railroad and steamer*	230 "
Total Distance	1,640 miles.

RETURNING *via* LAKE CHAMPLAIN.

New York to Montreal, *via* Niagara Falls	839 miles.
Montreal to Saratoga Springs	213 "
Saratoga Springs to New York	182 "
Total Distance	1,234 miles.

NEW YORK TO MONTREAL, *via* SYRACUSE and OSWEGO.

New York to Syracuse, *railroad route*	298 miles.
Syracuse to Oswego, " "	35 "
Oswego to Cape Vincent, or the "Thousand Islands," *steamboat route*	60 "
Thousand Islands to Ogdensburgh	65 "
Ogdensburgh to Montreal	120 "
Total Distance, New York to Montreal	578 miles.
Returning *via* Lake George and Saratoga Springs	400 "
Total Distance, round Trip	978 miles.

GRAND PLEASURE EXCURSION
FROM NEW YORK TO NIAGARA FALLS, TORONTO, MONTREAL, ETC.

PLEASURE travelers leaving New York at 7 o'clock A.M., or 6 o'clock P.M., by steamboats running on the Hudson River, can leave Albany almost immediately after their arrival, and proceed direct to *Schenectady*, 17 miles; *Utica*, 95 miles; *Rome*, 109 miles; or *Syracuse*, 148 miles from Albany, *via* New York Central Railroad.

At Schenectady the *Saratoga and Schenectady Railroad* commences and extends north to Saratoga Springs, 22 miles.

At Utica the *Black River and Utica Railroad* commences and extends north, 16 miles, to Trenton Falls, and thence to Boonville, a total distance of 35 miles. The above railroad, when finished, will run to Clayton, situated on the St. Lawrence River, 109 miles from Utica.

At Rome commences the *Watertown and Rome Railroad*, extending northward to Cape Vincent, 97 miles, forming a direct line of travel to Kingston and other places in Canada.

At Syracuse the New York Central Railroad is intersected by the *Syracuse and Binghamton Railroad* and *Oswego and Syracuse Railroad;* the latter railroad running north to the city of Oswego, 35 miles. Fare from Albany to Syracuse, $3. Usual time, 6 hours. Fare from Syracuse to Oswego, $1. Usual time, one hour and thirty minutes.

Travelers can proceed by railroad to *Rochester*, 81 miles from Syracuse, and there take a steamer for Toronto or Lewiston, or proceed direct through Lockport to the *Suspension Bridge* or *Niagara Falls*. From Niagara Falls, passengers desiring to go to Montreal or Quebec are conveyed by steamer from Lewiston or Niagara, Can., through Lake Ontario to *Kingston* or *Cape Vincent*, and thence down the St. Lawrence River

15*

Another new and favorite mode of traveling for those who wish to avoid the lake travel is to proceed to *Toronto*, and take the cars of the *Grand Trunk Railway* for Kingston. There take an American or British steamer for *Montreal*.

Steamers of a large class run daily from Oswego morning and afternoon. The morning boats leave Oswego for Sacket's Harbor, Kingston, Ogdensburgh, etc.; while the afternoon boats run direct to Charlotte, at the mouth of the Genesee River, and from thence direct for Toronto, Lewiston, etc., affording travelers a choice of routes if going *west* to Detroit, Chicago, etc., or if proceeding *north* to Kingston, Montreal, etc. Pleasure travelers are also conveyed direct to Niagara Falls, Buffalo, etc.

SACKET'S HARBOR, 45 miles from Oswego, is the first place at which the passenger boats stop to land and receive passengers; usual time, 3 hours.

KINGSTON, 40 miles farther, is usually reached in about the same time, where passengers can stop, or proceed direct down the St. Lawrence River, passing the "Thousand Islands" and magnificent rapids by daylight.

The American steamers, on leaving Kingston, run through the *Kingston Channel* to Clayton or French Creek, and thence to Ogdensburgh. The British steamers run on the north or *Canadian Channel*, stopping at Gananoque, Brockville, Prescott, etc., on the downward and upward trips.

Kingston being the best point for pleasure travelers to start from in order to see the "*Thousand Islands*" to advantage, we subjoin the following description of the trip to Prescott and Ogdensburgh, performed in June, 1857. The American steamers leave Kingston at about 3 o'clock P.M., descending the St. Lawrence, stopping at Ogdensburgh, 62 miles; while the British mail line of steamers leave at 6 o'clock A.M., running through to *Montreal*, 180 miles, by daylight.

On leaving Kingston the steamer runs between Howe and Grand Islands, both belonging to Canada, for a distance of about 15 miles. When at the foot of the former island, the steamer veers westward, passing through a beautiful group of small islands, and approaches GANANOQUE, 20 miles from Kingston. Several light-houses or beacons have recently been erected by the Canadian authorities to mark this intricate channel.

Other beautiful groups of islands are passed below Gananoque, when the *Fiddler's Elbow* is approached, 12 miles distant. Here is a light-house and another group of small islands.

ALEXANDRIA BAY, 34 miles below Kingston, is passed in sight on the right, the British steamer passing through the middle channel of the river. This favorite summer resort is reached by the American line of steamers.

The *Sisters* and *Scotch Bonnet* are a pretty group of islands situated in the middle channel, some 8 or 10 miles above Brockville. Here the stream of the river begins to narrow, and soon the labyrinth of islands are passed by the descending steamer.

The pleasure is greatly enhanced by an observing traveler to vary his routes, when an opportunity offers, in voyaging through the Lakes and down the St. Lawrence River, thus not only affording an opportunity to see the different points of interest on the route, but also see a different class of passengers—the Southern planter, the Northern financier, and the English or French Canadian resident, each possessing distinctive characters; while the intelligent ladies are always alike attractive.

BROCKVILLE, 52 miles below Kingston, is a fine Canadian town, situated immediately below the commencement of the Thousand Islands. The *Brockville and Ottawa Railroad*, now in progress of construction, will afford a direct and speedy route to the Upper Ottawa country.

PRESCOTT and OGDENSBURGH, 12 miles below Brockville, are important towns situated opposite each other, being closely connected by two steam ferries. Here navigation for sail vessels may be said to terminate, while steamers descend the rapids with the utmost safety.

For a further description of the Rapids of the St. Lawrence, see pages 169 and 174.

TRIP FROM MONTREAL TO QUEBEC.

On arriving at Montreal, one of the most important and interesting towns in Canada, the traveler has a choice of hotels, where every desired comfort can be obtained. The drive round the city and the mountain is one of great interest, and should be enjoyed by every intelligent traveler. The objects of interest are numerous and picturesque.

On leaving Montreal by steamer, or *via* the *Grand Trunk Railway*, the journey is one of varied interest; by the latter route passing over the Victoria Bridge, one of the grandest structures of its kind in America. If by steamer, after leaving the wharf, *St Helen's Island*, a military depôt, is soon passed, being in part covered with a rich growth of forest-trees, while the fort and buildings on the north end are seen to advantage.

A number of low islands are next passed on descending the stream, when the beautiful village of Varennes is soon reached and passed, situated on the right bank of the stream. Here is a mineral spring of some celebrity and a good public house.

The north point of the island of Montreal and northern branch of the Ottawa River are passed about 16 miles below Montreal, where are to be seen several picturesque islands, concealing in part the mouth of the Ottawa.

Here the St. Lawrence assumes its most majestic appearance for a stretch of several miles, the stream being from two to four miles in width—flowing onward in majestic grandeur with here and there a square-rigged sail vessel and immense timber rafts, such as are alone seen on the lower St. Lawrence being on their way to Quebec from the Ottawa River.

Before reaching Sorel, or William Henry, the stream contracts to about one mile in width, with more elevated banks. The river Richelieu, the outlet of Lake Champlain, enters the St

Lawrence at *Sorel*, or *William Henry*, 45 miles below Montreal, this being the first regular landing for the Royal Mail Line. Here is situated an old and handsome town, enlivened by English and French residents and the busy Yankee, who is slowly making his way into the lower Province of Canada.

After leaving Sorel a number of islands are again passed, and the steamer soon enters the broad waters of *Lake St. Peter*, an expansion of the St. Lawrence. Here again the square-rigged vessels, the timber rafts, and the more fleet steamer may often be seen threading their way up or down the river.

Three Rivers, 90 miles below Montreal and 80 miles above Quebec, is an old and important town, being advantageously situated at the mouth of the river St. Maurice, on the left bank of the river.

This is considered the head of tide-waters on the St. Lawrence, although the *Richelieu Rapids* are below, where is a strong current when the tide is receding, the river flowing over a rocky and dangerous channel for several miles—the stream alternately running to the right and the left, with banks somewhat elevated. *Point aux Trembles*, on the left bank, is a bold headland, which, when passed, the stream again widens for a number of miles—the shores for the entire distance of 170 miles being dotted with picturesque residences of the French habitans and churches of the Roman Catholic persuasion.

Cape Rouge, 10 miles above Quebec, is another interesting point, situated on the left bank of the river. Next comes in sight Point Levi and the frowning fortress of Quebec—then opens the Lower Town, with its numerous shipping, its steam-tugs, and ferry-boats—altogether affording, during the summer months, one of the most grand and enlivening scenes to be witnessed on the continent of America.

Without entering into a description of Quebec, which is fully described in its proper place, we will allude to the hotels now open for the accommodation of tourists. Russell's Hotel in Palace Street, Upper Town, is an old, popular house; while the St. Louis Hotel, kept by W. Russell, Lewis Street, near the

Durham Terrace, is a new and popular resort for pleasure seekers visiting Quebec.

There are several other good hotels in both the Upper and Lower Town, while Norman's Victoria Hotel at Point Levi, opposite Quebec, is also a favorite resort for both English and American visitors. It is situated near the terminus of the Grand Trunk Railway, from whence steamers are almost constantly crossing to Quebec, affording an opportunity to see the fortress and city, together with the adjacent country, from Cape Rouge to the island of Orleans.

The trip from Quebec to the Lower St. Lawrence and Saguenay Rivers is fully described in another part of this work. See page 253.

RETURN TO MONTREAL.

ON leaving Quebec for Montreal, *via* Grand Trunk Railway, passengers can proceed at 6 A.M. or 4 P.M., crossing the St. Lawrence by steamer to Point Levi, one or two miles distant. Near the depôt is situated the Victoria Hotel, a well-kept public house, surrounded by handsome grounds.

This is a most speedy route, the cars going through from city to city in six hours; 170 miles. The first station is the *Chaudiere Junction*, 8 miles from Point Levi; here the Chaudiere River is passed a few rods above the romantic falls on this stream, the spray arising from the waters alone being visible from the cars. For the next 40 or 50 miles the country is level and uninviting, with only a few residences in sight, being for the most part clothed with a stunted forest.

STANFOLD, 55 miles from Point Levi, is a small settlement surrounded by good farming land, which continues until *Warwick*, *Danville*, and *Richmond* are reached and passed. At the latter station the passenger trains usually connect with trains from Portland and Montreal, making this an important point on this great railway of Canada. Passengers bound for the White Mountains or Portland Me there change cars.

After leaving Richmond for Montreal, the line of the road descends toward the St. Lawrence, passing through several thriving villages.

St. Hyacinthe, 30 miles from Montreal, is handsomely situated on the Yamaska River, about 40 miles above its entrance into the Lake St. Peter.

St. Hilaire, 17 miles from Longueuil, is another delightful village, situated near Beloeil Mountain, a bold eminence rising from the plain to near one thousand feet in height, being plainly seen from Montreal. A most beautiful lake lies near its summit; the outlet flows westward into the Sorel River.

Other hills or mountains are seen in this vicinity besides the one above mentioned. *Mount Rouge* and *Mount Johnson* rise on the south, while *Boucherville Mountain*, also adorned by a most beautiful lake, lies a few miles northwest of St. Hilaire, forming altogether a most interesting and picturesque group of hills or mountains, being visible from the St. Lawrence River for many miles, which, in connection with *Mount Royal*, on the island of Montreal, are most grand and attractive objects to the observant traveler.

The *Sorel* or *Richelieu River*, the outlet of Lake Champlain, is next passed, and the traveler soon arrives at *Longueuil*, where a commodious steam ferry-boat plies regularly to and from Montreal, landing near the center of the city, where cabs and carriages are always to be found in readiness running to the different hotels.

The Grand Trunk Railway also affords the most speedy and direct route to the White Mountains of New Hampshire, as well as to the Ottawa River and Upper St. Lawrence and Lake country.

Montreal to Island Pond, Vt.............. 143 miles.
Montreal to White Mountains, N. H........ 201 "
Montreal to Portland, Me................. 292 "

Montreal to Prescott, C. W............... 113 miles.
Montreal to Ottawa City, *via* Prescott.... 167 "
Montreal to Toronto, C. W................ 333 "

MONTREAL TO BOSTON AND NEW YORK.

Passengers can leave Montreal for Boston or New York, and proceed, *via Champlain and St. Lawrence Railroad*, to Rouse's Point, N. Y., a distance of 45 miles, where they have the choice of proceeding by steamer to Plattsburgh, Burlington, etc., or take the cars of the *Vermont and Canada Railroad*, and proceed direct through by rail to Boston or New York, or any intermediate station.

Trains of cars also run twice daily from Montreal, *via Montreal and Lachine* and *Montreal and New York Railroads*, direct to Plattsburgh, N. Y., a distance of 62 miles, here connecting with steamers running to Burlington, Ticonderoga, and Whitehall.

On arriving at Burlington by any of the above routes, passengers have the choice of proceeding by steamer, or take the cars of the *Vermont Central Railroad*, if bound for the White Mountains or Boston; while the *Rutland and Burlington Railroad* runs both toward Boston and New York, forming a link in the great line of railroads running from the Eastern and Northern States into Canada.

On leaving Burlington by steamer, proceeding toward Whitehall, a most magnificent view is obtained, in a clear day, of the *Green Mountains* of Vermont and the *Adirondack Group* of New York, lying in the counties of Essex and Clinton. The latter are the most elevated peaks, rising to the height of 5,467 feet above the ocean; while the Mansfield Mountain peak of Vermont rises to the height of 4,279 feet, there being lesser peaks on both sides of the lake in full view. The surface of Lake Champlain is elevated 90 feet above tide-waters of the ocean, while Lake George is elevated 243 feet—there being a fall of 153 in the outlet of the latter lake within the distance of 4 miles.

Lake Champlain and the landings on its shore are fully described in a preceding part of this work. See page 201.

RAILROAD ROUTES.

ROUTES OF TRAVEL FROM MONTREAL TO BOSTON

RAILROAD ROUTE via VERMONT CENTRAL and NORTHERN (N. H.) RAILROADS.

MONTREAL to ROUSE'S POINT, N. Y.	44 miles.
Rouse's Point to Montpelier, Vt.	82 "
Montpelier to White River Junction*	62 "
White River Junction to Concord, N. H.	69 "
CONCORD to BOSTON	73 "

Total Distance..................330 miles.

MONTREAL TO BOSTON, via BURLINGTON, RUTLAND, AND BELLOWS FALLS.

MONTREAL to ROUSE'S POINT, N. Y.	44 miles.
Rouse's Point to Burlington, Vt.	56 "
Burlington to Rutland, Vt.	67 "
Rutland to Bellows Falls.	52 "
(Passing over the Green Mountains.)	
Bellows Falls to Fitchburg, Mass.	64 "
FITCHBURG to BOSTON	50 "

Total Distance..................333 miles.

ROUTES OF TRAVEL FROM MONTREAL TO NEW YORK, via THE VERMONT CENTRAL AND CONNECTICUT VALLEY RAILROADS.

MONTREAL to ROUSE'S POINT, N. Y.	44 miles.
Rouse's Point to White River Junction	144 "
(Passing over the Green Mountains.)	
White River Junction to Bellows Falls	40 "
(Passing down the Connecticut Valley.)	
Bellows Falls to Springfield, Mass.	95 "
Springfield to New Haven, Conn.	62 "
NEW HAVEN to NEW YORK	76 "

Total Distance..................461 miles.

* Connects with Railroad Route to the White Mountains, and Roads running South to Springfield, and New Haven.

RAILROAD ROUTE, via ROUSE'S POINT, BURLINGTON, RUTLAND, AND TROY, TO NEW YORK.

MONTREAL to ROUSE'S POINT, N. Y.	44 miles.
Rouse's Point to Burlington, Vt.	56 "
Burlington to Rutland, Vt.*	67 "
Rutland to Troy, N. Y.	84 "
Troy to Albany, (Railroad or	6 "
ALBANY to NEW YORK, Steamboat Route)	144 "

Total Distance.....................401 miles.

ROUTE FROM MONTREAL AND QUEBEC TO THE WHITE MOUNTAINS AND PORTLAND, ME., via THE GRAND TRUNK RAILWAY.

Passengers cars leave Montreal and Quebec, twice daily, for Portland, connecting at RICHMOND, C. E., 73 miles from Montreal; from thence proceed southeasterly through Sherbrooke, an important town of Canada, to ISLAND POND, Vt. Here is a large public-house for the accommodation of travelers, where every desired luxury and comfort can be found.

The road continues through Vermont and New Hampshire, until the WHITE MOUNTAINS are reached and passed; the cars stopping at GORHAM to land and receive passengers. Here is a well-kept hotel, called the *Alpine House*

STAGES leave Gorham on the arrival of the cars for the *Glen House*, passing up the valley of Peabody River, a mountain stream, which affords many picturesque and romantic views.

The Grand Trunk Railway passes through the Copper and Gold Region of Canada East, affording tourists a fine opportunity to explore the surrounding country, being alike celebrated for a healthy climate and rich mineral productions.

ACTON, C. E., 50 miles from Montreal, is one of the most noted mineral localities where copper is found, while deposits of gold extend over a large region of country along the line of the Grand Trunk Railway. The Chaudiere River and its tributaries are the most noted localities for gold, while the St. Francis River, Magog River, and Massawippi River, and streams flowing into the above rivers, are supposed to contain rich deposits of the precious metal.

Passengers leaving Portland, Me., are afforded an equally favorable opportunity to visit the *White Mountain* region.

---

* Railroad Route to Boston, *via* Bellows Falls.

WHITE MOUNTAINS OF NEW HAMPSHIRE.

"NOTHING in the United States so nearly approaches the wild scenery of Switzerland as the Alpine region of New Hampshire. More loveliness may be found among the beautiful valleys and villages of New England—the traveler may better realize his visions of the picturesque in the varied scenery of the Hudson—may be filled with greater astonishment as he stands, deafened, at the side of Niagara—may find more to excite his wonder in the Great Lakes, or mighty St. Lawrence, and awe-inspiring Saguenay—more to gratify his love of the beautiful and quiet combined, around the shores and on the silver waters of Lake George; but if he would see nature in ' her dwelling-place of magnificence and power'—if he would behold ' the beautiful, the grand, and the sublime in commingled harmony,' let him turn his steps toward this ' MOUNTAIN METROPOLIS,' and thread his way among its winding gorges, or stand alone upon its solitary turrets.

"No distance here lends enchantment to the view. It is not the height merely that impresses and overpowers the beholder; it is the wonderful structure and conformation of these rocky masses, so forcibly reminding the traveler of the more gigantic ALPS. It is the wild and stupendous congregation of mountains—everywhere, 'pile upon pile, peak basing peak,' rise the everlasting hills; while Mount Washington. like an enormous pyramid, overtops the whole—fitting throne of the Indian's God.

"Art here has acknowledged its inferiority, and reverently stood aloof. The ever busy hand of man has here felt its utter weakness, and shrunk from contact with the handiwork of God.

> "All here is nature, God alone could blend
> Wood, wind, and wave in melody so sweet;
> He, he alone, the rocky cliffs could bend,
> And pour so bright a river at their feet."

"Leave, then, ye seekers after pleasure and comfort, the dusty thoroughfares of the city; flee from the hot and crowded

Springs, where pride and envy and disease congregate; away from the busy, jostled haunts of man; away to this mountain-land, and strengthen your enfeebled frames with exhilarating draughts of pure mountain air, and refresh your care-worn souls with Nature, untarnished from the hands of God.

> " Go forth into the fields,
>   Ye dwellers in the city's crowded mart,
> Go forth, and know the influence nature yields
>   To soothe the wearied heart.
>
> " Leave ye the feverish strife,
>   The jostling, eager, self-devoted throng;
> Ten thousand voices, waked anew to life,
>   Call you with sweetest song."

"A visit to the White Mountains, which once occupied so large a space of time, as to make it impossible to many, and, at best, a hurried one to all, is now made available to every one, by the facilities and the cheapness of the many conveyances at the option of the traveler."

ASCENT TO MOUNT WASHINGTON

Starting from the ALPINE HOUSE, situated on the line of the Grand Trunk Railway, a ride of eight miles by stage or private conveyance takes passengers to the GLEN HOUSE, situated at the base of Mount Washington. The Carriage Road, finished in 1861, now forms the safest and most speedy mode of conveyance to the top of the mountain, the distance being eight miles in a circuitous route from the Glen House. The ascent can be made on foot, on horseback, or in a light covered wagon; whichever way may be preferred, parties can start from either hotel, the charges being the same. This carriage road, a triumph of engineering skill, furnishes the best road in the whole mountain region; the average grade being twelve feet in one hundred, and the steepest grade in any part is sixteen feet in one hundred for a short distance.

For the first three or four miles of the way, the road winds among the trees of the forest, which cover the sides of all the mountains, permitting only occasional glimpses of the mountain scenery around. At "the Ledge," the road emerges from the forest, and the grandeur of the ascent here begins. On leaving the Ledge, the road winds along the very verge of the deep ravine between Mounts Washington, Clay, and Jefferson, the upper end of which is called the Great Gulf. Here are experienced sensations peculiar to high altitudes; the wind sweeps almost unobstructed across the mountain peaks.

A most grand and surprising view is here afforded of Mounts Adams, Jefferson, and Madison; they rise up almost perpendicularly from the enormous gulfs at the right hand of the road, and are visible from base to crown.

During the last part of the ascent, the view of the world below enlarges; and, when arrived at the summit, a stupendous view is presented to the gaze of the beholder. "A widespread horizon of nearly six hundred miles bounds the prospect! The lesser mountain peaks stand on every side as sentinels over the prisoned valleys of New-England!" Here stands the "*Tip-Top House*," and the "*Summit House*," both being united under one management, where guests can be comfortably supplied with refreshments and lodging. The time in making the ascent from the Glen to the peak of Mount Washington is about three hours.

A carriage road has also been constructed, running from near the Crawford House, in the Notch, to the base of Mount Washington on its west face, thus reducing the distance which it is necessary to accomplish on foot or horseback from nine miles to about three miles. The distance from the Crawford House to the Glen House, passing over the summit of Mount Washington, is seventeen miles by the usual traveled route.

The following is a description of an ascent to Mount Washington from the WHITE MOUNTAIN HOUSE:

"Having for the first time ascended to the summit of the White Mountains of New Hampshire, I will give you, for the information of your readers, an account of the most exhilarating and sublime excursion the country affords. At nine o'clock A.M. I left the public house in company with a guide, three ladies, six gentlemen, and a lad ten years of age each provided with a good horse to ride. After proceeding about three miles, for the most part through a dense forest, crossing and recrossing several times the head-waters of the Ammonoosuc River, we diverged to the right from Fabyan's bridle road to Mount Washington, and commenced ascending Mount Pleasant, elevated about 5,000 feet above the ocean. The road now became very steep for two or three miles, when the ascent was overcome and we stood on the top of Mount Pleasant. Here we struck Crawford's bridle road, running from the Notch House, four miles distant, we having come about six miles, which took us three hours to accomplish. We here encountered a chilly blast of wind, which brought all the overcoats and shawls into requisition. On the top of Mount Pleasant we encountered nothing but naked rocks, having for some time previous been above the region of vegetation. The route now pursued leads over the summits of Mounts Franklin and Monroe, toward Mount Washington, all being elevated from five to six thousand feet above the ocean, and overlooking numerous other mountain peaks.

"The *Lake of the Clouds*, situated near the summit of Mount Monroe, is a small body of beautiful clear water, which supplies the head stream of the Ammonoosuc River. This little current immediately begins its descent, and dashes in a headlong course of several thousand feet into the valley below; in its course uniting with several other mountain torrents, which soon form a considerable stream.

"After a toilsome jaunt of four and a half hours, having traveled about nine miles, we arrived at the summit of Mount Washington, having for two hours been above all signs of vegetation, except occasionally a few plants of an Alpine character—nothing but flying clouds to be seen in every direction—when they would in part clear away and reveal to sight one of the most grand and extensive views imaginable. Then could be distinctly seen rocks piled on rocks, and innumerable mountain peaks in the distance, with occasional bodies of water and silvery streams flowing through the valleys. Our horses were left about half a mile from the summit, although horses are sometimes taken to the very top; here was spread a cloth on a huge rock, and a bountiful repast furnished by our obliging guide, the contents of a well-filled pair of saddle-bags.

"After remaining on the summit one hour, we commenced our downward journey, which was all, except about one mile, performed on horseback—the party preferring to walk over the most precipitous descent. The first three miles are a steep descent, then come about three miles of swampy ground, the remaining three miles being a good carriage or bridle road."

HEIGHT OF THE PRINCIPAL MOUNTAINS IN NEW ENGLAND.

MAINE.	Feet above the sea.		Feet above the sea.
Katahdin Mountain	5,300	Kearsage Mountain	3,067
Bald "	4,000	Carr's "	3,581
Ubeeme "	4,000	Pequaquet "	3,367
Outop "	4,000	Guns ock "	2,447
Abraham "	3,387	Ossipee "	2,361
Aroostook "	3,000	Red Hill, near Central Harbor	2,000
Baker's "	3,000		
Bigelow "	3,400	**VERMONT.**	
Speckled "	3,000	Mansfield Mt., (the Chin)	4,279
		Camel's Hump	4,183
NEW HAMPSHIRE.		Shrewsbury Mountain	4,086
Mt. Washington, *White Mts*	6,285	Mansfield Mt., (the Nose)	3,93
" Adams "	5,800	Kington Peak	3,924
" Jefferson "	5,700	Equinox Mountain	3,706
" Madison "	5,400	Ascutney "	3,320
" Monroe "	5,300		
" Gray "	5,200	**MASSACHUSETTS.**	
" La Fayette "	5,200		
" Carter "	4,900	Saddle Mountain	3,505
" Franklin "	4,900	Bald Peak "	2,624
" Pleasant "	4,800	Spruce Hill	2,588
" Moriah "	4,700	Clarksburg Mountain	2,272
" Clinton "	4,400	Becket "	2,194
" Jackson "	4,100	French's Hill	2,239
" Webster "	4,000	Perry's Peak	2,059
White Face Mountain	4,100	Wachuset Mountain	2,018

Numerous other peaks of the White Mountains rise from 3,000 to 4,000 feet above the ocean level, presenting, from the summit of Mount Washington, a most sublime view, during a clear day, the scene being varied by cloud effect and the change of seasons. For further description, see "EASTMAN'S WHITE MOUNTAIN GUIDE BOOK."
Maine, New Hampshire, and Vermont may be regarded as a mountainous section of country; also the western part of Massachusetts. The *Green Mountains* of Vermont are, however, the only continuous range; the others may be regarded as groups and isolated mountains, rising in solitary grandeur from among surrounding hills.

PRINCIPAL HOTELS AT THE WHITE MOUNTAINS.

Name.	Proprietors.	Location.
Alpine House	Mr. Hitchcock	Gorham Station.
Crawford House*	Gibbs & Co	At the Notch.
Flume House		Near Franconia Mts.
Glen House †	J. M. Thompson	Near Mt. Washington
Mt Crawford House		Near Mt. Crawford.
Profile House	Richard Taft	Near Mt. Lafayette.
Tip-Top House	J. R. Hitchcock	Top Mt Washington.
White Mountain H'se	G. T. Bradrook	N'r Ammonoosuc Falls.

---

* A bridle road runs from this house to the summit of Mount Washington.
† A carriage road runs from this house to the Tip-Top House, 8 miles.

LAKE WINNIPISIOGEE AND THE WHITE MOUNTAINS.

THE *Boston, Concord and Montreal Railroad*, running from Concord to Wells River, N. H., forms the most direct and favorite route to Lake Winnipisiogee and the White Mountains; the usual time being twelve hours' ride from Boston to the Crawford House, or ten hours to Franconia Notch. or Conway.

CARS make connections from Boston, leaving *Boston* and *Lowell*, or *Boston* and *Maine Depôts*, connecting at Concord, N. H., affording a choice of *three* routes to the WHITE MOUNTAINS.

1. Leaving the Cars at the Weirs, and taking the steamboat to Centre Harbor, (dine) and by Stage arrive at Conway same evening, ten hours from Boston, proceeding to the Mountains next day.

2. Leaving the Cars at Plymouth, (dinner) and proceeding to Franconia Notch by Stage, 24 miles, arriving same evening, ten hours from Boston.

3. Leaving the Cars at Littleton, the head of the White Mountains Railroad, and proceeding by Stage to Crawford House, the point of departure for ascending MOUNT WASHINGTON, arriving same afternoon at 7.30 P.M., and at Profile House, Franconia Notch, at 5.30 P.M.

This route affords the best opportunity of visiting the romantic LAKE WINNIPISIOGEE, on the waters of which the beautiful Steamboat LADY OF THE LAKE, Capt. Sanborn, is constantly plying between Weirs, Centre Harbor, and Wolfboro. Excellent Hotels, not surpassed in New England, will be found at all points on this route

☞ Passengers entering the Mountains by one of the above routes, can return by either of the others, as preferred.

PORTLAND.

This City is very advantageously situated on a peninsula at the western extremity of Casco Bay, distant 108 miles from Boston, 60 from Augusta, the capital of the State, 293 from

Montreal, and 570 from Washington. The city presents a beautiful appearance from the sea and the islands in the bay, as it rises like an amphitheater between two hills. It is regularly laid out and handsomely built, and has some fine public edifices, among which are a new exchange building, constructed of granite in the most substantial manner; a spacious city hall; a court-house and jail, and 20 churches; a customhouse, 10 banks, a theater, and an atheneum containing a library of several thousand volumes. The present population is about 30,000. On an eminence called *Mount Joy*, on which Fort Sumner formerly stood, there is an observatory 82 feet in height, being elevated 226 feet above the ocean, commanding a fine view of the harbor and the adjacent country. *Casco Bay* is seen lying to the east, studded with islands and rocky islets, said to amount to 365 in number. On the north is a body of water called Back Cove; the city is immediately on the southwest, and presents a splendid appearance in connection with the harbor and shipping. Cape Elizabeth lies on the south, 3 miles distant, where is located Cape Cottage, a much frequented public house and delightful place of resort during warm weather. *Fort Preble* stands two miles southeast, and commands the ship channel in connection with *Fort Scammel*, situated on an island. Beyond it lies the broad Atlantic Ocean, where, during the fall months of September and October, numerous small vessels are seen engaged in taking mackerel. *Mount Washington*, the highest peak of the White Hills of New Hampshire, distant 90 miles, may be seen on a clear day by looking through the glass here used in the observatory, which is a large and excellent instrument of the kind. Few places exceed Portland in point of location. Having an extensive back country, its trade is large and important; the principal articles of export are lumber, fish, and country produce. The trade with the West Indies is very great, also with Boston and New York, and Southern ports.

Portland, for beauty. picturesqueness, and variety of scenery in its vicinity, is deservedly noted. As a watering place it is justly celebrated. Nowhere on the Atlantic coast can seekers after health and pleasure more fully realize their expectations.

PRINCIPAL HOTELS IN PORTLAND.

American House, Congress Street; Elm Tavern, Federal Street; United States Hotel, corner Congress and Federal streets; besides many others of less note in different parts of the city.

STEAMBOAT AND RAILROAD ROUTES.

A line of Steamers runs from Portland to Boston, 108 miles; to Hallowell, 61 miles; to Bangor, 140 miles; to Eastport, 230 miles, and to St. Johns, N. B., 290 miles; stopping at many of the intermediate ports.

RAILROADS.

Length.

Portland, Saco and Portsmouth Railroad.......... 52 miles.
Grand Trunk Railway, to Montreal and Quebec....293 "
Portland and Kennebec Railroad, to Skowhegan.... 97 "
Maine Central Railway, to Bangor................138 "
York and Cumberland Railroad................. 18 "

The State of MAINE, alike celebrated for its healthy climate, sea-bathing resorts, and picturesque scenery, is annually visited by thousands of tourists, seeking health and pleasure.

RAILWAY STATIONS IN BOSTON.

Stations.

Eastern Railroad.................Causeway Street.
    Gloucester Branch.........   "   "
Boston and Maine Railroad........Haymarket Square.
    Newburyport Branch.......   "   "
    Manchester & Lawrence R. R. "   "
Boston and Lowell Railroad.......Causeway Street.
    Nashua & Lowell, and Concord R. R.............. "   "
Fitchburg Railroad...............Causeway Street.
    Cheshire Railroad.........   "   "
    Vermont and Massachusetts   "   "
Boston and Worcester R. R........Cor. Beach & Lincoln Sts.
    Western Railroad.......... "   "   "
    Norwich and Worcester R. R. "   "   "

Boston and Providence R. R........Pleasant St., op. Elliot St.
New Bedford & Taunton R. R.   "   "   "
Stonington & Providence R.R.   "   "   "
Old Colony, Fall River and Newport
    R. R....................Cor. Kneeland & South Sts.
Cape Cod Railroad..........   "   "   "
South Shore Railroad.......   "   "   "

RAILROAD ROUTES, DIVERGING FROM BOSTON, EAST,
NORTH, AND WEST—DISTANCES, FARES, Etc.

ROUTES.	Miles.	Fare.
Boston to Salem, via Eastern Railway............	16	$0 50
Newburyport, " "	36	1 10
Portsmouth, N. H., " "	56	1 70
South Berwick Junction, via Port Saco and P. R. R......................	70	2 10
Saco, Maine, " "	95	2 50
Portland* " " "	108	2 50
Brunswick, " via Portland and Kennebec R. R......................	135	3 60
Bath (Br. R. R.), Maine, " " "	144	3 75
Gardiner, " " " "	161	
Augusta, " " " "	168	4 25
Waterville, " " " "	186	5 00
Skowhegan, " " " "	205	5 75
Bangor, via Maine Central Railroad.....	241	

Usual Through Time, 12 hours.

Boston to Reading, via Boston and Maine Railway..	12	0 35
Lawrence,† " " " "..	26	0 80
Haverhill, " " " ..	33	1 00
Exeter, " " " ..	50	1 40
Dover,‡ N. H., " " " ..	68	1 80
Great Falls, Br., " " ..	74	1 95
South Berwick Junction, " ..	74	2 05
Saco, Maine..............................	99	
Portland,§ Maine...............	112	2 60
Danville Junction, via Maine Central Railroad..............................	140	
Lewiston, " " "	147	3 10

* Trains connect with cars on Grand Trunk Railway, running to the White Mountains, Montreal, and Quebec.
† Passenger Cars run from Boston to Concord, via Lawrence.
‡ Cars run via Dover to Alton Bay, on Lake Winnipisiogee.
§ Connect with Trains on Grand Trunk Railway.

RAILWAY STATIONS IN BOSTON.

ROUTES.   Miles.   Fare.

Boston to Waterville, Me., *via* Maine Central R. R., 195 $5 10
        Newport,   "   "   "   "   ..   223
        Bangor,   "   "   "   "   ..   250   6 60

Usual Through Time, 12 *hours*.

At Bangor, connects with *Bangor, Oldtown* and *Milford Railway*, and Stages running Eastward.

Boston to Lowell, *via* Boston and Lowell R. R...... 26 $0 80
        Nashua, N. H., *via* Nashua R. R....... 39   1 25
        Manchester, N. H., *via* Concord R. R.... 55   1 85
        Concord, N. H.   "   "   73   2 35
        Weirs Station,* *via* Boston, Concord and
          Montreal Railway.................. 106
        Plymouth,†   "   "   "   "   124
        Haverhill,   "   "   "   "   157
        Wells River,   "   "   "   "   166
        Littleton, *via* White Mountain R. R...... 183
        Franconia Mts., by Stage 12 miles...... 195
        White Mountains, by Stage 22 miles..... 205

Usual Through Time, 12 *hours*.

Boston to Concord, N. H., via Boston & Lowell R. R., 73   2 35
        Franklin, *via* Northern (N. H.) R. R.... 92   2 95
        West Lebanon,   "   "   "   142   4 15
        White River Junction,‡ Vt., *via* Vermont
          Central R. R...................... 143   4 15
        Royalton,   "   "   "   163   4 95
        Northfield,   "   "   "   197   6 25
        Montpelier,   "   "   "   205   6 60
        Waterbury, §   "   "   "   214   7 00
        Essex Junction,   "   "   "   218   7 75
        Burlington,   "   "   "   247   8 00
        St. Albans, Vt., *via* Vermont & Canada R., 264   8 50
        Rouse's Point,‖ N. Y.,   "   "   "   287   9 00

---

* A Steamer runs from this Station to Centre Harbor, Wolfboro, etc., on Lake Winnipisiogee.

† Stages leave Plymouth on the arrival of the Cars for Franconia Notch and the White Mountains.

‡ Connects with the Conn. and Passumpsic Rivers R. R., running North, and with the Sullivan and Conn. River Railways, running South.

§ Passengers leave at this Station for Mansfield Mountain House.

‖ Connects with Northern (Ogdensburgh) Railroad, 118 miles in length.

RAILWAY STATIONS IN BOSTON.

ROUTES.	Miles.	Fare
Boston to St. John, Canada, via Champlain and St. Lawrence R.	308	$
Montreal, " " "	331	10 50

Usual Through Time, 15 hours.

	Miles.	Fare
Boston to Groton Junc., via Fitchburg Railroad	35	1 10
Fitchburg, " " "	50	1 55
Keene, N. H., via Cheshire R. R.	92	2 95
Bellows Falls,* Vt., via " "	114	3 70
Ludlow, Vt., via Rutland & Bur. R. R.	141	
Rutland, † " " " "	166	5 70
Middlebury, Vt., " " "	199	6 95
Burlington, ‡ " " " "	234	8 00
Essex Junction, Vt. "	243	
St. Albans, Vt., via Vermont & Canada R.	269	8 50
Rouse's Point, N. Y., via " " "	292	9 00
Montreal, Can., via Champlain & St. Lawrence Railroad	336	
Ogdensburgh, N. Y., via Northern Railr'd.	410	10 00

Usual Through Time, 20 hours.

	Miles.	Fare
Boston to Worcester, via Boston and Wor. R. R.	44	1 35
Springfield, § via Western Railway	98	2 80
Pittsfield, " " "	151	4 00
Albany,‖ N. Y., via " "	200	5 00
Utica, N. Y., via New York Central R.R.	295	7 50
Rome, " " " "	310	7 80
Syracuse, N. Y., " " "	348	8 55
Rochester, " " " "	429	10 35
Lockport, " " " "	485	
Buffalo, ¶ " " " "	498	11 75
Niagara Falls,** via " " "	506	11 75

Usual Through Time, 20 hours.

---

* Connects with the Sullivan Railroad and Connecticut River Railroads.
† Passenger Cars run to Saratoga Springs, Troy, etc.
‡ Steamers run from Burlington to Plattsburgh, Rouse's Point, etc.
§ Through Trains run direct to New York, via New Haven.
‖ Connect with Trains for Troy and Saratoga Springs.
¶ Connect with Lake Shore Railroad for Cleveland, etc.
** Connects at Suspension Bridge with *Great Western Railway* of Canada, for Detroit, Chicago, etc.

STEAMBOAT AND RAILROAD ROUTES
FROM N. YORK TO BOSTON, AND THE WHITE MOUNTAINS

The **Fall River Line of Steamers** leave New York daily (Sundays excepted), at 5 P.M., from Pier No. 3, North River, for Newport, R. I., and Fall River, Mass., connecting with the *Old Colony and Newport Railroad*, running to Boston. Distance, 234 miles. Fare, $5. Usual through time, 13 hours.

The **Stonington Line of Steamers** leave New York daily (Sundays excepted), at 5 P.M. from the foot of Cortlandt Street, North River, for Groton and Stonington, Conn., connecting with the *Stonington and Providence Railway*. From Providence cars run over the *Boston and Providence Railway* to the city of Boston. Distance, 220 miles. Fare, $5. Usual time, 13 hours.

☞ From Boston passengers are conveyed by various routes to the **White Mountains** of New Hampshire, Portland, Montreal, Quebec, etc.

The **Norwich Line of Steamers** leave New York daily (Sundays excepted), at 5 P.M. from Pier No. 39, North River, for Allyn's Point and Norwich, Conn., connecting with the *Norwich and Worcester Railroad*, and with the *Boston and Worcester Railroad*, running to the city of Boston. Distance, 232 miles. Fare, $5. Usual time, 13 hours.

☞ From Worcester passenger trains run direct to Concord, N. H., and from thence to the **White Mountains**, affording a delightful and speedy route of travel. Distance from New York to the White Mountains, about 400 miles.

The **New York** and **New Haven Railroad,** in connection with other railroads in Connecticut and Massachusetts, running up the valley of the Connecticut River, also forms a speedy mode of conveyance to the **White Mountains.** Passenger Depôt, corner Fourth Avenue and Twenty-seventh Street.

New Jersey Steamboat Co.
PEOPLE'S LINE.

STEAMBOATS LEAVE FOR

ALBANY,

daily, at SIX o'clock, P.M. (Sundays excepted), from wharf foot of Cortlandt Street, and in connection with the

NEW YORK CENTRAL RAILROAD,
for Buffalo, Suspension Bridge, Cleveland, Detroit, and all Western and Northern cities.

THE STEAMERS
ST. JOHN,.........Capt. W. H. Peck,
AND
HENDRIK HUDSON, Capt. S. J. Roe,

composing this line, are in all respects fitted and equipped with an especial view to safety and comfort.

THROUGH TICKETS

can be had at the office on the wharf, and baggage checked to all stations on the New York Central Railroad, and the principal cities West.

Freight received as usual, and forwarded with dispatch, and at reduced rates.

For particulars, apply at the office of the Company, on the wharf, foot of Cortlandt Street.

EVENING STEAMBOAT LINE
FOR
ALBANY and TROY.

CONNECTING AT TROY WITH RENSSELAER AND SARATOGA RAILROAD, AND TROY AND BOSTON RAILROAD FOR

Saratoga Springs,	Williamstown, Mass.	Port Kent, N. Y.,
Moreau, L. George,	North Adams, "	Plattsburgh, "
Fort Edward, N. Y.,	Brandon, Vt.,	St. Albans, Vt.,
Whitehall, N. Y.,	Middlebury, Vt.,	Rouse's Point, N. Y.,
Castleton, Vt.,	Vergennes, "	Ogdensburgh, "
Rutland, "	Burlington, "	Montreal, Can.

THE NEW AND FIRST-CLASS STEAMERS

FRANCIS SKIDDY, W. H. Christopher, Commander,
TUESDAY, THURSDAY, AND SUNDAY:

C. VANDERBILT, G. O. Tupper, Commander,
MONDAY, WEDNESDAY, AND FRIDAY,

At **6** o'clock, P. M., from Pier **15**, North River,
FOOT OF LIBERTY STREET.

☞ This is the only River Line that connects and Checks Baggage through to Saratoga and the North.

G. R. MALLORY, Agent, New York.

DAY BOATS
BETWEEN
NEW YORK & ALBANY,
LANDING AT

30th Street, N. York; West Point; Newburgh; Poughkeepsie; Rhinebeck; Catskill; and Hudson.

Connecting at Albany with the New York Central Railroad for all points West, and Northern Railroads and Steamers on Lake Champlain to Saratoga, Montreal, and all points North.

These Steamers are fitted with State Rooms. Breakfast and Dinner on board.

THE STEAMBOATS

DANIEL DREW, Captain J. F. Tallman,
MONDAY, WEDNESDAY, AND FRIDAY;

CHAUNCEY VIBBARD, Capt. Hitchcock,
TUESDAY, THURSDAY, AND SATURDAY,
From Foot of Debrosses Street at Seven o'clock A.M.

☞ Returning, leave Albany Daily, from the foot of Hamilton Street, at 9 A.M , arriving in New York at 6 P.M.

At Hudson, these Steamers connect with the Cars for Lebanon Springs and Boston, arriving at the Springs at $7\frac{1}{2}$ P.M. Trains leave Albany at 5.15 P.M. for Utica, and at 6 and 11.15 P.M for Buffalo, Niagara Falls, and Suspension Bridge.

☞ Baggage to Central and Northern Railroads delivered Free.

☞ Tickets sold on board to all points West and North. Baggage Checked to all points.

STONINGTON LINE STEAMERS,

1864.  1864.

FOR

BOSTON,

Via Groton, Stonington, and Providence,

Inland Route—the shortest and most direct—carrying the Eastern Mail. The Steamships

PLYMOUTH ROCK, Captain J. C. Geer,

AND

COMMONWEALTH, Capt. J. W. Williams,

in connection with Stonington and Providence, and Boston and Providence Railroads, leave New York daily (Sundays excepted) from Pier No. 18 North River at 5 P.M., and Groton at 8.30 P.M., or on arrival of the mail train which leaves Boston at 5.50 P.M.

The **Plymouth Rock,** from New York—Monday, Wednesday, and Friday. From Groton—Tuesday, Thursday, and Saturday.

The **Commonwealth,** from New York—Tuesday, Thursday, and Saturday. From Groton—Monday, Wednesday, and Friday.

Passengers proceed from Groton, per railroad, to Providence and Boston, in the Express Mail Train, reaching said places in advance of those by other routes, and in ample time for all the early morning lines connecting North and East. Passengers that prefer it remain on board the steamer, enjoy a night's rest undisturbed, breakfast, if desired, and leave Groton in the 7 15 A.M. train, connecting at Providence with the 10.40 A.M. train for Boston.

Fare from Providence to Newport, Fifty Cents.

☞ A Baggage Master accompanies the Steamer and Train through each way.

For baggage, berths, state-rooms, or freight, apply on board the steamer, or at the Freight Office, Pier No. 18 North River, or at the office of the Company, No. 115 West Street, corner of Courtland Street. **M. R. SIMONS, Agent.**

For State Rooms, apply at HARNDEN'S EXPRESS, No. 65 Broadway, N.Y.

LAKE GEORGE.

THE
STEAMER MINNEHAHA

Makes daily trips through the Lake, connecting with the boats on Lake Champlain, Montreal, Quebec, and Niagara, and the railway to Saratoga, Troy, Albany, and New York. The Minnehaha leaves her dock, at the Fort William Henry Hotel, every morning, Sundays excepted, at half past 7 o'clock—steams down the Lake among the islands, and through to Ticonderoga, connecting with Lake Champlain steamers going north and south; returning in the afternoon, upon the arrival of the Lake Champlain steamers, to her dock at the Fort William Hotel at 6 o'clock.

☞ Passengers by the Hudson River Railroad (two trains daily) arrive at the Lake in time for Tea same day; by the Hudson River steamers (night boats) in time for Dinner the next day.

THE NEW AND ELEGANT STEAM-YACHT
HIAWATHA

Is placed at the disposal of the guests, and will leave her dock at a moment's requisition, for any point on the Lake. She is also particularly available for moonlight, pic-nic, and fishing excursions.

N.B.—Telegraph now finished to the office, connecting with all Lines through the State.

LAKE CHAMPLAIN.

THE NEW AND SPLENDID STEAMERS
OF THE
Champlain Transportation Company,
VIZ.,

AMERICA..........................Capt. MAYO,
CANADA.... .... "   FLAGG,
UNITED STATES..................... "   ANDERSON,

Will make Two Daily Lines between WHITEHALL and ROUSE's POINT (Sundays excepted).

Leave Whitehall at 10.45 A.M. and 8.45 P.M., on arrival of the Morning and Evening Trains from the South and West; arrive at Burlington at 5 P.M. and 4 A.M., and at Plattsburgh and Rouse's Point, mornings and evenings, in time to connect with Trains for MONTREAL and OGDENSBURGH.

Passengers who leave New York by the Evening Boat will arrive at Montreal and Ogdensburgh the next evening. Those who leave New York by the 11 A.M. Train, Hudson River Railroad, will arrive at Whitehall at 8.45 P.M., and Montreal next morning at 9 o'clock, and Ogdensburgh at 1 o'clock P.M.

GOING SOUTH—Leave Rouse's Point every morning and evening, on arrival of the Trains from Montreal and Ogdensburgh, and *via* Plattsburgh, Burlington, and Ticonderoga, arrive at Whitehall at 5 A.M. and 4.30 P.M., connecting with Trains for the South and West.

THE NEW AND BEAUTIFUL STEAMER
MONTREAL..........................Capt. MAYO,

Will make Daily Trips between Burlington, Port Kent, Port Jackson, and Plattsburgh.

☞ These Boats are not excelled, either in speed, neatness, or comfort, by any other Boats afloat.

Lake Ontario and River St. Lawrence.

ONTARIO STEAMBOAT CO.

1864.   1864.

AMERICAN EXPRESS LINE.

BAY STATE, ... Capt. J. J. MORLEY.
ONTARIO, ... Capt. J. B. ESTES.
ALEXANDRA, ... Capt. J. N. BOCKUS.

Forming a Tri-Weekly Line between

TORONTO AND MONTREAL.

Touching at **CHARLOTTE** (Rochester) Mondays, Wednesdays, and Fridays, at 10 A.M., for

Oswego, Sacket's Harbor, Kingston, Clayton, Alexandria Bay, Brockville, Morristown, Prescott, Ogdensburgh, Montreal, and Quebec.

Connecting at Sacket's Harbor with Stage for Watertown, and at Kingston with the steamer Bay of Quinte for Belleville and Picton, and with the Grand Trunk Railway, both East and West, connecting at Ogdensburgh with the splendid new steamer ALEXANDRA, for Montreal and Quebec, and Northern Railroad for Boston and all points East: at Prescott, with Prescott and Ottawa Railroads for Ottawa.

☞ Trains leave Buffalo from New York Central Railroad, Exchange Street Depot, at 6.45 P.M., and connect with Steamers at Charlotte (Rochester Landing).

Tickets can be purchased at the Company's Office, opposite Erie Street Depot; at the Niagara Falls Depot; and at the Union Ticket Office, No. 17 Exchange Street, Buffalo.

H. N. THROOP, Gen. Sup't.   M. RANDALL, Agent.

ADVERTISEMENTS.

Lakes Huron and Superior.

THE MAGNIFICENT UPPER CABIN, ROYAL MAIL STEAMER

ALGOMA,

D. McLEAN, Master,

Will leave COLLINGWOOD for

Owen Sound, Shebawananing, Little Current, Bruce Mines, Sault Ste. Marie, Michipicoten, and Fort William, as under:

Leaving Collingwood for Owen Sound and Sault Ste. Marie, and intermediate ports, every THURSDAY, at Noon, on arrival of Toronto trains.

June..........	2,*	9,	16,*	23,*	30*
July..........	7,	14,*	21,	28,*	..
August........	4,	11,*	18,	25,*	..
September....	1,	8,*	15,	22,*	29
October.......	6,*	13,	20,*	27,	..
November.....	3,*	10,	17,	24,	..

* Runs to Fort William, North Shore Lake Superior.

RETURNING, leaves Sault Ste. Marie for Collingwood and intermediate ports—

June..........	7,	13,	21,	27,	..
July..........	5,	11,	19,	25,	..
August........	2,	8,	16,	22,	30
September....	5,	13,	19,	27,	..
October.......	3,	11,	17,	25,	31
November.....	8,	14,	21,	28,	..

This trip of more than one thousand miles along the north shore of Lakes Huron and Superior, embracing scenery which for grandeur and beauty is not equaled on this continent, presents to the tourist for pleasure or health—including the splendid Trout Fishing in the numerous rivers and among the thousands of islands, more real attractions than can be found on any other route!

The Algoma is a new and powerful Double-engine, Side-wheel Steamer (built expressly for this route last season), is fitted up with large Double State Rooms the whole length of the vessel; and has accommodation for over One Hundred Passengers.

☞ Pleasure Parties from Sault Ste. Marie, for Montreal or Quebec, will be taken at **Reduced Rates of Fare**, connecting at Toronto with Royal Mail Line of magnificent upper cabin Steamers, leaving daily at Three o'clock P.M.; also with Capt. Milloy's splendid new Steamer CITY OF TORONTO, for Niagara Falls, Buffalo, New York, and Boston.

☞ For further information regarding Passages or Freight, apply at the Office of the NORTHERN RAILWAY COMPANY; or at the Office of the LAKES HURON AND SUPERIOR STEAM NAVIGATION COMPANY, 50 Front Street, Toronto.

Geo. Ewart, Gen. Agt.   E. M. CARRUTHERS & CO.

OTTAWA RIVER MAIL STEAMERS.

1864.  1864.

MONTREAL TO OTTAWA CITY,
DAILY (SUNDAYS EXCEPTED).
THROUGH IN TEN HOURS!

The splendid new fast-sailing Steamers,
PRINCE OF WALES.......Capt. H. W. Shepherd.
QUEEN VICTORIA ....Capt. Bowie.

A TRAIN LEAVES the BONAVENTURE STREET DEPOT MONTREAL, EVERY MORNING (Sundays excepted) at 7 o'clock, to connect at LACHINE with the Steamer "PRINCE OF WALES" (Breakfast) for CARILLON, passing through Lake St Louis, St. Anne's Rapids, and Lake of Two Mountains. From Carillon by Railroad to Grenville, join the Steamer "QUEEN VICTORIA" (Dinner) for Ottawa City.

Downward, the Steamer "QUEEN VICTORIA" leaves Ottawa City at 6.30 A.M., Passengers arriving at Montreal at 4.30 P.M. in time for the Quebec Steamers.

The comfort and economy of this Line are unsurpassed, while the Route passes through one of the most picturesque districts in Canada, and is the most fashionable for Tourists.

Parties desirous of a pleasant trip can obtain Return Tickets from Montreal to Carillon, valid for one day, at single fares.

Passengers for the celebrated CALEDONIA SPRINGS will be landed at L'Original, where Coaches are in readiness to convey them to the Springs.

☞ Further information, as well as Return and Excursion Tickets, may be obtained at the office, 83 Great St. James Street, next door to the American Church, at the Bonaventure Street Depot, or on board the Steamers.

R. W. SHEPHERD, Manager.

GRAND EXCURSION

TO THE FAR-FAMED

RIVER SAGUENAY!

AND

SEA-BATHING

AT

MURRAY BAY AND CACOUNA!

THE MAGNIFICENT IRON STEAMER

"MAGNET," Captain J. B. Fairgrieve,

(Running in connection with the Steamers of the Richelieu Company) will leave Napoleon Wharf, Quebec, every Tuesday and Friday morning during the Season, at 8 o'clock, for the River Saguenay to Ha! Ha! Bay, calling at Murray Bay, River Du Loup, and Tadousac.

☞ No expense or inconvenience in exchanging boats at Quebec; in every instance, the Steamers are brought alongside of each other.

This splendid Steamer is built in water-tight compartments, of great strength, and equipped with every appliance for safety, and acknowledged to be one of the best sea-boats afloat. She is fitted up with large Family State Rooms, most comfortably furnished, and in every respect second to none on the Canadian waters.

Return Tickets good for the Season at Reduced Fare, or any information may be obtained on application at the office, 21 Great St. James Street.

ALEX. MILLOY, Agent.

MONTREAL, *June*, 1864.

NEW YORK CENTRAL R.R.

FOR ALL PLACES IN THE
WEST, NORTH, AND CANADA.

 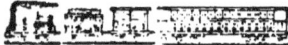

Time of Leaving the City of New York:

7.00 A.M. From Hudson River Railroad Depot, Chambers Street, (via Albany or Troy), arriving in Buffalo and Niagara Falls at 10.15 P.M., connecting for all points West.

7.00 A.M. From foot of Desbrosses Street, near Canal, North River, elegant new DAY BOATS, connecting at Albany with Evening Trains, arriving in Buffalo and Niagara Falls at 6.00 A.M., connecting for all points West.

10.00 A.M. From Hudson River Railroad Depot, Chambers Street, arriving in Buffalo and Niagara Falls at 6.00 A.M., connecting for all points West.

10.00 A.M. From Harlem Railroad Depot, corner Twenty-sixth St. and Fourth Avenue, arriving in Buffalo and Niagara Falls at 6.00 A.M., connecting for all points West.

4.00 P.M. From Hudson River Railroad Depot, Chambers Street, arriving in Rochester at 7.45 A.M.; Buffalo and Niagara Falls at 11.00 A.M.; connecting for all points West.

5.00 P.M. (Daily) From Harlem Railroad Depot, corner Twenty-sixth Street and Fourth Avenue, arriving in Rochester at 7.45 A.M.; Buffalo and Niagara Falls at 11.00 A.M.; connecting for all points West.

6.00 P.M. (Daily) From Hudson River Railroad Depot, Chambers Street, arriving in Buffalo and Niagara Falls at 11.00 A.M., connecting for all points West. ☞ SUNDAY NIGHTS this train starts from Thirtieth St. at 6.22 P.M.

6.00 P.M. (Daily) From foot of Cortlandt Street, PEOPLE'S LINE, elegant New Steamers, connecting with the 7.15, 9.00, and 10.00 A.M., and 12.30 P.M. trains from Albany, arriving in Buffalo and Niagara Falls same evening.

10.40 P.M. From Hudson River Railroad Depot, Chambers Street, with Sleeping Cars attached, arriving in Albany at 6.30 A.M.; Buffalo and Niagara Falls at 8.00 P.M.; connecting for all points West.

Elegant **SLEEPING CARS** attached to all **Night Trains**, and **SMOKING CARS** to Day Trains on this Route.

☞ Baggage by this Route is checked to all principal points West.

C. B. GREENOUGH, **C. VIBBARD,**
Passenger Agent, 289 Broadway, N. Y.   General Sup't, Albany.

GREAT NORTHERN RAILROAD

AND

STEAMBOAT ROUTE.

New York to Albany, Troy, Saratoga Springs, Lake George, Burlington, Montreal, etc., via Rensselaer and Saratoga, and Saratoga and Whitehall Railroad, and Lake Champlain Steamers.

Passengers leaving New York, Troy, and Albany, by Day Line, will take boat at Whitehall at 10.50 A.M., and on the passage through Lake Champlain will have an extensive view of the Adirondacks of New York and the Green Mountains of Vermont—will pass near the old Forts of Crown Point and Ticonderoga—arriving at Rouse's Point at 8.45 P.M., in time for cars to Montreal and Ogdensburgh SAME EVENING.

Passengers for Northern and Eastern New England will leave boat at Burlington 4.45 P.M., and take the train of the Vermont Central Railroad at 8 P.M., which is provided with elegant Sleeping Cars, passing through Montpelier, Concord, Lowell, Nashua—arriving at Boston at 8 A.M.; or, lodging at Burlington, leave at 7.25 A.M. for the White Mountains, connecting with the roads to all the principal places in New England SAME DAY.

Passengers leaving New York, Troy, Albany, by Night Line, will take boat at Whitehall at 8.45 P.M., reach Burlington at 3.45 A.M., and Plattsburgh at 5.30 A.M.; and from either place take cars, arriving at Montreal at 9.00 A.M., and Ogdensburgh at 12 M.

FARE AS LOW AS ANY OTHER ROUTE.

THROUGH TICKETS

Can be obtained at all the Ticket Offices of the HUDSON RIVER RAILROAD; M. CANFIELD, Pier 15, foot of Liberty Street, New York; on board HUDSON RIVER STEAMERS; UNION DEPOT, Troy, N. Y.; NORTHERN ALBANY RAILROAD DEPOT, Albany.

General Office, 239 Broadway, New York.

Troy and Boston Railroad.

GREAT NORTHERN U. S. MAIL ROUTE FOR
Rutland, Burlington, St. Albans, Rouse's Point, Montreal, Ogdensburgh, and Boston.

A NIGHT LINE BETWEEN TROY, MONTREAL AND BOSTON
NEW AND SPLENDID SLEEPING CARS.
Through to Montreal in Ten Hours and a Half, without Change of Cars!

Passengers leaving Troy by this route at 8 A.M., will reach Rouse's Point and Montreal nearly three hours in advance of those leaving by Boat Line at 7 30 A.M. Passengers leaving Troy by Fast Express Train at 12.30 P.M. will arrive at Burlington and all points North same time with those leaving five hours earlier by any other line. Fare as low as by any other route.

Trains leave UNION DEPOT, Troy, Daily (Sundays excepted), as follows:

8.00 A.M., Mail, *via* Western Vermont and Rutland and Washington Roads, arriving at Rutland, 11.40 A.M.; Bellows Falls, 2.12 P.M.; Fitchburg, 5.05 P.M.; Boston, 7 30 P.M.; Burlington, 4.00 P.M.; St. Albans, 6.00 P.M.; Rouse's Point, 7.00 P.M.; Montreal, 9.00 P.M.; Ogdensburgh, 12.00 night.

12.30 P.M., Express, *via* Western Vermont Road, arriving at Rutland, 3.45 P.M.; Burlington, 6.00 P.M.; St. Albans, 7.25 P.M.; Rouse's Point, 9.00 P.M.; Montreal, 11.00 P.M.

4.45 P.M., Accommodation, for North Adams, Bennington, and all stations on Rutland and Washington Railroad, due at Rutland, 9.00 P.M. Trains leave next A.M. for East, 4.00; for North, 4.30.

10.00 P.M., Sleeping Car Express, *via* Western Vermont Road, arriving at Rutland, 1.15 A.M., Burlington, 4.05 A.M.; St. Albans, 5.40 A.M.; Rouse's Point, 7.00 A.M.; Montreal, 9.30 A.M.; Ogdensburgh, 12 noon; Boston, 7.30 A.M.

NEW YORK TO TROY, MONTREAL, ETC.

This Road connects with **Steamers** from **New York,** and the **Hudson River Railroad,** forming a direct and speedy route of travel from **New York** to **Montreal.**

I. V. BAKER, Sup't, TROY, N. Y.

GREAT CENTRAL ROUTE,
CARRYING THE GREAT U. S. MAIL.

Great Western Railway
OF CANADA,
BETWEEN
NIAGARA FALLS, SUSPENSION BRIDGE, AND DETROIT,

Forming, with its connections, the shortest and best route between the Atlantic and the Mississippi. Three Through Express Trains each way daily. Luxurious sleeping cars attached to each night train. Smoking cars to all day trains.

All the Passenger Coaches on this road have attached to them a ventilator, by means of which the interior is kept cool and entirely free from dust in summer, and uniformly warm in winter.

As the trains pass across the magnificent Suspension Bridge, the finest views of Niagara Falls and Niagara River can be obtained.

No other railroad line West that passes within 23 miles of Niagara Falls and Suspension Bridge.

American funds received at par for Through Tickets and sleeping-car berths, and at all refreshment rooms.

☞ Baggage checked through to all important points.

Fare as low as any other route.

☞ Through Tickets by this route are for sale at all the principal Ticket Offices in the United States and Canada.

THOMAS SWINYARD, Gen. Manager, Hamilton, C. W.
JAMES CHARLTON, General Agent, Hamilton, C. W.

AGENTS.

GEO. E. JARVIS,
   273 Broadway, New York.

P. K. RANDALL,
   21 State St., Boston.

T. N. DERBY,
   Ogdensburgh, N. Y.

T. D. Barton,
   175 Washington St., Buffalo, N. Y.

1864. To Tourists and Travelers. **1864.**

NEW AND IMPORTANT ARRANGEMENT.

GRAND TRUNK
RAILWAY,

AND
ROYAL MAIL LINE
OF
THROUGH STEAMERS.

1864.  **1864.**

NIAGARA FALLS to MONTREAL,
QUEBEC, RIVER SAGUENAY, WHITE MOUNTAINS,
PORTLAND, BOSTON,
LAKE GEORGE, SARATOGA,
CITY OF NEW YORK,
ETC., ETC., ETC.   *(See next page.)*

ADVERTISEMENTS.

THE FOLLOWING MAGNIFICENT UPPER CABIN STEAMERS COMPOSE THE LINE:

GRECIAN, (new iron)...Capt. C. Hamilton.
PASSPORT, (iron).....Capt. Kelley.
CHAMPION,..........Capt. D. Sinclair.
KINGSTON, (iron).....Capt. T. Howard.
MAGNET, (iron).......Capt. J. B. Fairgreaves.
BANSHEE,............Capt. H. Swales.
CITY OF TORONTO, (new) Capt. D. Milloy.

NO TRANSHIPMENT AT OGDENSBURGH.

☞ The only line by which Passengers can retain their State Rooms through the entire trip, and passing the scenery of **The Thousand Islands, and Rapids of the River St. Lawrence by Daylight.**

This great route possesses peculiar advantages over any other, as by it parties have their choice of conveyance between Niagara Falls and Quebec, over the whole or any portion of it, without being obliged to decide when purchasing their tickets, consequently should the weather prove unfavorable, passengers may avoid Lake Ontario by taking the Grand Trunk Road to Kingston, and from thence by one of the above Steamers, making close connections. No extra charge for Meals and State Rooms.

☞ The only route to the White Mountains by which parties can ascend the far-famed Mount Washington by the Carriage Road.

The **Steamer Magnet,** commencing 1st July, leaves Quebec for the far-famed Saguenay every Tuesday and Friday, A.M. Also Trains on the GRAND TRUNK RAILWAY leave Point Levi daily, for River du Loup, at which point they can also take the Saguenay Steamer.

AMERICAN MONEY TAKEN AT PAR FOR TICKETS
by this Line, which can be obtained at most of the principal cities in the United States. Arrangements have also been made with the proprietors of the principal hotels at Toronto, Montreal, and Quebec, to take American Money at par, charging New York hotel rates.

ALEX. MILLOY, Gen. Agt.,	E. P. BEACH, Gen. Agt.,
ROYAL MAIL LINE STEAMERS,	GRAND TRUNK RAILWAY,
Office, Gt. St. James St., Montreal.	279 Broadway, New York.

1864. 1864.
GRAND TRUNK RAILWAY
SEA BATHING
PLEASURE EXCURSION TICKETS.
TADOUSAC, RIVIERE DU LOUP, CACOUNA, PORTLAND, AND THE WHITE MOUNTAINS.

RETURN TICKETS, valid until November 1st, will be issued on and after the 15th June, at the following Reduced Rates :—

FROM	TO Tadousac and back.	TO Riv. du Loup and back.	TO Portland and back.
DETROIT, ...	$25 00	$23 00	$24 00
TORONTO, ...	20 00	18 00	20 00
KINGSTON, . . .	14 50	12 00	16 00
MONTREAL, . . .	8 50	6 00	10 50
QUEBEC, ...	5 50	3 00	12 00

TADOUSAC, which is beautifully situated at the mouth of the Saguenay River, is considered to be one of the most salubrious places on the St. Lawrence.

The Tadousac Hotel Company have erected a commodious Hotel, which has been elegantly furnished and fitted up in a manner to afford to guests the greatest possible comfort. The accommodation is most ample, and charges moderate.

☞ A Steamer will run daily between Tadousac and Riviere du Loup, and three times a week up the Saguenay River to Ha! Ha! Bay.

At Cacouna, the Hotel accommodation for visitors has been greatly increased.

A regular Line of Stages will run between Riviere du Loup and Cacouna.

☞ For further information, Time Tables, and Tickets, apply to the agents of the Grand Trunk Railway.

E. P. BEACH, *General Agent*
   279 Broadway, New York.

C. J. BRYDGES,
Managing Director.

EASTERN RAILROAD.

BOSTON AND PORTLAND.

Trains leave PORTLAND for BOSTON, arriving at the new station on Causeway Street, at

8.45 A.M. and 3.00 P.M. in Summer,
8.45 A.M. and 2.30 P.M. in Winter.

These Trains arrive in Boston at 1.45 and 8.00 P M. (7.30 P.M. in Winter), in season to connect with Trains for

NEW YORK AND THE WEST.

Trains leave BOSTON for PORTLAND, at

7.30 A.M. and 3.00 P.M. in Summer,
7.30 A.M. and 2.30 P.M. in Winter,

Connecting with Railroads, Steamboats, and Stages, to all parts of

MAINE AND CANADA EAST.

FREIGHT TRAINS

Daily, each way, leaving Portland and Boston at 5.00 P.M.
Freight Office in Boston, 25 Merchants Row.

The Eastern Railroad, which is the great United States Mail Route between Boston and the East, connects at Brock's Crossing with the Great Falls and Conway Railroad, and at Portland with the Maine Central, Androscoggin, and Portland and Kennebec Railroads, for Augusta, Waterville, Farmington, Bangor, etc. Also with the GRAND TRUNK RAILWAY, for the WHITE MOUNTAINS, MONTREAL, QUEBEC, etc., and with Steamers for Eastport and St. Johns, N. B.

J. PRESCOTT, Sup't, BOSTON.

BOSTON AND MAINE RAILROAD.

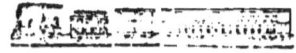 

The BOSTON AND MAINE RAILROAD, connecting with the Portland, Saco, and Portland Railroad through to PORTLAND.

This route is deservedly popular with travelers to and from the State of Maine. The Station in Boston being located on Haymarket Square, is very nearly in the center of business.

Passengers leaving Boston, cross Charles River by a bridge to Somerville, passing the Massachusetts State Prison on the right at the crossing of the Fitchburg Railroad in Charlestown; also, the Bunker Hill Monument in the distance; thence the road crosses Mystic River to Malden, the Medford Branch diverging on the left. At South Reading Junction the South Reading Branch (to Salem) and the Newburyport Railroad diverge; the last-named road is operated by the Boston and Maine Railroad Company, and is a pleasant and expeditious route to the fine old seaport town of Newburyport.

South Reading and Reading are large villages to be seen on the right as you pass on to Wilmington (Salem and Lowell Railroad crosses here), Ballardvale, and Andover. The next place is South Lawrence, opposite the thriving manufacturing city of Lawrence, on the Merrimac River. Trains cross the river below the dam with passengers for the city, and to connect with the Concord, Manchester, and Lawrence Railroad for Manchester, Concord, and the WHITE MOUNTAINS.

Passing through Andover to Bradford (Junction of the Newburyport Railroad), and then crossing the Merrimac, the large town of Haverhill is reached, which is the center of an extensive boot and shoe manufacturing business.

The towns of Atkinson, Plaistow, Newton, East Kingston, Exeter, South Newmarket, Newmarket Junction (passengers for Portsmouth, Manchester, and Concord change cars here), New Market, Durham, Madbury, N. H., are successively passed until we reach the town of Dover, the seat of a large manufacturing business and junction with the Dover and Winnipiseogee Railroad, over which road passengers for the Lake and White Mountains are conveyed to Alton Bay, there connecting with the Steamer *Chocorua* for Wolfsboro' and Centre Harbor.

Rollinsford is the next town, and is the junction of the branch to Great Falls, three miles.

After passing Salmon Falls we come to South Berwick Junction, connecting there with the Portland, Saco, and Portsmouth Railroad, continue on to North Berwick and Wells, Kennebunk, Kennebunk-port, Biddeford, Saco, and Scarborough, to PORTLAND, Maine.

Passengers for towns on the Grand Trunk and Maine Central Railroads keep their seats until they reach the Grand Trunk Depôt. Passengers for the Kennebec and Portland Railroad change cars at the Portland, Saco, and Portsmouth Railroad Depôt. At Portland, connect with Steamers for Bangor, Eastport, Calais, and St. John, N. B.

27

GREAT PLEASURE ROUTE,

VIA THE
Vermont Central R.R. Line,
TO
Mount Mansfield, White and Franconia Mountains, Lake Champlain, Lake George, Saratoga, Niagara Falls, Lake Ontario, Thousand Islands, Rapids of the River St. Lawrence, Montreal, Quebec, Saguenay River, etc., etc.

This Route passes through the Valley of Vermont, which has the most Splendid Scenery in New England!

MANSFIELD MOUNTAIN
is the highest land in Vermont, being about 5,000 feet high, giving a magnificent view of the whole range of the Green Mountains, and scenery that is not excelled in the Union.

The VERMONT CENTRAL LINE is the most direct Route between Boston and Montreal, and Quebec; between Boston and Ogdensburgh, Niagara Falls and Canada West; between New York and Montreal, either *via* Springfield and Connecticut River Railroad, or *via* Albany, Troy, or Saratoga.

Tickets for this line will be on sale in Boston, New York, Philadelphia, Baltimore, Washington, etc., etc., giving

Round Trips at Reduced Rates,
which will be advertised in the papers.

For any further information, apply at the

GENERAL AGENCY, NO. 5 STATE STREET, BOSTON.

S. H. FISHER, Trav. Agt.   L. MILLIS, Gen'l Agt.
BOSTON, May 23, 1864.

International Steamship Co.

DESIRABLE PLEASURE ROUTE
FOR
EASTPORT and CALAIS, Me.; ST. JOHN, N. B.; HALIFAX, N. S.; and CHARLOTTETOWN, Prince Edward Island.

THE SUPERIOR NEW SEA-GOING STEAMERS

NEW ENGLAND,
CAPT. FIELD; and
NEW BRUNSWICK,
CAPT. WINCHESTER,

leave Commercial Wharf, BOSTON, every Monday and Thursday morning at 8 o'clock; and PORTLAND same evening at 5 o'clock, for EASTPORT, Me.; and ST. JOHN, N. B. Returning, leave ST. JOHN same days.

At EASTPORT the Steamers connect with the Steamer QUEEN, for St. Andrew's, N. B.; from thence per Railway for Houlton and Woodstock Stations—also Calais and St. Stephens: at ST. JOHN with the European and N. A. Railway for Shediac, and from thence per Steamers for Prince Edward Island and Pictou, N. S., north shore New Brunswick, and Quebec, Canada. Also at St. John with Steamers for Fredericton, N. B., Digby and Windsor, N. S., and from thence per Railway for Halifax, N. S.

Fares.—Boston to Portland, $1 50; Eastport, $5 50; Calais, $6 50; St. John, N. B., $6 50; Halifax, N. S., $10 00.

J. B. COYLE, General Agent, PORTLAND, ME.

RICHELIEU COMPANY'S
DAILY ROYAL MAIL LINE
OF STEAMERS
BETWEEN
MONTREAL AND QUEBEC.

THE LARGE UPPER SALOON STEAMERS,

MONTREAL..............................Capt. COTTE,
EUROPA................................. " LAPELLE,

Leave Montreal and Quebec daily (Sundays excepted), every evening, affording to passengers a delightful trip between these two places of interest to all Tourists in Canada, stopping at SOREL, THREE RIVERS, and BATISCAN.

The comfort and economy of this Line are unsurpassed, while the Route passes through one of the most picturesque districts in Canada, and is the most fashionable for Tourists.

American Money taken at current rates.

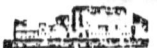

MONTREAL TO THREE RIVERS.

Steamer THREE RIVERS, Captain Joseph Duval.
Steamer NAPOLEON, Captain Robert Nelson.

Steamer VICTORIA, Capt. C. Davelny, runs between Montreal and Sorel, C. E.

Steamer CHAMBLY, Capt. F. Lamoureux, runs between Montreal and Chambly, C. E.

Steamer TERREBONNE, Capt. L. H. Roy, runs between Montreal and L'Assumption.

Steamer L'ETOILE, Capt. P. E. Malhoit, runs between Montreal and Terrebonne.

☞ For further information apply at the Office, No 29 Commissioners Street, Montreal.

J. B. LAMERE, *General Manager*, MONTREAL.

CLIFTON HOUSE, NIAGARA FALLS—CANADA SIDE.

UNION HALL,
SARATOGA SPRINGS.

This well-known Hotel is pleasantly located on the west side of Broadway, opposite the celebrated Congress Spring, and commands a view of the beautiful park connected with it.

By the addition, just finished, of a handsome brick building two hundred and forty-one feet long, by fifty-five feet wide, and five stories high, it is much the largest Hotel in the place, having a front of over one thousand feet, and can accommodate over one thousand guests. In extent and completeness the Dining Hall, Kitchen, and Laundry are unsurpassed in this country.

The court inclosed by the buildings forms a lawn of several acres in extent, intersected with well-shaded walks. Here a fine band of music, belonging to the house, contributes to the enjoyment of the guests every afternoon.

The management of UNION HALL, we trust, will meet with the approval of all who may honor us with their patronage.

LELAND & CO., Proprietors.

STANWIX HALL,
Corner of Broadway and Maiden Lane,
ALBANY, N. Y.,

AT THE JUNCTION OF THE NEW YORK CENTRAL, HUDSON RIVER, HARLEM, EASTERN AND NORTHERN RAILROADS.

F. RIDER,
Formerly of West Point; St. Germain, New York; and Pavilion, Rockaway, L. I.,

Respectfully informs the public generally that he has leased the above well-known Hotel, and refurnished, greatly improved, and put it in complete order, in every department, as a

FIRST-CLASS HOTEL,

F. R. assures his friends and the public that no exertion will be wanting on his part to merit a continuance of that patronage he has hitherto so liberally enjoyed.

FORT WILLIAM HENRY HOTEL.

The FORT WILLIAM HENRY HOTEL is situated on the site of FORT WILLIAM HENRY, adjoining FORT GEORGE and the old French Burying and Battle Grounds. The house is furnished in a style not surpassed by any city hotel. The building is 337 feet in length, with rear wing of 250 feet, and has

Handsome Accommodations for 500 Guests.

The rooms are airy, large, and in Suits or Private Parlors, as may be desired. Water is brought from a mountain spring, one mile distant, and carried to every part of the house, where are furnished

COLD AND WARM BATHS.

The Public Parlor is 87 by 42 feet, fronting on the Lake, and magnificently furnished. The house is brilliantly lighted with gas, made on the premises, and guests will therefore not be subject to any disagreeable smoke or smell from oil or camphene.

A CELEBRATED BAND

Is engaged for the season, and will perform upon the Piazzas during the day at dinner, and in the Public Parlor until 11 o'clock P.M., for those who wish to while away an hour in dancing.

LAKE GEORGE is celebrated for its fine trout, Oswego bass, pickerel, and other fish, which are served up daily at this hotel.

A Livery Stable is connected with both houses, together with an abundance of stable and barn room. Persons wishing to bring their horses and carriages to the Lake, can have private stables and carriage-houses. The drives on the Lake Shore and through the surrounding country are unsurpassed.

Steamers from New York to Albany and Troy have inclosed apartments for horses and carriages. Parties can leave New York at six P.M., with horses, etc., and arrive at the Fort William Hotel on the succeeding day. The driving distance from Troy to Lake George is 52 miles, over a good turnpike road.

ST. LAWRENCE HALL,
GREAT ST. JAMES STREET,
MONTREAL.

H. HOGAN, PROPRIETOR

This First-Class Hotel (the largest in Montreal) is situated on Great St. James Street, in front of the French Cathedral, or Church Ville Marie, Notre Dame Street, immediately adjacent to the Post Office, Place d'Armes, and Banks; is only one minute's walk from the Grey or Black Nunneries; New Court House, Reading Rooms, Champ de Mars (where the troops are reviewed), Mechanics' Institute, Bonsecours Market and Fashionable Stores

St. Lawrence Hall has long been regarded as the most popular and fashionable Hotel in Montreal. It has been under the charge of its present proprietor over ten years. The building presents a front of some 300 feet on Great St. James Street, with a depth of over 300 feet, and has over 300 apartments, every one of which is lighted by gas.

DONNEGANA'S HOTEL,
NOTRE DAME STREET,
MONTREAL.

ST. JULIEN & McKEOGH,
PROPRIETORS.

OTTAWA HOTEL,
GREAT ST. JAMES STREET,
MONTREAL.

S. BROWNING, PROPRIETOR.

RUSSELL'S HOTEL
PALACE STREET, QUEBEC.

The above comfortable and well-known establishment, having been thoroughly renovated and refitted during the winter recess, is re-opened for the reception of guests. The undersigned confidently hopes that this establishment, in connection with the

ST. LOUIS HOTEL (late Clarendon),

will afford ample accommodation not only to his numerous friends and patrons during the approaching

SESSION OF PARLIAMENT,

but also to the traveling community during the coming business and pleasure season.

WILLIS RUSSELL, Proprietor.

QUEBEC, May, 1864.

QUEEN'S HOTEL,
TORONTO, C. W.

CAPTAIN THOMAS DICK, PROPRIETOR.

This House is beautifully situated on FRONT STREET, near the Railway Station and Steamboat Landings, and commands an extensive view of the Harbor, Islands, and Lake.

☞ Carriages and trusty porters in attendance on the arrival of all Trains and Boats.

THE RUSSELL HOUSE,
OTTAWA, C. W.

The undersigned, proprietor of the above-named Hotel, begs leave to acquaint his numerous friends and the traveling public, that he has repainted and newly furnished throughout this commodious establishment, in the management of which, by strict personal attention to his business and guests, he hopes to deserve encouragement and support.

OTTAWA, June, 1864. **JAMES A. GOUIN.**

ADVERTISEMENTS.

THE AMERICAN HOUSE, Hanover Street, Boston,
Is the Largest Hotel in New England. Telegraph in the house to all parts of the Country. LEWIS RICE, PROPRIETOR.

CONGRESS SPRING.

Congress Spring.

Much spurious Mineral Water is sold as

"Congress Water,"

by unprincipled persons, who, when they dare not use THAT name, call it "Saratoga Water," although Saratoga is only the name of the town where the Spring is situated.

To protect the public from such impositions we have all the corks branded with C. & W.'s stamp,

"CONGRESS WATER."

☞ Congress Water Orders addressed to

CLARKE & WHITE,
AT THEIR SOUTHERN DEPOT,

No. 98 Cedar Street, New York,

OR AT

Saratoga Springs,

WILL BE PROMPTLY ATTENDED TO.

CONGRESS SPRING WATER

As analyzed by Dr. JOHN H. STEEL, at the Spring.

	Grains
Chloride of Sodium	385,000
Hydriodate of Soda	3,500
Bi-Carbonate of Soda	8,982
Bi-Carbonate of Magnesia	95,748
Carbonate of Lime	98,099
Carbonate of Iron	5,075
Silex and Alumina	1,500
Hydro-bromate of Potash, a trace	000
Solid contents in a gallon	597,943
Carbonic Acid Gas	.811
Atmospheric Air	7
Gaseous contents in a gallon	318 cubic inch.

Analysis made in London by Sir HUMPHREY DAVY and Professor FARADAY from Congress Water bottled seven Months.

	Grains
Chloride of Sodium	385.44
Hydriodate of Soda	4.02
Carbonate of Lime	116.00
Carbonate of Magnesia	56.80
Oxide of Iron	64
Carbonate of Soda	56
Hydro-bromate of Potash, a trace	00
Solid contents in a gallon	563.46

CLARKE & WHITE,
Proprietors of Congress Spring.

EMPIRE SPRING WATER.

The EMPIRE SPRING was purchased by D. A. Knowlton in 1861, and was placed in the hands of a Stock Company in 1863. This water is better adapted to general use than any other Mineral Water on this continent. It is more widely efficacious as a remedial agent than the water from any other mineral spring. This opinion is sustained by eminent medical men, and, what is still more important, by the actual experience of thousands. The public are fast becoming convinced of this, for it is a well-known fact that the owners of Congress Spring have sold a very large amount of water for years, and yet the Revenue Tax paid by that Spring the last twelve months proves that in some of the best business months the Empire Spring Company have sold and shipped more water than the Congress.

SARATOGA SPRINGS, *June 8th*, 1864.

D. A. KNOWLTON,
Pres't Saratoga Empire Spring Co.

☞ SOUTHERN DEPOT 18 John St. New York.

SARATOGA WATER-CURE,
ON BROADWAY,
Opposite the "Congress Spring Park."

OPEN ALL THE YEAR.

THIS IS ONE OF THE LARGEST WATER-CURES IN THE COUNTRY,
ACCOMMODATING ABOUT TWO HUNDRED GUESTS.

It is pleasantly located. The rooms, especially in the brick part, are large, airy, and well furnished. Persons visiting the Springs, either for health or recreation, can be accommodated with a quiet home, good wholesome food, experienced medical advice, and other facilities for restoration and enjoyment, which would make their stay here pleasant and profitable.

N. BEDORTHA, M.D., Proprietor and Physician.

www.ingramcontent.com/pod-product-compliance
Lightning Source LLC
Chambersburg PA
CBHW021203230426
43667CB00006B/537